D1327217

Israel and the World Economy

Israel and the World Economy

The Power of Globalization

Assaf Razin

The MIT Press
Cambridge, Massachusetts
London, England

© 2018 Massachusetts Institute of Technology

All rights reserved. No part of this book may be reproduced in any form by any electronic or mechanical means (including photocopying, recording, or information storage and retrieval) without permission in writing from the publisher.

This book was set in Palatino by Westchester Publishing Services. Printed and bound in the United States of America.

Library of Congress Cataloging-in-Publication Data

Names: Razin, Assaf, author.
Title: Israel and the world economy : the power of globalization / Assaf Razin.
Description: Cambridge, MA : The MIT Press, 2018. | Includes bibliographical
   references and index.
Identifiers: LCCN 2017023963 | ISBN 9780262037341 (hardcover : alk. paper)
Subjects: LCSH: Israel—Economic conditions—20th century. | Israel—Economic
   conditions—21st century. | Globalization—Economic aspects—Israel. |
   Israel—Emigration and immigration—Economic aspects. | Global Financial
   Crisis, 2008–2009.
Classification: LCC HC415.25 .R385 2017 | DDC 337.5694—dc23
LC record available at https://lccn.loc.gov/2017023963

10 9 8 7 6 5 4 3 2 1

In good memory of my son, Ofer Razin

Contents

Preface

Globalization—the integration of markets in goods, services, and capital whose pace accelerated in the 1990s with the fall of communism, the consolidation of the European single market, and growing openness of China and India—is currently under attack in Europe and the United States. The disintegration of the former Communist Bloc allowed full integration of central Europe into the world economy. The fall of the Berlin wall brought up the unification of Germany. In the 2000s both Russia and China became members of the WTO. Israel's successful globalization-based economic path is consistent with the enthusiasm with which policymakers around the world pushed forward the globalization wave.

However, globalization and new-technology forces accelerated the decline of low-tech manufacturing industries, the rise of the financial centers, and also the surge in migration. Brexit may have been the first wave of anti-globalization and rising populism that gushes over most advanced nations. Then came the 2017 chaotic change of guards in the United States. Meanwhile, European countries straightjacketed inside the confines of the single currency area—Germany, France, the Netherlands, Spain, Poland, and others—witness the anti-EU forces gather strength.

Israel provides a counterexample to the anti-globalization view, both with respect to goods and international capital flows, and to immigration flows. The state of Israel, founded in 1948, benefited immensely from the post-1945 world economic order with globalization at its center. Steadily reforming its financial and commercial institutions and becoming increasingly globalized in trade, labor market, and finance, Israel became a member of the Organization for Economic Cooperation and Development (OECD) in 2010. Currently, Israel's is a thriving economy, integrated tightly into the world economy, with a remarkable

technological prowess. The Israeli economy is a remarkable development success story. A middle-income economy in the midst of a hyperinflation in the early 1980s, Israel grew into one of the most thriving
economies in the world—and this despite the ongoing national security
challenges, which tend to drain resources from investment projects.

This book's objective is twofold: First, the book provides rigorous
analysis of some of the major globalization episodes during the decades-
long emergence of the economy of Israel. Second, it brings out theoreti-
cally and empirically based arguments as to how globalization played
a crucial role in advancing Israel's economic progress. Economists can
learn from the unique case of a globalized economy that takes advantage
of tailwinds arising from international trade, labor mobility, international financial links, and at the same time push up against globalization
headwinds, such as those triggered by the 2008 global financial crisis.
A general lesson that comes out is that once a gradual opening up
process is set, time-consistent macroeconomic policy is adopted, and
well-regulated institutional setup is put in place, the economy will be
able to ride on growth-enhancing globalization flows and also to weather
globalization's chilly storms.

The book addresses several unprecedented economic episodes. They
have rocked the global economy during the past several decades, and
turned out to be inflection points in the development of Israel's economy.
Some of these extraordinary events, external as well as domestic, are

(1) the collapse of the Soviet Union, and the massive wave of high-skill
immigration to Israel that followed;

(2) the Great Moderation in inflation and output-employment fluctuations in the advanced economies, and the convergence of Israel's inflation to the low world inflation rates;

(3) the 2008 global financial crisis (epicentered in the United States,
spreading violently to Europe), and the surprising robust performance
of the Israeli economy;

(4) the rise of the Asian markets, recently opened up to Israel's exports,
which also became an abundant source of foreign direct investments
into Israel;

(5) the global information technology surge, and its spillovers
to the fast-developing high-tech sector in Israel, aided by high skill
immigration;

(6) Israel's West Bank occupation challenges, and the cascade of Palestinian uprisings stretching over the last few decades;

(7) the brain drain of top Israeli talents, assisted greatly by Israel's advanced higher-education system and helped by the pro-skill bias immigration policies in Europe, Australia, and North America;

(8) the rise in income inequality and social polarization.

The book provides a theoretical and empirical analysis of these game-changing events, evaluates their role in Israel's remarkable development, and compares these developments to groups of developed and emerging market economies in similar circumstances. To gain broader perspective, the book also looks back into Israel's recent history. Governed by a populistic regime in the 1980s, Israel's economy moved quickly to messy hyperinflation. As with economic populism elsewhere (this brings to mind Latin America's populism) the surging government spending and mandated wage hikes produced a temporary "sugar high," to be followed by a crash. Because they are unsustainable, populist policies cause people to shift spending from uncertain future to the present, when the economy is temporarily booming. Beneath the surface, however, the country's economic potential is deteriorating, financial disorders appear, and its financial institutions crash. It was a remarkable political economy episode when the hyperinflation was beaten down and regulatory institutions emerged. Indeed, it took Israel two to three decades to put its policy-making institutions in order.

Israel's fast development came, however, at the cost of rising income inequality and social polarization—fertile grounds for political upheaval. Israel now has the most unequal distribution of income among OECD countries, and its public education has declined from one of the best to one of the worst in the OECD. Israel's income redistributive policies from rich to poor, from healthy to sick, and from young to old currently are significantly less comprehensive in scope, compared to the European systems. The situation has been worsening over the last decades. Israel has an unusually high fertility rate among the developed economies. The problem is that the exceptionally high fertility among ultra-Orthodox Jews and the Arab minority is the main reason for Israel's flagging labor-force participation. In addition, high fertility diminishes Israel's skill attainment of the labor force. Growing income inequality in all advanced economies, which in the last two decades has also taken a sharp upward turn in Israel, has a potential for setting off social divide and political polarization.

The book ventures to marry macroeconomic theory with empirical evidence. It does so in a way that could be enlightening to the specialist and at the same time digestible for the nonprofessional reader. There could be at least three potential groups of readers: a) policy makers, academic and nonacademic researchers (from international institutions, banks, etc.) and students interested in the Israeli economy; b) students taking advanced undergraduate courses in International Economics and in Development Economics; and c) policy makers and academic and nonacademic researches interested in the effects of globalization.

On a personal note, I feel that with this book I am closing a circle. My first official involvement with economic policy in Israel was in 1979. I had then a short stint in the Israeli government, witnessing firsthand the emergence of the hyperinflation crisis. Subsequently, I have been consulting for various government bodies and commissions, occasionally making media and press commentaries, and I have been monitoring events up close. Following the exodus of Jews from the collapsing Soviet Union, and the first Palestinian intifada, two game-changing events, I wrote *The Modern Economy of Israel: Malaise and Promise* with Efraim Sadka (University of Chicago Press, 1993). Twenty-five years later, with the benefit of hindsight, I return to the same old subject of inquiry: reviewing past and present, and where Israel is heading going forward.

I have benefitted from generous cooperation with, and feedback from, several colleagues: Chapter 3 draws heavily on a joint work with Efraim Sadka. Chapters 1 and 5 draw partly on a joint work with Steve Rosefielde. Chapter 10 partly draws on a joint work with Jackie Wahba. Insightful conversations and email correspondences with Guillermo Calvo, Alex Cukierman, Paul de Grauwe, Jeff Frieden, Reuven Gronau, Moshe Hazan, Elhanan Helpman, Leo Leiderman, and Ronny Razin are gratefully acknowledged. Helpful comments and suggestions from three anonymous reviewers, skillful research assistantship provided by Tslil Aloni, and research funding from the Sapir Center at Tel Aviv University Eyal Ben-David, and the Falk Institution at the Hebrew University are all thankfully accepted.

Assaf Razin
Eitan Berglas School of Economics
Tel Aviv University
December 2017

Wise Words

The study of economics does not seem to require any specialized gifts of an unusually high order. Is it not, intellectually regarded, a very easy subject compared with the higher branches of philosophy or pure science? An easy subject at which few excel! The paradox finds its explanation, perhaps, in that the master-economist must possess a rare combination of gifts. He must be mathematician, historian, political leader, philosopher—in some degree. He must understand symbols and speak in words. He must contemplate the particular in terms of the general and touch abstract and concrete in the same flight of thought. He must study the present in the light of the past for the purposes of the future. No part of man's nature or his institutions must lie entirely outside his regard. He must be purposeful and disinterested in a simultaneous mood; as aloof and incorruptible as an artist, yet sometimes as near to earth as a politician.

Keynes (1924, 321–322)

Prologue

Israel has had a remarkable development, emerging from a low-income, high-inflation developing economy in the 1970s to a medium- to high-income advanced economy in the 2000s, while being increasingly integrated into the world economy in trade, in supply chains, and through financial links. At the same time, the global economy has been buffeted by several unprecedented economic events during the past four decades. I attempt to provide a rigorous analysis of the impact of these events on Israel's development, institutions, and economic policies.

Globalization is currently facing some challenging political tests, more than in the past decades. Migration is the core of the emerging economic nationalism. Jeff Sachs (2017) puts it succinctly when he says, "If people were told that they could move, no questions asked, probably a billion would shift around the planet within five years, with many coming to Europe and the US. No society would tolerate even a fraction of that flow. Any politician who says, 'let's be generous,' without saying 'we're not going to let the doors stand wide open' will lose." Rational and generous policy that also resonates politically will not eliminate national borders altogether. Rather, it will elicit calls for limits on the flow of migrants. The core of the wall-building coalition in the United States consists of white males with low educational attainment. Low-income citizens were also far more likely to support Brexit in the United Kingdom. The call for a "points-based" immigration system from the Brexit campaign was an explicit call to increase the skill composition of UK immigrants. Israel's Law of Return not only enables free immigration but also grants returnees immediate citizenship. For a researcher, it is like a laboratory experiment of how free migration can function without noneconomic forces and anti-migration rules.

Brexit may have been a leading indicator of anti-globalization and rising economic nationalism. Continental Europe has not followed through, so far. There is still the looming problem of settling the Middle East refugees in the EU. The political backlash against trade treaties in the United States has put off multilateral trade agreements such as the Transatlantic Trade and Investment Partnership (a United States–EU trade deal), the Trans-Pacific Partnership (a United States–Asia trade deal), and more. The open-border model, which governed the global economy for more than seventy years, is under threat. However, the acceleration of finance, technology, and telecommunication and global supply chains makes the reversal from globalization self-defeating. Against this background, it is desirable to bring to the fore how Israel has been able to advance the political-economy process of globalization, notwithstanding domestic and external crises.

Israel's globalization story provides a counterexample to the current trends.[1] Several unprecedented economic episodes have buffeted the global economy during the past few decades. These episodes have had transforming effects on Israel's economy: the collapse of the Soviet Union, and the massive wave of high-skill immigration to Israel that followed; the Great Moderation in inflation and decreased employment fluctuations in the advanced economies, which helped open emerging economies converge to the world inflation rates; the 2008 global financial crisis, whose epicenter was in the United States but which spread violently to Europe; the rise of the Asian markets as export targets and as new origins for outward foreign direct investment; and the global information technology surge and its spillovers, reinforced by foreign direct investment. Brain drain of top talents has also been encouraged, enabled by the pro-skill immigration rules in advanced countries on the demand side and facilitated by Israel's highly advanced higher education system on the supply side.

The Great Moderation in advanced economies occurred from 1985 to 2007, during the low-inflation era when the Federal Reserve and other advanced economies' central banks provided a broadly stable macroeconomic environment to facilitate rational private-sector choice. Israel avidly globalized during this period, and its inflation decelerated from three-digit rates in the 1980s to the low single-digit range as its financial sector became more and more globally integrated.

Curbing inflation has been a struggle for Israel for many years, since the very beginning of the state. After several failed efforts to stop the eight-year-long hyperinflation, Israel's national-unity government implemented a successful stabilization program. Still, the inflation rate stuck persistently to the low two-digit levels until spillovers from the Great Moderation in advanced economies put entrenched inflation off. Israel climbed down from three-digit rates to two-digit rates, and the inflation rate later converged to the advanced countries' rate.

The 2008 global depression crisis came to the world as a surprising outcome. Pre-2008 macroeconomic models did not adequately capture the features of real-world business cycles: small recessions that occur in the interval between deep and long depression-recessions. All this was because traditional macroeconomic models ignored the role of financial intermediaries. These financial institutions were treated simply like a neutral conduit between savers and investors, and not as a source of crisis by themselves. This deficiency may have been remedied, but uncertainties remain. These are crucial for comprehending the 2008 global financial crisis and its aftermath. Israel and the global economy may generally have difficulty coping with the Great Recession, the Eurozone crisis, and perhaps secular stagnation in some of the advanced economies, especially in Europe.

Migration has become a huge political-economic issue. There are several problems with the argument that immigrants are an unmitigated economic boon. One is that almost any major economic event like a large-scale immigration has far-reaching distributional effects, very much like a big cut in trade barriers.[2] Another is the fiscal burden arising from low-skill immigrants. In contrast, high-skill immigration brings with it fiscal gains, especially for an aging society. In general, immigration enriches the workforce, allowing for a more finely graded specialization, which raises average productivity and living standards. Diverse workforces are likely to be more productive, especially in industries in which success depends on specific knowledge, such as computing, health care, or finance. Indeed, Israel's migration episode came with a rise in labor productivity coupled with a rise in income inequality. Absorption of immigrants in Israel is strikingly different from the European experience. It is more similar to the experiences in Australia, Canada, and the United States.

The exodus of Soviet Jews to Israel in the 1990s also had an impact on income inequality and the political balance of power. I describe the extraordinary experience of Israel, which received three-quarter of a million migrants from the former Soviet Union (FSU) within a short time. This wave was distinctive for its large skilled cohort, which raised disposable income inequality, but no rise in market income inequality. That is, the welfare state took a sharp regressive turn. Part

I of the book analyzes these events. The unique experience of Israel is markedly different from recent immigration experiences in the United States and Europe, where anti-globalization forces reign supreme. Today's western societies are sharply divided, be it 51:49 or 49:51—a reflection of deep social divisions that are accentuated by large-scale migration flows.

To highlight Israel's top-quality performance, the book considers parallel globalization episodes of other success stories. Ireland entered the 1950s as a very poor postcolonial society. However, it realized major successes by its integration into the EU and it reached an elite hi-tech status. Ireland was able to attract from the rest of the world (other than the EU) massive Foreign Direct Investment (FDI), thanks to being a tax-sheltered gate to the EU massive markets. The emerging market economies, China, Vietnam, India, and Indonesia, abandoned autarky in favor of export-led growth in the mid-1980s. Suddenly, and with little warning, more than a third of the world's population joined the postwar globalization parade, powerfully effecting global demand everywhere, including Israel. Israel has significantly pivoted its trade to the emerging East Asia markets.

Dovetailing with immigration in the 1990s and the global information-technology surge was the unprecedented growth of Israel's high-tech sector. Innovation requires scale, and scale requires trade. An isolated small economy cannot be a center of innovation. The incentives of entrepreneurs to invest effort and resources in generating valuable services are related to the ability to use the resulting knowledge repeatedly, on a large scale, over time. Foreign direct investment provides critical incentives to be able to use scale economies, so as to leap from the precarious innovation stage at the confines of a small economy to the execution stage, by utilizing the world markets. The globalization of an economy is crucial for its nascent high-tech industry to develop, and flourish. The book then turns to investigate the implications of the global information and communication technology (ICT) surge on the nascent high-tech industry in Israel, and on economy-wide productivity growth. While the long-term benefits of the ICT technological surge are palpable, in the short run, the simultaneous wave of financial liberalization contributed heavily to the surge in development and global economic growth from 1985 to 2008. However, the deregulation turned out to be a two-way street. It spurred entrepreneurship, investment, and technological progress, and the global technology surge spread into Israel's nascent high-tech industry. However, the surge also created a fertile environment for asset speculation and leveraging, with dire consequences when the dot-com crisis erupted.

The book surveys major flaws in the socioeconomic fabric. It addresses Israel's brain drain of top professional talents. Brain drain is evidently the flipside of intensive globalization interactions and skill-biased immigration rules in advanced economies. Talent outflow is reinforced by the top level of Israel's academic institutions, and entrepreneurship increases the supply of skilled workers that is also channeled, partly, into the state-of-the-art, high-tech industry. Advanced science and technology institutions that are off the global centers suffer from resource squeeze, as they bring to the world a growing supply of Israeli scientists who seek and find their opportunities elsewhere. The book goes on to compare these developments to representative emerging market economies and illuminates similarities and differences among the various experiences.

Fast technological developments and globalization come in the case of Israel at the cost of a rising income inequality. Israel's welfare redistributive policies have deteriorated.

Sizeable communities exist with high fertility rates. Indeed, international ranking of Israel's economy in terms of the population growth rates puts Israel at the very top among advanced economies. The high fertility rate among the Jewish ultra-Orthodox and the Israeli Arabs, and the lack of proper investment in children in the periphery to prepare them for the labor market, raises the dependency ratio, undermines the skill level of the labor force, and raises the fiscal burden of Israel as a welfare state. Even though the skill attainment of the labor force is currently high, the demographic trends, if not reversed, could severely lower future GDP growth and weaken Israel's international competitiveness.

This book highlights the role played by globalization in mitigating, not eliminating, the cyclical effects of the Palestinian uprising and points to its uncertain future consequences. However, the inconvenient circumstances of the Israeli-Palestinian conflict boil down to its uncertain long-term implications. The almost intractable conflict comes together with combustible internal conflicts. The concern is about international political-economic isolation and explosive internal conflicts that tear the social and economic fabric.

In other words, the unresolved Palestinian-Israeli conflict poses serious long-term challenges for Israel's economic place in the world because of the danger of international political-economic isolation and internal conflicts. There is also uncertainty about the possibility of cuts in trade and financial links for an economy that is currently integrated into the world financial and trade networks.

The common theme of the book is the power of globalization. Once well-regulated institutional setup and time-consistent macroeconomic policy are put in place, the economy is capable of riding on top of globalization flows and weathering outside storms. The book provides a rigorous analysis of the powerful role globalization has played in the remarkable development of the Israeli economy.

I   Historical Background

Israel's nascent market-economy–based regime has been the dominant rule, with strong protection of human and civil rights, free media, and freedom of speech. It set Israel apart from most of the new nation states which gained their independence after World War II. It enabled the development of a powerful civic society, transparency in the government, and competition in the private sector. That is, from the start Israel built institutions to protect democratic ways of life, as common in western democracies, to reinforce its developing market economy. Its courts enforce contracts and property rights in ways that are largely independent of who is before them. Taxes are calculable on the basis of an arithmetic algorithm, not on person-to-person deals. Companies and governments buy from the cheapest bidder. An evolving regulation system follows previously promulgated rules. In the economic arena, the state's monopoly on the use of force is used to enforce contracts and laws and to secure property rights. This model of capitalism has hardly been a norm among developing and emerging market economies. Larry Summers (2016) observes that in the developing world many market economies operate what might be called ad hoc or deals-based capitalism: "Economic actors assume that they have to protect their property and do their own contract enforcement. Tax collectors use discretion in assessing taxes. Companies and governments buy from their friends rather than seek low-cost bids. Regulators abuse their power. The state's monopoly on the use of force is used to enrich and satisfy the desires of those who control the apparatus of the state." Israel, in contrast, is a remarkable example of rule-based capitalism.

This introductory part of the book comprises two defining episodes in Israel's economic history: first, the populistic-government–triggered 1980s hyperinflation and its remarkable conquest by a national unity government; second, the unique immigration experience. Israel's "Law of Return" is a unique example of free migration among almost all other economies which typically adopt immigration quotas.

1 Swell and Retreat of High Inflation

Inflation accelerated in the 1970s, rising steadily from 13 percent in 1971 to 111 percent in 1979.[1] Some of this higher inflation was "imported" from the world economy, instigated by extreme oil price rises in 1973 and 1979. Inflation kept gathering pace. From 133 percent in 1980, it leaped to 191 percent in 1983 and then to 445 percent in 1984, threatening to become a four-digit figure within a year or two. After several failed efforts, the successful phase of the stabilization of the Israeli economy began with the heterodox program introduced in July 1985. The initial success of the stabilization program included a decrease in inflation, from 445 percent in 1984 to 185 percent in 1985 and 20 percent in 1986. There was also an increase in real economic activity, with the annual growth in business-sector product per capita rising from 0.4 percent in 1984 to 4.3 percent in 1985 and 3.6 percent in 1986. But, in the second half of 1987, the economy slid into recession, an aftershock event. However, inflation did not converge to advanced countries' inflation.[2]

Israel's hyperinflation crisis is visible in figure 1.1. Following the 1977 political-economic regime switch, inflation spiked (that is, the inflation rate acceded the 50 percent per year) and was stopped only by the 1985 inflation stabilization program.

Figure 1.2 describes the price level and the exchange rate paths for the inflation-rising period in the wake of the hyperinflation crisis, and the aftermath of the 1985 stabilization program.

The figure demonstrates the accelerated path of inflation and the lagging path of exchange-rate depreciations in the 1980s. It highlights the sharp flattening of inflation that took place immediately after the implementation of the 1985 stabilization-policy package. All along, the exchange-rate–managed depreciations fell short of inflation; therefore, the real exchange has been markedly appreciated throughout the

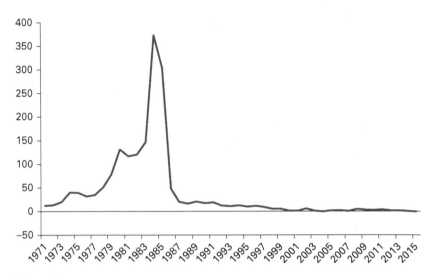

Figure 1.1
Annual inflation rate, 1970–2015 (percentage).
Note: CPI inflation. *Source*: OECD Stats.

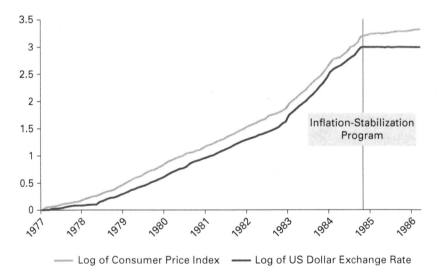

Inflation-Stabilization
Program

——— Log of Consumer Price Index   ——— Log of US Dollar Exchange Rate

Figure 1.2
Price level and exchange rate, 1977–1986. *Source*: Bank of Israel.

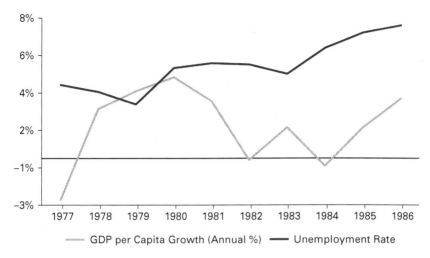

Figure 1.3
Output growth and unemployment, 1977–1986. *Source*: Israel CBS, World Bank.

period. The real-exchange-rate appreciation naturally corresponds also to the rise in unemployment, and to output growth decline. Real exchange rate (RER) misalignment refers to a situation in which a country's actual RER deviates from the RER that would prevail in the absence of price rigidities. Using an international panel data set (which includes observations from Israel), Razin and Collins (1999) find that real-exchange-rate overvaluation, like the one that Israel experienced during the entire period of hyperinflation, significantly stifles demand-triggered output growth.

Figure 1.3 describes the path of major output and employment indicators. The figure shows severe slackness in economic activity during the hyperinflation crisis, leading to unprecedented unemployment.

Economic activity was impacted severely by the swelling credit frictions because the inflation crisis undermined the functioning of credit institutions. Banks and financial market regulation also failed during the 1980s. At the time, bank stocks accounted for more than 90 percent of all issued stocks in the stock market. Their monopoly power in the stock market allowed the large banks to build up low-cost loan portfolios and give them out to borrowers, with poor selection and poor monitoring. Central bank oversight of commercial banks was almost nonexistent. Israel's Securities and Exchange Commission was powerless, legally and administratively. Massive stock issues allowed banks to increase their available capital as a source of investments, loans, and so on. To get market participants to continue investing in the large bank's stock, the government began buying back its own stock. On October 6, 1983, known as the "Black Thursday," an onslaught of banks' stock sales brought down the stock market. The largest banks became state owned through a swift bailout.

1.1 Political Inflection Point and Economic-Regime Switch

The economic crisis started to develop when the opposition party, Gahal (now Likkud), gained power for the first time since independence. The political upheaval in 1977, the so-called *Maapach*, was a game changer for economic policy in Israel. The newly elected government abruptly switched away from a long-running economic regime, which had been able to maintain fiscal discipline in the presence of strong external shocks (the Yom Kippur War and the first oil crisis). Monetary policy was moderately accommodative, underpinned by a fixed exchange rate regime and shielded from capital flights by capital controls. Notwithstanding the oil price shock, inflation was in the low double digits.[3]

A useful way to understand the framework within which the economic policy was conducted prior to the political regime switch, and afterward, is to think about the basic trilemma in international finance.[4] In international finance, the trilemma stems from the fact that, in almost every country, economic policy makers would like to achieve the following goals: First, make the country's economy open to international capital flows, because by doing so the policy makers of a country enable foreign investors to diversify their portfolios overseas and achieve risk sharing. The country also benefits from the expertise brought by foreign investors. Second, use monetary policy as a tool to help stabilize inflation, output, and the financial sector in the economy. This is achieved as the central bank can increase the money supply, reduce interest rates when the economy is depressed, and reduce money growth, and raise interest rates when it is overheated. Moreover, the central bank can serve as a lender of last resort in case of financial panic. Third, maintain stability in the exchange rate. This is because a volatile exchange rate, at times driven by speculation, can be a source of broader financial volatility, which makes it harder for households and businesses to trade in the world economy and for investors to be able to plan.

The problem, however, is that a country can only achieve two of these three goals. In order to maintain a fixed exchange rate and capital mobility, the central bank loses its ability to control the interest rate or, equivalently, the monetary base—its policy instruments—as the interest rate is anchored to the world interest rate by the interest rate parity, and the monetary base is automatically adjusted. This is the case of individual members of the European Monetary Union. In order to keep control over the interest rate or, equivalently, the money supply, the central bank has to let the exchange rate float freely, as in the case of the United States. If the central bank wishes to maintain both exchange rate stability and control over the monetary policy, the only way to do it is by imposing capital controls, as in the case of China.

Following the 1977 political change in Israel, the economic regime switched from pegged exchange rate, capital controls, and fiscal discipline to loosely managed exchange rate, relaxed controls on outgoing capital flows, and fiscal laxness. Right from the beginning, the new government lifted some capital controls without putting safeguards in place; that is, no prudent financial and banking regulatory measures existed. Intensive shifts in demand and supply for foreign exchange followed almost instantly. Key to the steady increase in inflation, the new populistic government also embarked on an uncontrolled path of fiscal expansion accommodated by monetary expansion. Exchange rate and capital flow fluctuations called for Bank of Israel to intervene, occasionally at first, and significantly later, in the foreign exchange market on a day-to-day basis to smooth out these fluctuations. A massive wave of capital flight caused over a few years a fast depletion of the stock of international reserves, which weakened the ability of Bank of Israel to intervene in the foreign exchange market. The exchange rate was at a free fall. In the context of the open economy trilemma, this means that a fixed exchange rate regime and perfect capital mobility must erode the ability of the central bank to stabilize employment and price fluctuations.[5] Therefore, Israel lost control over inflation. Lax safeguards brought stock market crashes. The lesson learned from the first-generation currency crisis literature is that such inconsistent set of policies become quickly unsustainable and lead to massive speculative attacks on international reserves, followed by rounds of financial and stock market crashes.

1.2   Political Deadlock Ends

Following almost eight years of the hyperinflation economic chaos, the Israeli voters brought about some major political rebalancing toward the political center. The newly established Unity government (Likkud plus Avoda) successfully implemented key stabilization measures, all of which required political consensus.[6] A new legislation (Khok Hahesderim) allowed the government to exercise tighter control over its spending and taxation. A new law forbade the central bank to monetize the budget deficit (Khok Iee Hadpassa) and ended the accommodating monetary policy. A tri-party agreement between the government, the Federation of Labor (Histadrut), and the association of private-sector employers stabilized the wage-price dynamics and enabled a sharp one-shot nominal devaluation that ended in a competitiveness-boosting real devaluation.[7] The exchange rate depreciation had not passed through to wages and prices, in high likelihood because the entire macro regime has changed, as in the modern expectations-based macroeconomic setup. The comprehensive program involved a deep cut in the government's budget deficit and the imposition of a severe upper limit on the rate of growth of total bank credit. It involves a one-shot rise in the prices of goods that were controlled by subsidies before the program.[8] Wage indexation was suspended temporarily. The fiscal measures helped cut the budget deficit from 12 percent of GDP in 1984 to 5.7 percent in the second half of 1985 to 2.6 percent in 1986.

Because of the credibility of the policy measures, backed by the tri-party agreement, and the greater independence of the central bank, inflation expectations adjusted rapidly to the policy steps.[9]

1.3   Inflation and Fiscal Revenues

Israel's high-inflation calamity amounted to a crisis of political and economic institutions. Failing economic governance made it essential for the government to raise revenue through money expansion. At the time when the newly elected government was catering to populistic demands, the printing press was used to finance the fast-expanding government spending and transfers.

In an essay published in 1969, Milton Friedman described what he believed to be a surefire mechanism that central banks could use, and populist government actually used, to generate inflation: "Drop currency straight from helicopters onto the population. If you keep doing this on a large scale the result would be hyperinflation." In accounting terms, helicopter money is a multistage process that we can imagine starting with the central bank crediting the Treasury's account. This means that the Treasury issues a bond to the central bank in exchange for an increase in their account balance. The next step in this description of helicopter money is that the Treasury distributes the money to individuals and firms. Therefore, helicopter money is *not* only monetary policy. It is a fiscal policy carried out with the cooperation of the central bank (see Cecchetti and Schoenholtz 2016).

Dividends from seigniorage (the profit made by a government by issuing currency) are derived from the exclusive ability of the central bank to issue bank notes. In addition, central banks can hold required reserves from commercial bank deposits, which pay no interest. Central banks can also inflate the non-indexed portion of the public debt and raise the real revenue intake with progressive tax schedule. But, how much can the central bank lower the consolidated-government fiscal burden depends not just on how actual inflation is consistent with expected inflation.

The central lesson from the Friedman (1971) is that steady-state seigniorage from a revenue-maximizing central bank is small.[10] But Israel, as well as previous historical episodes, offers a counter example. Indeed, Edi Karni (1983), made rough calculations and found significant seigniorage revenue generated by Israel's hyperinflation. In a related context, Cukierman (1998a) brings evidence for a significant share of revenue attributable to seigniorage in the 1920s' German hyperinflation, where the monotonous increase in inflation as well as in the rate of high-powered money growth continued throughout the entire hyperinflation period.[11]

Time inconsistencies on the part of the central bank in producing these spikes are due to harmful incentives. They lead policymakers to implement inflation levels that they may eventually come to regret. These incentives are no rarity; they are very common in economies that do not have the instruments to reach a first-best equilibrium. Moreover, these incentives cannot be ruled out, even under rational expectations in such a time-inconsistent setup. On this issue, Calvo (2016) writes:

Repeated use of surprise inflation is unlikely to be successful in increasing seigniorage, because the public will start to expect a rate of inflation larger than the one that optimizes steady-state revenue from inflation. Thus, eventually the economy may land on the excessive-inflation territory highlighted in Friedman (1971). However, this is not due to an elementary economics error on the side of the central bank, as Friedman's results might lead us to conclude. An inflation spike is, in the short run, one of the cheapest and most expeditious manners for securing additional fiscal revenue. Moreover, this "carrot" is always there. As noted, though, a problem arises if the government repeatedly reaches out for the carrot. However, even in this case, the evidence presented in Friedman (1971) does not prove that authorities were making an error. To assess that, one needs information of how quickly the public catches up with the inflation-spike strategy.

Even in the time-inconsistency paradigm,[12] however, there is room for policy. One could try to neutralize the harmful incentives if the central bank was banned from extending loans to the fiscal authority. This is why the 1985 Israel inflation stabilization package included the nonprinting item "Chok Iee Haadpasa," which prevented the Bank of Israel from purchasing government treasuries directly from the treasury.

What are the fiscal implications of deep-rooted inflation expectations, before hyperinflation is stopped?

To understand the economic mechanism, imagine a simple economy where there is a stock of public debt denominated in domestic currency, D.[13] We denote one-period nominal interest rate by i. Then, the next-period full service of the government debt (i.e., principal plus interest) will be $(1+i)D$. We choose the units of measurement so that the present price level is equal to one, and assume that the real interest rate is equal to zero. We also denote the one-period expected inflation rate, π^e, so that, inclusive of the inflation premium, the nominal gross interest rate is $i = 1 + \pi^e$, and the next-period price level is equal to $1 + \pi^e$. If the government surprises market participants by setting the actual inflation rate to zero, so that the actual bond-return gross return is equal to one, the actual real burden of servicing the next-period debt is equal to

$(1 + \pi^e)D$.

On the other hand, if the government fulfills the private sector–entrenched inflationary expectations and sets the actual inflation equal to expected inflation, the real burden of the debt is just D.

Thus, the temptation to *not* stop inflation in its tracks may be irresistible.

Similarly, if the government surprises market participants by abrupt stopping of hyperinflation in the presence of entrenched inflation expectations, the fiscal burden of a public sector wage bill and subsidies to basic food must rise. Therefore, the government may hesitate to do so.

To overcome this difficulty there must be a full-fledged social agreement between the government, savers (who hold government bonds), public sector wage earners, and recipients of food subsidies. To fix the inflated outlays on debt service, wage bill, and subsidies, some major redistribution of income must accompany the inflation-halting step. This is in essence the lesson from Israel's inflation stabilization policy.

The credibility of the stabilization program can be gauged by its effect on inflationary expectations. Sargent (1999) argues that high inflation can be stopped quickly, and at a low cost. His argument is that inflationary expectations are quick to adjust when the economic regime shifts considerably.[14] But, he ignores the fiscal burden and the income distribution that follow. Cukierman (1988b) reports that except for a brief period, when the public feared that the government will not be able to prevent the initial large one-shot (policy-induced) price shock from spreading, inflationary expectations started to decline sharply and steadily within months after the implementation of the 1985 stabilization policy. Six months later there was no significant difference between actual and expected inflation.

1.4   A Balance-of-Payments Crisis

Inflation crises are often intertwined with balance-of-payments crises. Budget deficits were the root cause of the balance-of-payments cum inflation crisis. The high-inflation period (1977–1985) coincided with a prolonged balance-of-payments crisis.[15] Large budget deficits make the inflation-employment trade-off acute, under the regime of pegged exchange rate and liberalized international capital flows; the pre-stabilization regime in Israel. In order to maintain a pegged exchange rate and liberalized capital mobility, the central bank lost its ability to control the interest rate. Both inflation and unemployment ensued. The stabilization package resulted in a regime switch; the government effectively shifted the regime from the first goal of the tri-lemma to the second goal, while being able to sharply reduce budget deficits.[16] Balance-of-payment crises occur when a country lifts restrictions on capital mobility (in Israel it begun in 1977) without the consolidation of its fiscal stance and regulatory institutions; especially those overseeing the financial intermediaries. If under these conditions the country is trying also to maintain a fixed exchange rate regime, it then unavoidably faces conflicting policy needs (such as fiscal imbalances, or a fragile financial sector) that need to be resolved by independent monetary policy.

1.5   Institutional Changes

Some of the macroeconomic institutional changes brought about by the inflation stabilization have lasted until these very days. The hyperinflation–cum–financial collapse episode has not reoccurred. Thanks to more disciplined monetary and fiscal policies, and well-regulated banks, the inflation rate converged to low rates, enjoyed by the advanced economies during the Great Moderation era.

In contrast, inflation stabilization programs adopted by other developing countries, especially in Latin America, proved not to have similar long-term durability. Argentina's stabilization program, relying on a rigid currency-board setup as its major pillar, was different. A lack of adequate budget discipline and, more important, inadequate bank regulations were some of the major weaknesses of the program. With a sovereign debt crisis and international capital flow reversal, all hell broke loose. The abruptly collapsed currency board and the run on the banks created a severe liquidity shortage. Sovereign debt default ensued. The world had cut Argentina from the international capital market. More than ten years later, prices are not stabile. The country was able only recently to have better access to the international capital markets. Chile's stabilization program, however, had long-lasting outcomes, similarly to the Israeli program.

In contrast to the crisis-management experience in Latin America, the Asian crisis has been a game-changing event that put the Asian Economies (particularly South Korea and Indonesia) on a durable growth track. To a large measure, the post-crisis restructuring of financial and monetary institutions enabled the entire region to escape the 2008 global crisis.

Appendix 1A: Balance-of-Payments Crises[17]

The gold standard and the 1944 Bretton Woods system (which established the International Monetary Fund [IMF] and the World Bank Group) created a world-wide fixed exchange rate system. Fixed and adjustable peg exchange rate mechanisms are no longer with us, as they were replaced in the early 1970s by flexible exchange rates. The branch of models, the so-called first-generation models of currency attacks, was motivated by a series of events where fixed exchange rate regimes collapsed after speculative attacks; for example, the early 1970s breakdown of the Bretton Woods global system. The proximate driving force:

the U.S. fiscal burden as a result of the Vietnam War. Israel's balance-of-payments crisis, driven by budget deficit, can also be understood by the first-generation crisis models.

Currency crises occur when a country is trying to maintain a fixed exchange rate regime with capital mobility but faces conflicting policy needs, such as fiscal imbalances or a fragile financial sector, that need to be resolved by independent monetary policy.[18] The Asian financial crisis that erupted in 1997 was a money-and-credit implosion induced by foreign capital flight. It began as a run on Asian banks by foreign short-term depositors and expanded into an assault on government foreign currency reserves, sending shock waves as far as the shores of Russia and of Argentina. Banks were decimated by acute insolvency. They did not have the cash on hand to cover mass withdrawals of short-term deposits because these funds had been lent long, sparking asset fire sales, slashed capitalizations, and credit and money contractions, which in turn triggered widespread business failures, depressions, and mass unemployment. The Asian economy, and later Russia and Argentina, witnessed the interplay between currency and banking crises, sometimes referred to as the *twin crises*, and balance-of-payments crises caused by currency mismatch in the balance sheet of the private sector. Similar crises include those in Mexico, Brazil, Argentina, and Chile in 1982; Sweden and Finland in 1991; Mexico again in 1995; Thailand, Malaysia, Indonesia, and Korea in 1997–1998; Argentina again in 2002; and the 2010–2013 episodes in Iceland, Ireland, Greece, Portugal, Spain, Italy, and Cyprus. The foundation for the crisis was laid by a massive inflow of foreign investment into the country. Massive portfolio capital inflows came to an abrupt stop with a sudden rush out and run on the banks. These financial crises exhibited a combination of the collapse of fixed exchange rate regimes, capital flows, financial institutions, and credit.

One basic mechanism, outlined in the new modeling of crises, is where unhedged foreign currency liabilities play the key role in causing and transmitting crises. One of the first models to capture this joint problem was presented in Krugman (1999). In his model, firms suffer from a currency mismatch between their assets and liabilities: their assets are denominated in domestic goods, and their liabilities are denominated in foreign goods. Then, real exchange rate depreciation increases the value of liabilities relative to assets, leading to deterioration in firms' balance sheets. Because of credit frictions, the deterioration in firms' balance sheets implies that they can borrow less and invest less. The novelty in Krugman (1999) is that the decrease in investment validates the depreciation in general equilibrium. This is because the decreased investment by foreigners in the domestic market implies that there will be a decrease in demand for local goods relative to foreign goods (the *transfer problem* in international trade), leading to real depreciation. Hence, the system has multiple equilibria with high economic activity, appreciated exchange rate, and strong balance sheets in one equilibrium, and low economic activity, depreciated exchange rate, and weak balance sheets in the other equilibrium.[19]

Chang and Velasco (2001) model the vicious circle between bank runs and speculative attacks on the currency. On the one hand, the expected collapse of the currency worsens banks' prospects, as they have foreign liabilities and domestic assets, and thus generates bank runs. On the other hand, the collapse of the banks leads to capital outflows that deplete the reserves of the government, encouraging speculative attacks against the currency. Accounting for the circular relationship between currency crises and banking crises complicates policy analysis. For example, a lender-of-last-resort policy or other expansionary policy during a banking crisis might backfire as it depletes the reserves available to the government, making a currency crisis more likely, which in turn might further hurt the banking sector that is exposed to a currency mismatch.

Israel's hyperinflation crisis in the early 1980s (see Chapter 1) had elements of currency crisis, credit crunch, and bank runs all in one mega crisis. The 2001 Argentina crisis had some similar elements.[20] An important aspect of financial crises is the involvement of the government and the potential collapse of arrangements it creates, such as an exchange rate regime. Many currency crises originate from the desire of governments to maintain a fixed exchange rate regime that is inconsistent with other policy goals. This might lead to the collapse of the regime. The literature on currency crises begins with the first-generation model, attempting to understand the basic mechanism underlying the early 1970s breakdown of the Bretton Woods global system. The literature continues with the second-generation model, attempting to understand the basic mechanism underlying the 1992 collapse of European exchange rate Mechanism Monetary, whereby the European exchange rates were to converge into a single currency. The third-generation models of currency crises connect models of banking crises and credit frictions with traditional models of currency crises. Such models were motivated by the East Asian crises of the late 1990s, where financial institutions and exchange rate regimes collapsed together, demonstrating the linkages between governments and financial institutions that can expose the system to further fragility.[21]

The first-generation models locate the causes of currency crises in unsustainable government policies driven by budget deficits. Consequently, pegged exchange rates are subject to a fatal attack by investors.[22]

The paper that started the vast literature of crises that are triggered by fiscal factors is Krugman (1979). He describes a government attempting to maintain a fixed exchange rate regime, but it is subject to a constant loss of reserves, due to the need to monetize persistent government budget deficits. These two features of the policy are inconsistent with each other and lead to an eventual attack on the international reserves of the central bank, which culminates in the collapse of the fixed exchange rate regime.

Flood and Garber (1984) extended and clarified the basic mechanism suggested by Krugman, generating the formulation of the lack of control by the monetary and fiscal authorities that undermines the fixed exchange rate system; the formulation has been widely used since then.

Let us provide a simple description of this model. Recall that the asset side of the central bank's balance sheet at time t is composed of domestic assets, $B_{H,t}$, and the domestic-currency value of foreign assets, $S_t B_{F,t}$, where S_t denotes the exchange rate (i.e., the value of foreign currency in terms of domestic currency). The total assets have to equal the total liabilities of the central bank, which are, by definition, the monetary base, denoted by M_t.

Because of fiscal imbalances, the central bank's domestic assets grow at a fixed and exogenous rate:

$$\frac{B_{H,t} - B_{H,t-1}}{B_{H,t-1}} = \mu.$$

Because of perfect capital mobility, the domestic interest rate is determined through the interest rate parity, as follows:

$$1 + i_t = (1 + i_t^*)\frac{S_{t+1}}{S_t},$$

where i_t denotes the domestic interest rate at time t, and i_t^* denotes the foreign interest rate at time t. Finally, the supply of money (i.e., the monetary base) has to be equal to the demand for money, which is denoted as $L(i_t)$, a decreasing function of the domestic interest rate.

The inconsistency between a fixed exchange rate regime, $S_t = S_{t+1} = \overline{S}$, with capital mobility and the fiscal imbalances is due to the fact that domestic assets of the central bank keep growing, but total central bank assets cannot change because the monetary base is pinned down by the demand for money from the public at large, $L(i_t^*)$, which is anchored by the foreign interest rate. Hence, the obligation of the central bank to keep financing the fiscal needs puts downward pressure on the domestic interest rate, which in turn puts upward pressure on the exchange rate. To prevent depreciation, the central bank has to intervene by reducing the inventory of foreign reserves. Overall, $\overline{S}B_{F,t}$ decreases by the same amount as $B_{H,t}$ increases, so the monetary base remains the same.

The problem is that this process cannot continue forever, as the reserves of foreign currency must have a lower bound. Eventually, the central bank will have to abandon the solution of the tri-lemma through a fixed exchange rate regime and perfect capital mobility for a solution of the tri-lemma through a flexible exchange rate, with stabilizing monetary policy (i.e., flexible monetary base or an equivalent domestic interest rate) and perfect capital mobility.

The question is as follows: What is the critical level of domestic assets $B_{H,T}$ and the corresponding period of time T at which the fixed exchange rate regime collapses? As pointed out by Flood and Garber (1984), this happens when the shadow exchange rate—defined as the flexible exchange rate under the assumption that the central bank's foreign reserves reached their lower bound while the central bank keeps increasing the domestic assets to accommodate the fiscal needs— is equal to the pegged exchange rate. This is depicted in figure 1A.1. Recall that the shadow exchange rate is the market-based exchange rate if the level of international reserves is set equal to zero at any point of time. The symbol $\overline{S}$ denotes the pegged exchange rate. The upper panel plots the shadow and actual exchange rates against the domestic assets. The bottom panel depicts the stock of international reserves also against domestic assets. Figure 1A.1 identifies the critical value, $B_{H,T}^*$, of the central bank's domestic assets that triggers abrupt depletion of foreign assets and the forced switch to a flexible exchange rate regime. At this critical value, international reserves deplete overnight by a successful speculative attack on the central bank's remaining stock.

While the first-generation model of currency crises focused on the government policies alone, later-generation analytical framework of currency crises essentially connects models of banking crises and credit

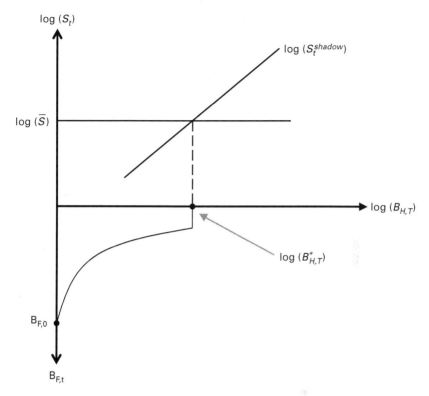

Figure 1A.1
International reserves and exchange rate: first-generation currency crisis. *Source*: Razin
(2015).

frictions with models of currency crises. Thus, they address the fragility
of financial institutions and the lack of regulation. Such models were
motivated by the East Asian crises of the late 1990s, where financial
institutions and exchange rate regimes collapsed together, demonstrating the linkages between governments and financial institutions that
can expose the system to further fragility. This is again relevant for the
current situation in Europe, as banks and governments are intertwined,
and the fragility of the system depends largely on the connections
between them.

2 Immigration Wave: Soviet Jew Exodus

Immigration has far-reaching economic and social consequences, including on the labor market, international trade, economic growth, the social and political structure, and so on (see, e.g., Lucas [2014] for a recent treatise), as has long been known. Between 1990 and 2012 almost twenty million people moved from Central, Eastern, and South-Eastern Europe to richer countries in Western Europe—about 8 percent of the population of Europe. This east–west migration accelerated after 2004 when eight Central European countries, including Poland, the Czech Republic, and Hungary, joined the EU.

More than a million migrants and refugees crossed into Europe in 2015 and 2016. Among the forces driving people to make the dangerous journey are the conflicts in Syria, Iraq, and Afghanistan. The vast majority—more than 80 percent—of those who reached Europe by boat in 2015 came from those three countries. Israel received almost one million immigrants, about 20 percent of Israel's population. In both episodes migration border restrictions were eased. In both the Israeli case and within the EU's borders the free movement of people is tied to the free movement of trade and capital. However, key differences between the two episodes, in addition to the relative size of the flow of migrants, are in the skill levels of the immigrants and the migrant-absorption policies that the receiving countries embraced.

The unique experience of Israel is vastly different for continuing the globalization historical effort, not only from the recent experience in Europe, but also from the U.S. experience. The core of the wall-building coalition in the United States is white males with low educational attainment. Low-income Brits were far more likely to support Brexit in the UK. The call for a points-based immigration system from the Brexit campaign was an explicit call to increase the skill composition of UK immigrants. How does one explain the recent anti-immigration sentiment by a simple argument based on first principles? Low-skilled immigrants compete for low-skill native jobs, and depress their wages. Furthermore, low-skilled immigrants are also more likely to be net beneficiaries from the typically generous welfare state, the burden of which low-skilled workers share. In contrast, high-skill immigrants may increase the productivity of the low-skilled population and are net fiscal contributors, which makes them a more attractive form of immigration. The low-skill segment of the destination-country established population. Therefore, net fiscal burden involves the discontent with immigration, and would push to tilt the composition of immigration toward high-skilled workers. Other groups are more likely to gain from low-skilled immigration. They increase the wages of high-skill workers and do not necessarily impose a fiscal burden on retirees, who no longer fund the welfare state. Therefore high-skill workers have supported the globalization course that advanced economies have taken, until the more recent wave of anti-immigration sentiment. In Israel, as we will see, the major political-economy effect of the 1990s–early 2000s migration wave is on income inequality through the downsizing of the welfare state. But, partly because of successful integration, no significant anti-migration sentiments emerged.

The exodus of Soviet Jews to Israel in the 1990s, especially its impacts on income inequality and the political balance of power, vivifies Lucas's findings.[1] Israel is already well known for the unique ways it absorbs immigrants, who in turn tend to arrive in waves triggered by external shocks. Each wave has its unique origin, distribution of skills, and often socioeconomic characteristics. Thus, the exodus of Soviet Jews in the 1990s adds useful insights into this ongoing experiment.

The importance of the Soviet Jewish exodus is perhaps best appreciated in historical perspective. Immigration to pre-state Palestine and to the state of Israel came in waves from the late nineteenth century onward.[2] During the pre-state era (prior to 1948), immigration was at times controlled by the British rulers.[3] However, immigration was free, and even encouraged, under the umbrella of the Law of Return. Table 2.1 suggests that immigration at times, especially in the nascent statehood and in the last wave from the former Soviet Union (FSU) constitutes about 20 percent of the established population.

The Soviet Jew immigration of the 1990s stands out from previous waves both because of its sheer volume and because of the economic motivation. The choice, albeit limited by immigration restrictions of the advanced countries in the West—Australia, Canada, Germany—was

Table 2.1
Immigration, 1922–2001

Period	Immigrants as a percentage of established population	Annual percentage growth rate of population
1922–1932	8.2	8.0
1932–1947	6.4	8.4
1947–1950	19.8	21.9
1950–1951	13.2	20.0
1951–1964	2.2	4.0
1964–1972	1.3	3.0
1972–1982	0.9	2.1
1982–1989	0.4	1.8
1989–2001	19.0	2.9

Source: Ben-Porath (1985) for the years 1922–1982; Central Bureau of Statistics (1992), Bank of Israel (1991) for the years 1982–2001.

between Israel and these countries, and the United States. In fact for a portion of would-be immigrants, Israel was a second choice.

2.1 The Origin

The disunion of the Soviet Union and the destruction of communism in the USSR in 1987–1991 triggered the recent wave of migration by Soviet Jews (figure 2.1) to various parts of the world, including Israel.

All the migrant destinations were controlled by the migration policies of the receiving countries, except Israel. Immigration into Israel is free by the Law of Return.

The primary driver of Jewish exodus from Russia between 1990 and 1996 was the Soviet Union's, and subsequently Russia's, economic collapse, often-dubbed *katastroika*. The Jewish community sensed the pain, anticipated the danger, and fled for this compelling reason, but also due to the twin threats of a military coup d'état and civil war. Both the demise of the Soviet Union and the following exodus in a macroeconomic jargon is a supply side shock, which triggers sizeable migration flows. The communist regime inaugurated a liberalization campaign in the political (*demokratizatsiya*), economic (perestroika), and social and international spheres (*novoe myshlenie*) that expanded the opportunities for many, including the Soviet Jews, to increase their welfare.[4] However, they were legally barred from leaving the country until the complete demise of the regime. The prospect of brighter tomorrows in

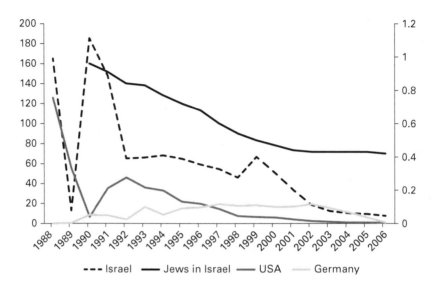

Figure 2.1
Emigration of Jews and their family members from the former USSR to Israel, the United
States, and Germany (left axis, thousands) and the fraction of Jews in Israel (right axis,
percent). *Source*: http://demoscope.ru/weekly/2012/0497/demoscope497.pdf.

more stable and advanced countries, reinforced by the mounting political, social, and economic turmoil that raised the risk of civil war, created
the specter of a military coup d'état, and threatened economic collapse.

The Soviet Union economy ceased growing in 1989 and then plum-
meted nearly 10 percent in 1990 as enterprise managers focused on
privatizing state assets to themselves (spontaneous privatization), liq-
uidating them, and transferring balances abroad instead of dedicating
them to current operations.[5] Interindustrial supplies, the backbone of
modern economies, were shattered because managers ignored their
contractual obligations to intermediate input users.

This was shock therapy in action without Sachs's conditionality.[6] In
theory, Soviet managers who had no experience designing and marketing products to satisfy consumer demand were expected to transform
themselves into efficient competitors under duress. However, they could
not do it. The reality was an economic depression that caused GDP to
fall between 37 and 50 percent between 1989 and 1998.[7] Full economic
recovery was not achieved until 2006.

The Soviet Union's crumbling sphere of influence in Central Europe
and East Germany, together with the successful secession of the Baltic

States, alerted the Russian Jewish community to the wisdom of carpe diem. A window of opportunity had opened, and Jewish émigrés of the 1990s chose to seize the day.

2.2 Migrant Characteristics

The professional, social, attitudinal, and behavioral characteristics of the 1990s Jewish exodus cohort proved to be distinctive. Immigrants came mostly from urban areas, with advanced education systems. Their skill (education) composition was heavily skewed toward high education levels, and they had relatively higher labor income (see table 2.2). Their share in the population was sizable—14.5 percent. Their average family size (2.32 standard persons) was lower than the national average (2.64 standard persons). This indicates fewer dependents. Most important was their higher education level and consequently their higher labor income. The average number of schooling years of the new immigrants was 14, compared to the national average of only 13.3.

Even more striking was the percentage of heads of households with bachelor's degrees: 41.1 percent among the new immigrants, compared to a national average of just 29.5 percent. The higher education level and the lower family size can presumably explain the income gap: the average labor income per standard person of the new immigrants was

Table 2.2
The Skill, Age, and Income of Immigrants from the FSU and the National Average, 1990–2011

	Immigrants from the FSU	National average (including immigrants)
Share of total population (%)	14.5	100
Household size (number of standard persons)	2.32	2.74
Schooling years of head of household (number)	14	13.3
Head of household with a bachelor's degree (%)	41.1	29.5
Gross monthly labor income per standard person (2011 NIS)	4,351	4,139

Source: Eilam (2014).

NIS 4,351, compared to a national average of only NIS 4,139. What is noteworthy is that this gap existed even though the new immigrants had lower work seniority than the established population. The educational achievement figures of the immigrants from the FSU are impressive compared to the EU-15. Relying on data from the International Organization for Migration (IOM) and the OECD, Razin and Sadka (2014) report that only 18 percent of the stock of immigrants in the EU-15 in 1990 and 24 percent in 2000 had tertiary education.

2.3 Catching Up

Cohen and Hsieh (2000) show that average effective wages of native Israelis fell and the return to capital increased during the height of the influx in 1990 and 1991. By 1997, however, both average wages and the return to capital had returned to pre-immigration levels due to an investment boom induced by the initial increase in the return to capital. As predicted by the standard intertemporal model of the current account,[8] the investment boom was largely financed by external borrowing. Furthermore, despite the high educational levels of the Russian immigrants, the Russian influx did not lower the skill premium of native Israelis. They explain this effect by the rise in total factor productivity during the 1990s, relative to stunningly low productivity increase through much of the 1970s and 1980s. Eckstein and Weiss (2004) developed a descriptive methodology for the analysis of wage growth of immigrants that is based on human capital theory. The sources of the wage growth are (1) the rise of the return to imported human capital, (2) the impact of accumulated experience in the host country, and (3) the mobility up the occupational ladder in the host country. Using data on established Israelis and immigrants from the former Soviet Union into Israel, they estimate Mincer-type wage equations jointly for the two groups. They find that in the ten years following arrival, wages of highly skilled immigrants grow at 8 percent a year. Rising return to skills, occupational transitions, accumulated experience in Israel, and an economy-wide rise in wages account for 3.4, 1.1, 1.5, and 1.5 percent each. They do not reject the hypothesis that the return for experience converges to that of natives and that immigrants receive a higher return for their unmeasured skills. We find that there is some downgrading in the occupational distribution of immigrants relative to that of the established work force.

2.4 Migration Waves and Growth: Bird's Eye View

One of the most distinctive features associated with the Aliyah waves (that is, immigration waves) is the high rates of economic growth.[9] See table 2.3.

Table 2.3 indicates that the Aliyah produced massive investments, both in residential structures and in nonresidential capital. These investments were so substantial that they increased the capital-to-labor ratio and facilitated economic growth, in some cases further aided by the remarkable human capital brought by the *olim* (immigrants to Israel). Except for the *olim* who came during the major wave of Aliyah immediately after the birth of the state of Israel, the education level of the *olim* generally exceeded that of the established population and thus contributed remarkably to overall productivity. It is also noteworthy that in general the massive investments in physical capital and infrastructures were financed by capital imports (reflected in persistent current account deficit), as the *olim* themselves fled their former homes almost penniless and credit constrained, so that they hardly saved. Table 2.3 shows, for instance, that during the years 1922–1931, when

Table 2.3
Aliyah and Growth, 1922–2015 (annual percentage growth rates)

Period	*Olim* as a percentage of established population	Population growth rate	Capital stock growth rate (excluding housing)	Housing stock growth rate	Per capita output growth rate (not cyclically adjusted)
1922–1931	9.5	8.0	—	—	7.8
1932–1946	15.6	8.4	—	—	3.0
1947–1949	37.7	21.9	—	—	—
1950–1951	26.1	20.0	—	—	10.0
1952–1963	19.4	4.0	12.8	11.6	4.9
1964–1971	8.3	3.0	8.7	7.7	5.5
1972–1982	7.6	2.1	6.1	7.7	0.8
1983–1989	2.7	1.8	3.1	4.0	3.1
1990–2001	16.5	3.0	7.0	4.7	2.5
2002–2007	1.9	1.8	2.4	2.5	1.9
2008–2015	1.8	2.0	3.4	3.2	1.3

Source: Ben-Porath (1985) for the years 1922–1982; Central Bureau of Statistics (2016) and Bank of Israel (2016).

the number of *olim* each year was about 9.5 percent of the established population, output increased at the whopping rate of about 16.4 percent per annum, so that output per capita increased by a remarkable 7.8 percent per annum. Similarly, during 1950–1951, when each year the *olim* amounted to about 26.1 percent of the established population, output increased by about 10 percent per annum. During the years 1952–1963, when the percentage of *olim* each year was about 19.4, output growth was steady, 4.9 percent per annum. In this period, capital stock growth rate was 12.8 percent and housing stock rose by 11.6 percent—a whopping investment boom. In contrast, during the years 1972–1982, when the percentage of *olim* each year was about 7.6, output per capita rose by the meager rate of 0.8 percent per annum (obviously, the oil price shock and the Yom Kippur War depressed output growth). In the later years, output growth was a declining trend; the percentage of *olim* each year was to 16.5, and output growth was meager 2.5 percent per annum.

Obviously, table 2.3 is only suggestive for the role played by immigration and the massive investment, which accompanied its big waves, in growing the economy. Evidently, the statistics in table 2.3 reflect the effects of business cycle fluctuations, external shocks, military conflicts, and the like, in addition to the migration waves.

3   Understanding Migration and Income Inequality

Today's Western societies are sharply divided—a reflection of deep social divisions that are accentuated by large-scale migration flows. This is not a fertile ground for populism, but rather nativism. Jeff Sachs (2017) put this succinctly when he said: "If people were told that they could move, no questions asked, probably a billion would shift around the planet within five years, with many coming to Europe and the US. No society would tolerate even a fraction of that flow. Any politician who says, 'let's be generous,' without saying—'we're not going to let the doors stand wide open' will lose." Rational and generous policy that also resonates politically will not eliminate national borders altogether. Rather, it will set calls for limits on flow of migrants. There are several problems with the argument that immigrants are an economic boon. One is that almost any major economic event like a large-scale immigration has far-reaching distributional effects, like a big cut in trade barriers.[1] The second is the short-term fiscal burden or the long-term fiscal gain, through the effects on age composition of the population, the skill composition of the labor force, and the progressivity of the fiscal tax-and-transfer system. Immigration enriches the workforce, allowing for a more finely graded specialization that raises average productivity and living standards. Diverse workforces are likely to be more productive, especially in industries where success depends on specific knowledge, such as computing, healthcare and finance. The migration episode in Israel came with a sharp rise in income inequality.[2]

   An intriguing research agenda has been the study of whether immigrants put downward pressure on wages, and thereby raise market-based income inequality. In theory they should, but empirical studies come to mixed conclusions. Borjas (2006) finds that although immigration did not depress overall wages between 1980 and 2000, it did hold down the pay of the low-skilled by 5–10 percent. However, Card (1990) finds that there was no significant effect. He is able to use the natural-experiment methodology for the unexpected surge in Cuban migrants to Miami in 1980.

Israel's experience with respect to the natural-experiment methodology is unique. The effects of the migration "shock" on the market-based inequality through wage gaps among different skill workers has not been rigorously looked at. The Soviet Jews exodus was not foreseen ahead of time. On a more impressionistic level, there is no sharp change in market-based inequality, at least as measured by the Gini coefficient. However, it is potentially explainable by forces that operate in many other immigration experiences. Countries receiving immigrants are typically welfare states, Israel included. Putting it differently, inequality in disposable income is significantly lower in a typical welfare state than in non-welfare-state market economies. Transfers and the taxes of a typical welfare state serve to reduce disposable income inequality.

3.1 Upward Intergenerational Mobility and Income Inequality

The second generation of Jews, whose parents immigrated from the FSU, experienced significantly higher upward mobility than all other ethnic groups. As documented by Aloni (2017), although the general association with parents' incomes within the FSU group is not very different compared to the population, their mobility relative to the national distribution is high, and the second generation finds its way even to the top percentiles. Table 3.1 shows the estimated probability of the second generation outranking the first generation in the full sample, and the groups' relative income rank convergence rates. Having higher probability to outrank their parents highly depends on the relative income position of the group in the population's income distribution; thus, for example, Ethiopian and Arab children exhibit high upward mobility. But, controlling for their initial position, FSU immigrants to Israel experienced the highest pace of upward mobility, while other groups converged to the mean slower.

Upward mobility is also indicated in figure 3.1. The figure shows the distribution of children of parents from the bottom decile. Comparing the FSU immigrants and the general population, the former experienced a greater upward mobility, with children reaching higher earning ranks, dispersing more evenly across the deciles.

Table 3.1
Intergenerational Mobility Indicators by Israeli Ethnic Groups

	Israel	Asia / N. Africa	Euro. / America	FSU	Ethiopia	Arab
Probability of outranking parents	40%	49%	37%	58%	75%	59%
Rank shift pace, controlling	−0.22	−0.02	—	2.69***	−4.58***	−6.92***
for initial family position	(0.17)	(0.15)	—	(0.16)	(0.49)	(0.16)

Notes: First row is the probability of the child reaching higher percentile in children's generation distribution compared to parents' average percentile in their income distribution. Second row is the regression results of child-rank on the population groups' dummies, controlling for parents' income rank using 100 percentile dummies. Base group is of families with Asian/North African origins. The sample is of children born between 1979 and 1982, matched to parents using administrative data.
Standard errors in parentheses; upper asterisks indicate ***$p < 0.01$, **$p < 0.05$, *$p < 0.1$.
Source: Aloni (2017).

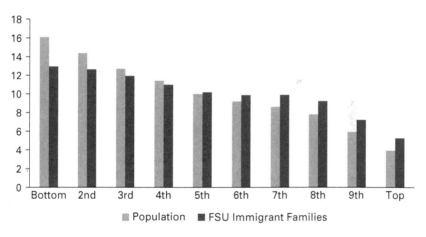

Figure 3.1
Earning deciles of children born to the bottom-decile parents. *Source*: Aloni (2017).

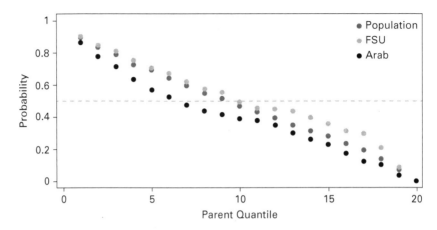

Figure 3.2
Probability of outranking parents by 5 percentiles by parents' quantiles.
Note: Each point represents the proportion to have a children's rank higher than parents'
by at least 5 percentiles, binned on parents' quantile. Population excludes FSU and Arab
population. The difference between FSU and Arab groups is significant in a 95 percent
significance level throughout. *Source*: Aloni (2017).

Figure 3.2 shows the probability of outranking parents by 5 percentiles, as a function of parents' rank. Comparing these two groups to the general population suggests an increasing polarization.

These documented facts that the FSU group has higher upward mobility, along with the fact that the Israeli-Arab group experienced slower upward mobility, may increase inequality. This is because the FSU first generation immigrants' income is high compared to the population, while Israeli-Arab families have a lower income mean. Israel's fast development, facilitated by the integration into the world economy, and the inflow of high-skill immigrants, came at a cost of growing income inequality, measured both by market-based and redistribution-based Gini coefficients. Currently, Israel, the United States, and the UK are at the top of market-forces–generated inequality; and they do less than other OECD countries to reduce the inequality through the redistribution of income.[3] See figure 3.3.

To gauge the size of income redistribution one can subtract the market-based Gini coefficient from the disposable income Gini coefficient. Israel's relatively high market-based inequality coefficient, shown in figure 3.3, is driven by the large, and increasing, share of two relatively poor minority groups in the population: ultra-orthodox Israeli Jews (primarily males), and the Israeli Arabs (primarily females),[4] stay out

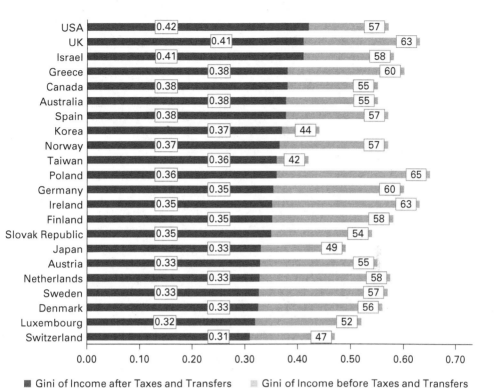

Figure 3.3
Income inequality and redistribution. *Source*: Gornick and Jäntti (2014).

of the labor force. The rise in the share of these groups in the total population is because the fertility rates among these minorities are much higher than the other groups in the population.[5] In addition, the emergence of highly educated, economically active large group of Israelis, reinforced by the high-skill immigration of Soviet Jews, made the upper tail of the distribution thicker. Israel is not an outlier in the OECD countries with respect to the market-driven (pre-tax and transfer) income inequality. However, figure 3.4 indicates the time dimension of inequality. Disposable-income inequality in Israel was roughly stable until the beginning of the 1990s and rose sharply thereafter, even though no such change occurred with respect to the market-generated inequality. Israel's level of redistribution of income falls short of many other OECD countries. A partial resolution of the issue, proposed by Razin, Sadka, and Swagel (2002), hinges on the political-economy effects

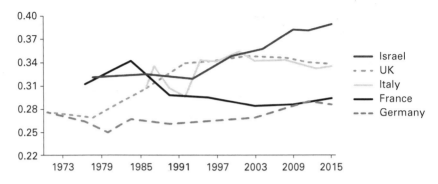

Figure 3.4
Disposable income inequality* in Israel and several EU-15 countries, 1973–2013.
*Gini coefficient. *Source*: Ben-David (2015).

of a rise in the dependency ratio. On the one hand, a higher dependency ratio means a larger pro-tax coalition, as the low income groups
are net beneficiaries of the transfers from those who actively participate
in the labor market. On the other hand, a higher dependency ratio puts
a higher tax burden on the people around the median voter, as it is
necessary to finance transfers to a larger share of the population. People
for whom the costs of higher taxes outweigh benefits shift to the anti-
tax coalition. Hence, the second factor dominates in many other rich
countries. That is, the political-economy equilibrium-tax rate declines
when the dependency ratio rises. This would be the case until society
ages enough so that the median voter is retired, at which point there
is a discontinuous jump in the tax rate and a corresponding increase
in the share of transfers. In other words, the increased share of the fiscal
net beneficiaries in the population may have two opposing effects on
redistribution policies. On the one hand, the political influence gained
by low-income groups is persistently on the rise. This means that
the median voter preferences shift over time in the direction of a more
generous welfare state.[6] On the other hand, if the median voter,
plausibly, does not belong to the low-skill and nonworking groups (as
is probably also the case in Israel), then the increased share of the
nonworking and the low skilled in the population may well lead policy
makers to lower taxes and transfers, because the increased fiscal burden
that results for the large share of "net beneficiaries" adversely affect
the median voter (who is a net contributor to the welfare system). The
later effect dominates in Israel. Consequently, the entire redistribution
system contracts.

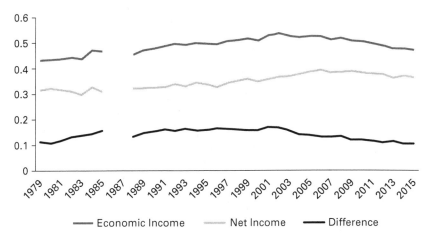

Figure 3.5
Total income, net income inequality and redistribution, 1979–2015*. *Notes*: The difference between total and net-income coefficients.
The years 1999–2002 do not include East Jerusalem population. The years 2012–2015 do not include the Bedouin population. *Source*: Dahan (2017).

Figure 3.5 demonstrates a strong rise in income inequality between 1990 and 2003. It is a combination of declining market inequality offset by a marked decline in redistribution. The implied more-than-a-decade-long fall in income redistribution follows the Soviet Jew immigration wave.

For the unique position of Israel as a welfare state among OECD countries, see figure 3.6, which highlights the low ranking of Israel in terms of its provision of social services per capita.[7] High defense expenditures may have crowded out social services more than in the other OECD countries. However, even though defense expenditures as a share of Israel GDP were following a distinct downward trend over the last thirty-five years, Israel diverges down in the provision of social expenditures, relative to the OECD countries. Figure 3.6 plots the social expenditure, per capita, for Israel against selected group of countries. Israel is at the bottom of the group.

3.2 Immigrants and the Political System

Immigrants may also shift the balance of politics among ethnic groups, economic classes, or age groups, or may generate a massive political backlash. In Israel the political backlash has been moderate, whereas the change in political balance was substantial. Israel's Law of Return

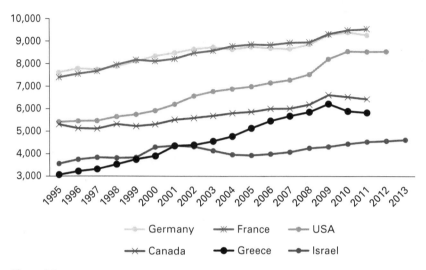

Figure 3.6
Social expenditures per capita, selected countries.
Note: Constant 2005 PPPs, in U.S. dollars. *Source*: OECD library.

grants returnees immediate citizenship and, consequently, voting rights. An early study by Avner (1975) found that the voting turnout rate of new immigrants had been markedly lower than that of the established population. This means that immigrants did not fully exercise their voting rights and did not therefore influence the political economy equilibrium in Israel as much as the established population.

A similar low voting turnout for migrants is reported also by Messina (2007) and Bird (2011) for Western Europe. However, a later study conducted by Arian and Shamir (2002) about voting turnout patterns of new immigrants to Israel in the 2001 elections reverses the earlier finding. The new immigrants in this study are predominantly from the FSU. Arian and Shamir find no marked difference in the voting turnout rates between these new immigrants and the established population. This is indeed a unique feature of the 1989–2001 immigration waves from the FSU. This is key to understanding the political-economy mechanism (see Razin, Sadka, and Swagel [2002b]).

Migration differs from the movement of other factor inputs (such as capital flows) in one fundamental way. Migrants become part of the society of the receiving country, including its evolving culture and politics. (The Swiss writer Max Frisch ironically declared: "We asked for workers. We got people instead.") A highly developed social welfare system in the receiving country may greatly complicate matters, as emphasized by Razin, Sadka, and Suwankiri (2011). While high-skilled and therefore high-wage migrants may be net contributors to the fiscal system, low-skilled migrants are likely to be net recipients, thereby imposing an indirect tax on the taxpayers of the destination country. Sooner or later, migrants may shift the balance of politics among ethnic groups, economic classes, or age groups, or may generate a massive political backlash. Migrants may change the nature of social interactions, with shifts in religion, ethnicity, and cultural practices.

3.3 Political-Economy Theory

To understand better the balance of the political-economic forces at play, one has to analyze them in a general-equilibrium setup. Razin, Sadka, and Swagel (2002b) compare the political equilibrium with and without voting by immigrants. Without immigrants' voting, unskilled (or skilled) immigrants raise (or lower) the fiscal burden, which reduces (or raises) redistribution. With Immigrants' voting, unskilled immigrants strengthen (or weaken) the pro-redistribution coalition, which rises (or reduces) redistribution.

Razin and Sadka (2016) provide such a stylized general equilibrium model with free migration, where wages are endogenous and redistribution policy is determined by (endogenously determined) majority voting.[8] They address the issue of how migration can reshape the political balance of power, especially between skilled and unskilled workers and between native-born citizens and migrants, and consequently the political-economic equilibrium redistribution policy of the welfare state. The general equilibrium model could provide insights as to how, in a "natural experiment" manner, an external supply-side shock triggers a wave of skilled migration. The shock then can change wages, migration flows, and political coalitions, so as to reshape the political-economy balance and the redistributive policies.

3.3.1 Human Capital Investment

There are just two types of workers: skilled (with a symbol S) and unskilled (with the symbol U). The wage per unit of labor of a skilled worker is w, whereas an unskilled worker earns a wage of ρw per unit of labor, where $\rho < 1$. All native-born citizens (N) are initially unskilled. However, a native-born citizen can acquire education at some cost (c) and becomes skilled. Individuals differ from one another through their cost of education: there is a continuum of native-born individuals, distinguished only by their cost of education. For notational simplicity, we normalize the number of native-born individuals to one. An individual is identified by her cost of education, so that an individual with a cost of c is termed a c-individual. We assume for simplicity that the cost of education is uniformly distributed over the interval $[o, \bar{c}]$.

All native-born individuals are endowed with E units of a composite good, the single good in this economy. All individual inelastically supply one unit of labor. If a c-individual acquires education and becomes skilled, their income[9] is (denoted by I_S^N)

$$I_S^N(c) = (1-t)w + b + (E-c)(1+r),$$

where t is a flat wage tax rate;[10] b is a uniform (lump-sum) per capita social benefit; and r is (the interest rate)—(the return to capital). If a c-individual decides not to acquire education and remain unskilled, their income (denoted by I_U^N) is

$$I_U^N = (1-t)\rho w + b + E(1+r). \tag{3.1}$$

(Note that $I_S^N(c)$ depends on c, whereas I_U^N does not.)

Thus, there is a cutoff level of cost, c^*, so that all c-individuals with $c \le c^*$ will choose to become skilled, and all the others (with $c \ge c^*$) will remain unskilled. This c^* is defined by

$$(1-t)\ w+b+(E-c^*)\ (1+r) = (1-t)\ \rho w + b + E(1+r).$$

Upon some rearrangement, the cutoff level of the cost of education, c^*, becomes

$$(1-t)(1-\rho)\ w = c^*(1+r).$$

That is, c^* is solved from the equality between the return to education and its cost. A c^*-individual is just indifferent between acquiring education (and thereby becoming skilled) or staying unskilled. Upon further rearrangement, c^* is defined by

$$c^* = \frac{(1-t)(1-\rho)w}{(1+r)}. \tag{3.2}$$

Note that c^* may well exceed E, which means that those c-individuals with c below but close to c^* (which is endogenous) actually *borrow* in order to acquire education. Naturally, the payoff in terms of the higher wage would more than offset the borrowing cost. For those individuals $E - c$ is negative.

Also, note that we are employing a static framework within which all economic and political processes occur simultaneously with no time dimension.[11] For instance, we do not distinguish between the time in which the education is acquired and the time when the earnings occur. Similarly, capital earns its return r at the same time it is employed.

The number of c-individuals with $c \leq c^*$ is the number of native-born skilled individuals. Denoting this number by n_S, it follows that

$$n_S = \frac{c^*}{\bar{c}}. \tag{3.3}$$

Then, the number of native-born unskilled individuals, n_U, is thus given by

$$n_U = 1 - n_S. \tag{3.4}$$

Aggregate investment in human capital (education), denoted by H, is then given by

$$H = \int_0^{c^*} c \cdot \frac{1}{\bar{c}} dc = \frac{(c^*)^2}{2\bar{c}}. \tag{3.5}$$

Therefore, the aggregate stock of physical capital, K, is equal to

$$K = E - H. \tag{3.6}$$

There are also two types of migrants: the skilled who can earn a wage w in the host country, and the unskilled who earn a wage of ρw in the host country. None of them has any initial endowment. The migrants come to the host country after they have already made and implemented the decision whether to acquire or not acquire education. Thus, it is exogenously given who is skilled and who is unskilled. In other words, the economy benefits from the skilled migrants because it does not have to pay for the cost of investment.

3.3.2 Income Groups
The income of skilled and unskilled migrants is, respectively,

$$I_S^M = (1 - t)w + b \tag{3.7}$$

and

$$I_U^M = (1 - t)\rho w + b. \tag{3.8}$$

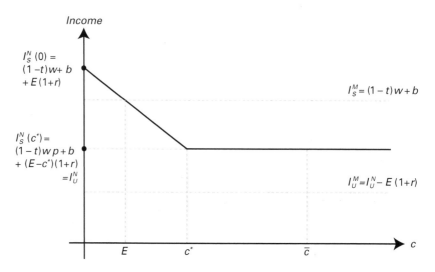

Figure 3.7
Income groups as function of cost of education.

The income of the native-born individual as a function of c is depicted in figure 3.4. Note that $I_S^N(c)$ declines in a straight line until it reaches c^*, where

$$I_S^N(c^*) = (1-t)w + b + (E-c^*)(1+r) = (1-t)\rho w + b + E(1+r) = I_U^N.$$

The labor income of the unskilled native-born individual and the unskilled migrants is the same, but the total income of an unskilled migrant, which is $(1-t)\rho w + b$, is definitely below the income of an unskilled native-born individual, the difference being the capital income enjoyed by the unskilled native-born individual, namely $E(1+r)$. The total income of a skilled migrant is definitely higher than the total income of the unskilled migrant, because of the higher wage earned by the skilled, whereas both have no other income. The income of the skilled migrant exceeds the income of the skilled native-born individual with $c > E$, but falls short of the income of the skilled native-born individual with $c < E$.

Figure 3.7 shows the income of a skilled migrant as $I_S^M = (1-t)w + b$, whereas the income of a skilled c-individual is $(1-t)w + b + (E-c)(1+r)$. Therefore, as long as $E-c$ is positive (i.e., the c-individual does not borrow in order to invest in human capital), then $I_S^N(c) > I_S^M$. However, if $E-c < 0$ (i.e., the individual borrows in order to invest in human capital), then the income of the skilled migrant $\left(I_S^M\right)$ is greater than the income of the skilled native-born individual $\left(I_S^N\right)$. In sum, we have the following ranking of incomes:

$$I_U^M < I_U^N = I_S^N (c = c^*) < I_S^N (c > E) < I_S^N (c = E) = I_S^M < I_S^N (c < E).$$

3.3.3 Supply of Immigrants

Recall that the country employs an unrestricted migration policy. We envisage an economy that allows any migrants to come. Thus, the decision whether to immigrate or no rests solely with the migrant. Each potential migrant has some reservation income, so that they will migrate if and only if they will be accorded a higher income in the destination country.

Due to various factors (such as skill, family ties, age, and so on), this reservation income is not the same, but there is rather a continuum of such reservation incomes. Distinguishing between the two skill groups, we then assume that there is an upward-sloping supply function for each skill group, depending on the income accorded to immigrants in the destination country. Denoting the number of skilled migrants by m_S, the supply function of skilled migrants is given by an iso-elastic function:

$$m_S = B_S \left(I_S^M\right)^{\sigma_S}, \tag{3.9}$$

where B_S and σ_S are some positive parameters. Similarly, the supply function of unskilled migrants is given by

$$m_U = B_U \left(I_U^M\right)^{\sigma_U}, \tag{3.10}$$

where m_U is the number of unskilled migrants and B_U and σ_U are some positive parameters.

3.3.4 Production and Factor Prices

We employ a Cobb-Douglas production function

$$Y = AK^{\alpha}L^{1-\alpha}, A > 0, 0 < \alpha < 1, \tag{3.11}$$

where Y is gross domestic product, A is a total factor productivity (TFP) parameter, and α is the capital-share parameter (and $[1 - \alpha]$ is the labor-share parameter). Symbol L indicates the total labor supply in efficiency units and is given by

$L = n_S + \rho n_U + m_S + \rho m_U.$ (3.12)

The competitive wage per efficiency unit of labor (w) and the competitive interest rate (r) are given by the marginal productivity conditions

$$w = (1 - \alpha)A\left(\frac{K}{L}\right)^{\alpha}$$ (3.13)

and

$$r = \alpha A\left(\frac{K}{L}\right)^{1-\alpha},$$ (3.14)

where we assume for simplicity that capital does not depreciate.

The model exhibits the standard gains from trade argument. (See Appendix 5A, which reminds us who are gainers and losers from the flow of skilled migrants.)

3.3.5 Income Redistribution System

We employ a very simple system of redistribution. Wages are taxed at a flat rate of t. The revenues are distributed by a uniform per-capita transfer, b.

We assume that the migrants qualify for all the benefits of the welfare state, and they are naturally subject to the state taxes. Therefore, the government budget constraint is as follows:

$twL = b(1 + m_S + m_U),$ (3.15)

assuming that the government has no other revenue needs, except for redistribution.[12] Note that it follows from equation (3.15) that t and b must be of the same sign. A positive wage tax (t) allows the government to accord a positive transfer (b) to all. A subsidy to wages (namely, a negative t) requires the government to impose a lump-sum tax (negative $-b$) on all. When t and b are positive, the tax-transfer system is progressive. When they are negative, the system is regressive.

With unrestricted migration, the flows of migrants m_S and m_U are determined by the migrants themselves, according to their reservation incomes (embedded in the supply functions [3.11] and [3.12]), and the income accorded to them in the host country. There are therefore only two policy variables—the tax rate and the social benefit b. However, as the government is constrained by a balanced budget (condition [3.16]), it follows that there is essentially only one policy variable; once t is chosen, all the other economic variables are determined in equilibrium, including the tax revenue (twL), the number of migrants (m_S and m_U), and b. Alternatively, once b is chosen, all the other economic variables are determined in equilibrium.

Choosing t as the single policy variable, we note that there remain 15 endogenous variables

$$w, b, r, c^*, I_S^M, I_U^M, n_S, n_U, I_S^N, m_S, m_U, H, K, Y, L.$$

There are also 15 equations in the model—(3.2)–(3.9) and (3.10)–(3.15)—from which the endogenous variables are to be solved.[13]

The policy variable is chosen by some natural and plausible version of a majority voting, as described below.

Upon observation, we can see from equations (3.2) and (3.3) that the direct effect of the tax-transfer policy on the incomes of the unskilled native-born individuals and the unskilled migrants is the same and works through the net wage income $(1-t)\rho w + b$. For the unskilled migrant this is the only effect of the tax-transfer system. However, for unskilled native-born individuals, there is also an indirect effect through capital income $I(1+r)$ (note that r depends on t); but this indirect effect is of a second-order magnitude compared to the direct effect.

Similarly, the direct effect of the tax-transfer policy on the incomes of the skilled native-born individuals and the skilled migrants is the same and works through the net wage income $(1-t)w + b$. Here again, there is also an indirect effect on the income of the skilled native-born individuals (but not on the income of the skilled migrants) through the capital income $(E-c)(1+r)$. Once again the indirect effect is of second-order magnitude.

Thus, all unskilled individuals (both native-born and migrants) are affected by the tax-transfer policy mainly through $(1-t)\rho w + b$, whereas all skilled individuals (both native-born and migrants) are affected mainly by $(1-t)w + b$. It is therefore natural that all the unskilled workers, whose wage is only ρw, would rather prefer to tax wage income and take advantage of all the skilled workers, whose wage is higher: w. Thus, the most preferred policy of the unskilled entails a positive tax and a positive transfer. Therefore, if the unskilled (both native-born and migrants) constitute a majority, then the political-economy equilibrium tax and transfer will be positive—a progressive tax-transfer system. However, due to the indirect effect, which applies only to the unskilled native-born individuals, the most preferred tax and transfer policy is not necessarily the same for the unskilled native-born individuals and the unskilled migrants. We then postulate that when the unskilled form a majority, then the tax-transfer policy chosen is the most preferred policy by the larger of the two subgroups (the unskilled native-born citizens or the unskilled migrants).

Similarly, the skilled (both native-born and migrants whose wage is higher than the unskilled) would opt to grant a subsidy to the wage, financed by a lump-sum tax. That is, they opt for negative t and b—a regressive tax-transfer policy. In this case too there is also an indirect effect that applies only to the skilled native-born individuals. Thus, the most-preferred tax-transfer policy is not the same for the two subgroups of skilled native-born individuals and skilled migrants. In this case too we postulate that the political-economy tax-transfer policy is the most preferred policy of the larger subgroup.

Note that the indirect effect of the tax-transfer policy, which works through the capital income $(E - c)(1 + r)$, is not the same for all members of the skilled native-born subgroup (because it depends on c). In this case, we assume that the median voter within this group prevails.

If we keep all other parameter values constant and increase only the parameter value of B_S, we can isolate the effect of a supply-side shock. That is, we give a positive shock to the supply of skilled migrants. We find that the number of skilled migrants (m_S) rises sharply. The skilled now constitute the majority $x_S + m_S > x_U + m_U$. As predicted, the political-economy tax-transfer policy now becomes regressive: t and b are negative. That is, there is a wage subsidy financed by a lump-sum tax. In addition, the skilled migrants form the larger of the two skilled subgroups, (i.e., $m_S > x_S$), and their most preferred tax-transfer policy now becomes the political-equilibrium tax-transfer policy. Furthermore, the politically dominant subgroup of skilled migrants drives out all unskilled migrants $(m_U = 0)$ by according them zero disposable income $\left(I_U^M = 0\right)$.

It is noteworthy that the unskilled native-born individuals were initially the politically dominant subgroup and dictated their most preferred progressive tax-transfer policy. Following the supply-side stock of skilled migration, the unskilled native-born individuals lose their dominance to the skilled migrants, who are now dictating their most preferred regressive tax-transfer policy. Nevertheless, the unskilled native-born individuals are better off, because the return to their capital income (namely, r) rises sharply (in unit of the all-purpose composite good). Even though the wage per efficiency unit falls, the sharp rise in the rate of interest more than compensates the native-born unskilled laborers for the wage decline. For the same reason, the skilled (native-born and migrants) are all better off. Thus, except for the unskilled migrants, who are driven out, all other income groups gain from the skilled-migration supply shock.

Note that the influx of skilled labor raises overall productivity of the labor force; consequently, it does also raise the tax revenue needed for shouldering the preexisting redistribution policy. This force works toward more generous-redistribution because it is fiscally less burdensome. Counteracting this pro-distribution force, however, is the rebalancing of the political coalition triggered by the increased share of higher-income skilled individuals in the voting population. The result is that the emerging decisive voter *reverses* the preexisting redistribution regime.[14]

It is worth explaining the model-specific forces that totally drive out the unskilled migrants in the wake of the skilled-migration supply shock. The model assumes perfect substitutability between skilled and unskilled labor in production: each unit of time of an unskilled worker is equivalent to ρ units of time of a skilled worker. Thus, unskilled migrants provide no productivity benefits to the skilled. At the same time, they constitute a fiscal burden Therefore, the new skill-dominant coalition drives them out altogether by pushing their disposable income all the way to zero. The assumed perfect substitutability in production does serve to highlight the anti–unskilled-migration forces within the ruling skilled coalition.

3.3.6   Implications
The model attempts to rationalize the sharp rise in income inequality following the Soviet Jew exodus shock. It allows us to explore how migration supply side shock alters immigration patterns and, at the same time, reshapes the political-economy balance. We develop a stylized political-economy model with free migration. Important political-economy mechanisms are at work: First, the influx of skilled immigrants depresses the incentives for unskilled migrants to flow in, though they are still free to do so. Second, the fiscal burden of redistribution policies diminishes from the viewpoint of the decisive voter. That is, the influx of skilled labor raises overall productivity of the labor force; consequently, it also raises the tax revenue needed for shouldering a redistribution policy. However, counteracting this pro-distribution force is the rebalancing of the political coalition, because of the share of the increase in the skilled workers in the population. Therefore, the emerging decisive voter reverses the preexisting redistribution regime,

notwithstanding the fall in the fiscal burden. Third, the unskilled native-born individuals may nevertheless become well off, even though they lose their political influence. To sum up, the model predictions are as follows: First, the shock depresses the incentives for unskilled migrants to flow in, though they are still free to do so. Second, tax-transfer system becomes less progressive. Third, the unskilled native-born citizens may well become well off, though they lose their political influence, which they had before the migration wave. All other native-born income groups are also made better off. The positive economics predictions seem consistent with data. The model helps interpret these results in a normative fashion.

The chapter describes the unique experience of Israel. Within a short period in the early 1990s Israel received scores of migrants from the FSU. A distinctive feature was the migrants' high labor skill. It caused a sharp new upward trend of disposable income inequality but without a parallel change in market income inequality. That is, the welfare state took a sharp regressive turn. This underscores the role played by the post-migration political balance, which triggered less redistribution.

Appendix 3A: Gains to Native-Born Individuals from Migration

Like international trade in goods, there are gains and losses from the opening of national borders to labor mobility. A simple figure (figure 3A.1) can serve to illustrate the gains from migration in our model. For concreteness, we illustrate the gains to the native-born citizens from low-skilled migration. For simplicity, we assume that there are no taxes and benefits.

The down-sloping curve in this figure is the marginal product of low-skilled labor. This curve is also the demand for this type of labor.

There are S native-born high-skill laborers. The free-migration number of high-skilled immigrants is

FM_s.

In a closed economy with no migration, the equilibrium high-skilled wage is w_S.

GDP is equal to the area OGAD, of which the area HGA goes to the high-skill native-born workers and the area OHAD goes to the low-skill native-born workers.

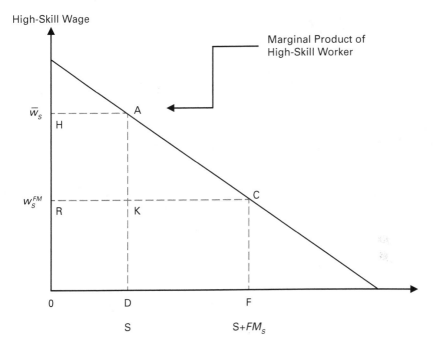

Figure 3A.1
The gains from a high-skill migration.

Suppose the high-skill migrants face a reservation wage of w_S^{FM} in their countries of origin, which is below the threshold $\overline{w}_S$. If we allow for a free migration, then FM_S high-skilled migrants will come. The equilibrium wage will be: w_S^{FM}. GDP increases to OGCF (for both native-born individuals and migrants), an increase measured by the area DACF.

A part of this increase (the area DKCF) goes to the low-skilled migrants, so that the total gains to all the native-born citizens is the area AKC. Note, however, that not all native-born individuals gain. The income of high-skill native-born individuals drops to the area ORKD, so that they lose the area HAKR. On the other hand, the income of the high-skill native-born individuals exceeds the loss to the low-skill native-born individuals.

Therefore, with a perfect, non-distortionary system of redistribution (via lump sums), the high-skilled native-born individuals can more than compensate the low-skilled native-born individuals, so that all native-born citizens can gain from migration.

Table 3A.1

The Effect of a Supply Shock of Skilled Migration: (a) Immigrants vote (b) Immigrants do not vote

	m_U	m_S	x_U	x_S	I_U^M	I_U^N	I_S^M	$\overline{I_S^{N^*}}$	w	r	t	b
(a) Immigrants Vote												
(a.1) Unskilled Majority (Unskilled Native-Born the Larger Sub-Group) Parameter Value of $B_s=1.2$	0.891	0.138	0.966	0.034	0.063	0.194	0.237	0.281	0.312	1.553	0.323	0.025
(a.2) Skilled Majority (Skilled Migrants the Larger Sub-Group) Parameter Value of $B_s=8.2$	0	1.106	0.966	0.034	0	0.202	0.263	0.334	0.228	2.940	-0.406	-0.058
(b) Immigrants do not Vote												
(b.1) Unskilled Majority (Unskilled Native-Born the Larger Group) Parameter Value of $B_s=1.2$	0.891	0.138	0.966	0.034	0.063	0.194	0.237	0.281	0.312	1.553	0.323	0.025
(b.2) Unskilled Majority (Unskilled Native-Born the Larger Group) Parameter Value of $B_s=8.2$	0.892	0.714	0.981	0.034	0.063	0.244	0.196	0.311	0.245	2.537	0.338	0.034

Note: In both (a.1) and (b.1) the unskilled native born is the decisive voter; in (a.2) the skilled migrant is the decisive voter; in (b.2) the unskilled native born is the decisive voter.

*Since the income of the native skilled population is not constant but a linear function of an individual's c, we report this group's average income. Notice that since the minimal income of a skilled native is equal to that of an unskilled native, we have that the income of the skilled immigrant lies in between them. Other (Common) Parameter Values:

$$B_U = 56, \ \rho = 0.18, \ \overline{c} = 2, \ E = 0.05, \ \alpha = 0.33, \ \sigma_S = \sigma_U = 1.5, \ A = 1$$

Note also that if the migration of high skill triggers either productivity gains (through external effects) or an increase in infrastructure investment (through policy effects) the marginal productivity curve would shift outwardly. Therefore, the wage of the highly skill under free migration need not fall.

Because a redistribution system (via wage taxation) is distortionary, the compensation possibilities are limited. It is not always the case that all native-born citizens gain from migration. A similar conclusion holds in the case of high-skilled migration.

A striking result in chapter 3 is that the migration supply shock benefits all income groups (except low-skill immigrants that are shrinking in numbers) despite the fact that income redistribution is diminished in scope and magnitude. See Appendix 3B.

Appendix 3B: Numerical Simulation of the Migration-Inequality Model

The migration-inequality model, motivated by the Israeli experience with the wave of skilled migration from the FSU, simulates the effects of a supply shock of skilled migration on the political-economy equilibrium tax-transfer policy.

We start with parameter values that entail the unskilled (both native-born and migrants) as a majority: $x_u + m_u > x_s + m_s$. This case is described in the first row in table 3A.1. As predicted, the political-economy tax-transfer policy is progressive: t and b are positive. Also, the unskilled native-born form a majority of the unskilled: $x_u > m_u$.

Other (common) parameter values:

$B_u = 56$, $\rho = 0.18$, $\bar{c} = 2$, $E = 0.05$, $\alpha = 0.33$, $\sigma_s = \sigma_u = 1.5$, $A = 1$

The political-economy tax-transfer policy is the most preferred policy by the unskilled native-born individuals.

We now keep all other parameter values constant and increase the parameter value of B_s. This supply-side shock triggers a wave of skilled migration. The results are shown in the second row of table 3A.1. The number of migrants (m_s) rose sharply from 0.14 to 1.11. The skilled now constitute the majority: $x_s + m_s > x_u + m_u$. As predicted, the political-economy tax-transfer policy now becomes regressive: t and b are negative. Also, the skilled migrants form the larger of the two skilled subgroups (i.e., $m_s > x_s$) and their most-preferred tax-transfer now becomes the political-equilibrium tax-transfer policy. Furthermore, as can be seen from the second row of table 3A.1, the politically dominant subgroup of skilled migrants drives out all unskilled migrants ($m_U = 0$), by according them zero income $\left(I_U^M = 0 \right)$. It is noteworthy that the unskilled native-born individuals were initially the politically dominant subgroup and dictated their most preferred progressive tax-transfer. Following the supply-side stock of skilled migration, the unskilled native-born individuals lose their dominance to the skilled migrants, who are now dictating their most-preferred regressive tax-transfer policy. Nevertheless, the unskilled native-born individuals are better off, because the return to their capital income (namely, r) rises sharply from 1.55 to 2.94 (in unit of the all-purpose composite good).

To underscore the role of migrant integration into the political process, we also simulate the model for a case where migrants do not vote at all (panel b in figure 3A.1). In this case, the skill-migration shock would strengthen the progressivity of the fiscal system and diminish the inequality in disposable incomes. The reason is that unskilled native born maintain their majority following the migration shock. When migrants are not allowed to vote following the migration shock, all income groups gain except unskilled migrants, who lose.

II Globalization, Disinflation, High Tech, and Foreign Direct Investment

The world's Great Moderation from 1985 to 2007 was the period when the Federal Reserve, and other advanced economies' central banks, provided a broadly stable macroeconomic environment to facilitate private sector economic decisions. In those twenty-two years, the rate of inflation in advanced economies rose above 5 percent for only three years and fell below 2 percent for only two years. GDP growth was relatively stable, and unemployment was low. During the Great Moderation, inflation around the world fell substantially. The average annual inflation rate among developing countries was 41 percent in the early 1980s and declined to 13 percent toward the end of the 1990s. Global inflation in the 1990s dropped from 30 percent a year to about 4 percent a year.

The Great Moderation enabled Israel to eradicate inflation, after more than a decade and a half of struggle.

4 The Great Moderation and Israel's Disinflation

The 1990s' globalization wave has swept emerging markets in Latin America, European transition economies, East Asian emerging economies, and Israel over the last decades. The 1992 single-market reform in Europe and the formation of the Eurozone were watersheds of globalization. Emerging markets, including China and India, likewise became significantly more open. Wynne and Kersting (2007) note that in the 1970s more than three quarters of industrial countries had restrictions of some sort on international financial transactions. By the 2000s, none did. Likewise, restrictions on these transactions among emerging markets fell from 78 percent in the 1970s to 58 percent in the 2000s. Israel was exposed intensively in the globalization forces and was able to exploit them to climb down from three-digit inflation rates in the early 1980s and double-digit rates in the late 1980s and early 1990s.

Economic integration of the world economy has been reinforced by the transition from communism to capitalism in the former Soviet Union. Spontaneous privatizers, including the military industrial complex (VPK), began mass sales of natural resources abroad. The USSR's entire strategic mineral reserves from the prolonged war were shipped out of Russia's far east ports to Asia, contributing to a decade-long plunge in natural resources prices, setting in motion a broad drop in energy products' inflation.

The Great Moderation refers to the significant reduction in business-cycle volatility starting in the mid-1980s, believed at that time to be permanent, in developed nations. Sometime during the mid-1980s major economic variables such as real GDP growth, industrial production, monthly payroll, and the unemployment rate began to decline in volatility. These reductions were primarily due to greater independence of the central banks from political and financial influences, which has allowed them to follow more consistently macroeconomic stabilization.

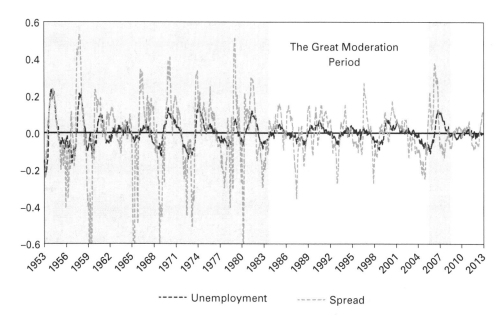

Figure 4.1
HP Filter de-trended unemployment rate, and five-year bond-yield (corporate/treasury)
spread, United States, 1953–2014.
Notes: De-trended unemployment rate obtains through HP-filter, in SD. Bond yield
spread is defined as the difference between two things: five-year treasury constant maturity rate, and Moody's seasoned Baa corporate bond yield, HP filtered, in SD. *Source*:
FRED (economic database of the Federal Reserve Bank of St. Louis), BLS, an extension
to Eckstein, Setty, and Weiss (2015).

Figure 4.1 describes deviations from the trend of the unemployment
rate and the bond-yield corporate-treasury spread for the period 1953–
2014. The figure highlights the significant reduction in the fluctuations of the unemployment rate and the bond-yield spread between
Baa corporation rates and the treasury rate—a sign of greater corporate
solvency.

Global inflation declined from 30 percent to 4 percent between
1993 and 2003. Rogoff (2003, 2004) hypothesizes that globalization—
interacting with deregulation and privatization—has played a strong
supporting role in the past decade's disinflation. An important feature
of openness relates to international labor flows. International migrants
constituted 2.9 percent of the world population in the 2000s, up from
2.1 percent in 1975. In some countries, changes have been more dramatic. In Israel in the 1990s, there was a surge of immigrants of up to
17 percent of the population, and the central bank achieved a sizable

decline of inflation. It is possible that the two events are related. In Spain in 1995, the percentages of foreigners in the population and in the labor force were below 1 percent and below 0.5 percent, respectively. At the end of 2006, these rates were around 9 percent and 14 percent.

By easing labor bottlenecks, migrants help to keep down prices of goods and services. Pass-through of world low inflation, and low interest rates, to domestic prices and interest rates, and the effects of migration on wages, are to be addressed by the standard Phillips curve analysis.[1]

Recall that the independence of central banks is a way to overcome dynamic inconsistency: Positive (expected) inflation leads to output, employment, and financial-market distortions. However, surprise inflation boosts employment and output through the Phillips curve mechanism. In the absence of central bank independence, the non-commitment of central banks leads to high expected inflation. Central bank independence is therefore a necessary condition for overcoming such dynamic inconsistency and consequently for weakening the inflation bias. Accordingly, Rogoff (2003, 2004) attributes the moderation in world inflation to a broad-based move toward having them run by more independent anti-inflation–oriented central bankers; similar developments happened also in Israel. The precursor of Israel's central bank independence was the no-printing clause in the 1985 stabilization program.

The increased competitiveness was a result of the interplay of globalization, deregulation, and a decreased role for governments in many economies. Given Rogoff's diagnosis, he foresaw continued disinflation and even deflationary pressures (which came into a stark relief in the Great Recession), arguing that the most important factor supporting worldwide disinflation has been the mutually reinforcing mix of a goods market and financial deregulation and globalization, and the consequent significant reduction in monopoly pricing power. These developments increased competitiveness and diminished the gains a central bank can reap via unanticipated inflation, because it reduces the gap between the economy's monopolistically competitive equilibrium and the more socially desirable competitive equilibrium. In addition, both theory and empirics suggest that economies that are more competitive have more flexible nominal prices, making smaller the Barro-Gordon–type output gain the central bank can achieve by inflating, and making them more ephemeral. In a standard, stylized political economy model, Rogoff then shows that it is easier to credibly sustain low inflation in a competitive economy than in a highly monopolistic one.[2]

Evidence of the effect of globalization on the Phillips curve is provided by Loungani, Razin, and Yuen (2001), Razin and Loungani (2007), and Clarida (2008). Previously, Romer (1993, 1998) and Lane (1997) showed that inflation and trade liberalization are negatively (significantly) correlated among the large (flexible exchange rate) OECD economies.

The core mechanism in the New Keynesian paradigm depends on the Phillips curve; that is, the trade-off between surprise inflation and the level of economic activity. The reason why the New Keynesian framework is capable of generating such a trade-off between inflation and economic activity is that producer-desired prices (once prices are adjusted) rise with the economy's output, when marginal costs slope upward due to diminishing returns to scale. Furthermore, when the labor supply increases, workers tend to experience increasing marginal disutility of labor efforts. The resulting increased real-wage demands must rise. Increased wage demands put an upward pressure on the marginal cost, and consequently on the producer-desired price setting.

Specifically, the big drivers of domestic inflation, as they are formulated in the Phillips curve, are (1) the price of imports and the exchange rate; (2) capacity pressures and labor market tightness in the domestic economy; (3) public expectations about future inflation, future exchange rates, and future foreign prices; and (4) the amount of trading world slack. The level of foreign wages is also important for countries open to labor mobility.[3] As we can see later, these work to reduce Israel's inflation to low one-digit rates.

Bean (2006) succinctly summarizes some key effects of globalization on the Phillips curve in the era of globalization:

One of the most notable developments of the 1990s has been the apparent flattening of the short-run trade-off between inflation and activity. The seventies were characterized by an almost vertical relationship in the United Kingdom, in which attempt to hold unemployment below its natural rate resulted in rising inflation. In the eighties, the downward sloping relationship reappears, as inflation was squeezed out of the system by the slack of the economy. However, since the early nineties, the relationship looks to have been rather flat. Three factors—increased specialization; the intensification of product market competition; and the impact of that intensified competition and migration on the behavior of wages—should all work to flatten the short-run trade-off between inflation and domestic activity.[4]

Evidently, changes in the foreign price pass into domestic inflation in the open-economy case even if the exchange rate depreciation trend does not change. If, in addition, the exchange rate depreciation tapers down, and once the foreign exporters to the home country are also given a chance to adjust prices in response to the moderation in the exchange rate depreciation, the home country import price inflation moderates as well. In the world of the Great Moderation the home country inflation abates.

Opening up of the economy to capital, goods, and labor mobility also flattens the Phillips curve. In the New Keynesian framework, Binyamini and Razin (2008) show how increased volume of trade in goods, greater financial openness, and labor migration affect the trade-off between output and inflation by flattening the Phillips curve. Minimizing the (utility-based) loss function implies moderate inflation, akin to the Great Moderation. They demonstrate analytically how the opening up of the domestic economy to trade in goods, international borrowing and lending, and migration flatten the Phillips Curve (see Appendix 4A). Every successive round of the opening up of the economy contributes to flattening the aggregate supply curve. The intuition is that when an economy opens up to trade in goods, it tends to specialize in production but to diversify in consumption. This means the number of domestically produced goods is less than the number of domestically consumed goods. Consequently, the commodity composition of the consumption and output baskets, which are identical if the trade account is closed, are different when trade in goods is possible. As a result, the correlation between fluctuations in output and in consumption (which is equal to unity in the case of a closed trade account) is less than unity if the economy opens up to international trade in goods. The decomposition of the utility-based Phillips curve to the various forces of migration, output gap, and real exchange rate is shown in an Appendix 1A. In words, these globalization forces work analytically as follows.

When the capital account is open, then the correlation between fluctuations in consumption and domestic output is further weakened; this is because with open capital accounts the representative household can smooth consumption through international borrowing and lending and thereby separate current consumption from current output. The inflation effects of shocks to the marginal cost are therefore reduced, because the fluctuations in labor supply are also smoothed, because of the consumption smoothing.

When the labor market is internationally closed to outward migration, wage demands faced by domestic producers are upward sloping, both under in-migration and under a completely closed labor market. However, when the labor market is open to in-migration, domestic producers face an expanded labor supply: additional to the skilled native-born labor supply (with upward-sloping wage demand), they also face a complementary unskilled foreign labor supply (with exogenously determined wage demand). That means that in-migration acts on the Phillips curve essentially like a domestic productivity shock.

There has been some evidence of greater restraints on domestic prices and wage growth in sectors more exposed to international competition, such as textiles and electronics. Chen, Imbs, and Scott (2004) analyzed disaggregated data for EU manufacturing over the period 1988–2000. They found that increased openness lowers prices by reducing markups and by raising productivity. In response to an increase in openness, markups show a steep short-run decline, which partly reverses later, while productivity rises in a manner that increases over time. If globalization reduces the markup, our model predicts that this effect by itself leads to a more forceful anti-inflation policy and lessens the attention given by the policy maker to the fluctuations in economic activity. One can conjecture that more frequent price updating steepens the trade-off between inflation and activity; however, to our knowledge, neither theory nor empirical evidence exists in support of any systematic relationship between globalization and frequency of price updating. Notably, Gopinath and Rigobon (2007) report that the time frequency of price adjustment of U.S. imported goods trended downward, on average, during the Great Moderation. Gopinath and Itskhoki (2008) exploit the open economy environment, which provides a well-identified cost shock—namely, sizeable exchange rate shocks. They use this identification method to test the effects of price-adjustment frequencies and pass-through. They demonstrate that high frequency adjusters have a long-run pass-through that is at least twice as high as low frequency adjusters in the data. Borio and Filardo (2007) present cross-country evidence in support of their contention that global factors have recently become empirically more relevant for domestic inflation determination.[5]

4.1   Israel Globalizes and Disinflates

There are several countries, including Israel, that went through a hyperinflation crisis in some stage of their development.[6] Following the 1977 change of guards at the government level (the political *Ha'Maapach*) in Israel, the newly elected Likud government abruptly eased its control over the economy, as detailed in chapter 1. In particular, capital controls largely lifted, initially bringing in short-term capital, which was followed by a reversal when the economy faltered. At the same time, a populist economic policy led to high budget deficits and big wage increases. The absence of constraining rules on actions of the central bank rendered it strongly accommodating the treasury in its expansionary monetary policy. With improper bank regulation, banks exercised Visut Menayot (propriety trading deals). They were on the verge of collapsing. Following the hyperinflation crisis in the early 1980s under the populist Likkud government, a major political restructuring in Israel toward the political center enabled a unity government (Likkud plus Avoda) to stabilize the economy. Indeed, some key measures requiring a political consensus were taken and new legislation helped to immunize, in part, the economy from similar extreme crisis features. In particular, a new legislation (Khok Hahesderim) allowed the government to exercise tighter control over the budget. A new law forbade the central bank to monetize the budget deficit (Khok Iee Hadpassa). A Tri-party agreement between the government, the Federation of Labor (Histadrut), and the association of private sector employers dampened the wage-price dynamics and enabled a sharp nominal devaluation that ended in a real devaluation.[7]

The macroeconomic changes, brought about by the stabilization program, have lasted until these very days. The hyperinflation episode has not reoccurred.[8] The 1985 inflation stabilization program laid the foundation for the increasing independence of central banks. Such independence is critical for the successful conquest of inflation (see chapter 1). We document how strong was the correlation between the convergence to advanced countries' inflation and the globalization process; both took a sharp upturn in the mid-1990s.

4.1.1   Convergence of Inflation Rates

Globalization—interacting with deregulation and privatization—has played a strong supporting role in Israel's disinflation. The moderation is due to a large extent to the increasing independence of the Bank of Israel, which conducts effective anti-inflation policies in the presence of worldwide disinflation.[9]

Figure 4.2 shows the convergence of Israel's inflation rate to U.S., German, and OECD rates. The inflation fall started after the 1985 inflation stabilization policy but converged to the low one-digit rates of advanced economies in the 1990s.[10]

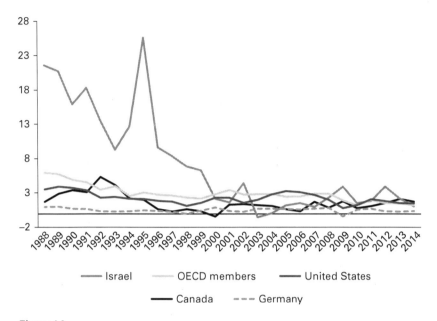

Figure 4.2
Inflation Rates (annual GDP deflator, percentage). *Source*: World Bank.

4.1.2   International Financial Integration
Full international financial integration requires that in the long run (when prices adjust to various shocks and markets clear) the following arbitrage equation holds:

$$1 + r_t^{US} = (1 + r_t^i)\frac{q_{i/US,t+1}}{q_{i/US,t}},$$

where i stands for Israel, Canada, Germany, and the United Kingdom; and q stands for the real exchange rate vis a vis the U.S. dollar:[11]

$$q_{i/US,t}^t = E_{i/US,t}\frac{P_{US,t}}{P_{i,t}},$$

In addition, E stands for the nominal exchange rate vis a vis the U.S. dollar, and P stands for the price level.

Figure 4.3 plots the graphs of the real interest rate, adjusted for real exchange rate changes; the yields on three-month government bonds for Israel, Canada, Germany, and the United Kingdom; and the yields on three-month U.S. government bonds. International financial integration generates more synchronized country-specific yields. Time series

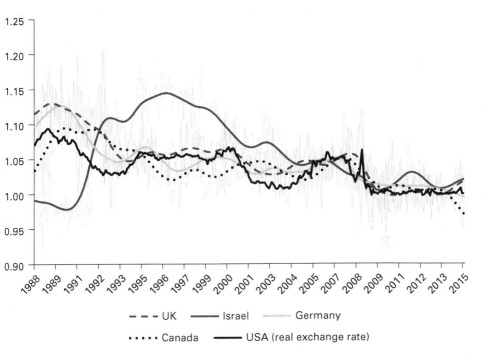

Figure 4.3
Gross real interest rate adjusted for real-exchange-rate changes (U.S. benchmark).
Note: Series are HP-filtered. Monthly data are shown in the background. *Source*: Stats Bureau, FERD, World Bank, real-exchange-rate adjusted, yields on three-month government bonds for Israel, Canada, Germany, and the United Kingdom, and the yields on three-month U.S. government bonds.

are filtered to wash out short-run idiosyncratic fluctuations. Figure 4.3 demonstrates strikingly that in the 1990s Israel's real interest rate, adjusted for real exchange rate (U.S. benchmark), converged to the U.S. real interest rate, which implies that Israel's financial markets integrated significantly into the world financial markets.

The flattening of the short-run trade-off between inflation and activity is apparent in figure 4.4. The scattered observations for 1990–2001, 2002–2011, and 2012–2016 indicate that the Phillips curve has flattened. Taking this evidence together with the convergence of inflation to the world inflation in figure 4.2, and the financial integration indicated by figure 4.3, one can conjecture that the flattening of the Phillips curve is in part due to globalization forces.

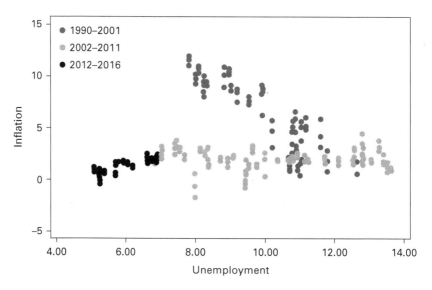

Figure 4.4
Inflationary expectations (derived from financial markets) and the rate of unemployment, 1990–2016. *Source*: Bank of Israel and the Israeli Central Bureau of Statistics.

4.2 Implications

The absence of constraining rules on actions of the Bank of Israel and on Israel's fiscal authority has induced strongly accommodative monetary policies and uncontrolled inflation. With improper financial sector regulation, (e.g., the so-called Visut Menayot) banks were on the verge of collapsing in the 1984 crisis. They were able to recapitalize, making their investment portfolios less risky over the next two decades, thanks to more rigorous bank regulations.

The 1990s globalization trends in Israel facilitated tighter controls on monetary and fiscal policies and triggered the great convergence to the low inflation rates of advanced economies. However, globalization abetted the increase of income (market-based) inequality. Improvements in the quality and range of financial services while broadening access to new financial services and products may narrowly improve the quality of financial services for high-income households with access to financial services (Greenwood and Jovanovic 1990). But such access to financial investments may not exist for low-income households. International financial liberalization helps lower the borrowing constraints of high-income households without changing the tight borrowing constraints of low-income households. Indeed, de Haan and Sturm (2016) bring new evidence that supports the argument that financial liberalization increases income inequality.[12]

Appendix 4A: Globalization and the Phillips Curve

Binyamini and Razin (2008) show how trade in goods, financial openness, and labor in- and out-migration affect the trade-off between output and inflation by successively flattening the Phillips curve. In the case of *perfect mobility of labor, capital,* and *goods,* the log-linear approximate aggregate supply curve (Phillips curve) is given by[13]

$$\hat{\pi}_t = \kappa \cdot \left[\frac{\omega_p \cdot n}{1 + \omega_p \theta} \cdot x_t + \frac{\omega_p \cdot (1-n)}{1 + \omega_p \theta} \cdot (\hat{Y}_t^F - \hat{Y}_t^N) + \frac{1}{1 + \omega_p \theta} \cdot \hat{w}_t^W + \frac{(1-n)}{n} \cdot \hat{q}_t \right]$$
$$+ \frac{(1-n)}{n} \cdot (\hat{q}_t - \hat{q}_{t-1}) + \beta \cdot E_t \left[\hat{\pi}_{t+1} - \frac{(1-n)}{n} (\hat{q}_{t+1} - \hat{q}_t) \right],$$

where $\hat{\pi}_t$ is the deviation of CPI inflation from its target; $x_t \equiv (\hat{Y}_t^H - Y_t^N)$ is the domestic output gap; $(\hat{Y}_t^F - \hat{Y}_t^N)$ is the difference between foreign output and domestic natural output; the parameter ω_p is the elasticity of the marginal cost with respect to producer's output, θ is the intraindustry elasticity of substitution, σ stands for the intertemporal elasticity of substitution, and β denotes the subjective discount factor. The term n denotes the mass (number) of domestically produced goods, w is domestic wage, and superscript F, N, and W denote foreign, natural, and world variable, respectively. The term $\kappa = \dfrac{(1-\alpha)(1-\alpha\beta)}{\alpha}$ captures the degree of price flexibility, and $(1-\alpha)$ is the probability of receiving a price-updating signal. The variable $\hat{q}_t$ is the real exchange rate, formally defined as

$$\hat{q}_t = \hat{\varepsilon}_t + \hat{P}_{F,t} - \hat{P}_t,$$

where $\hat{P}_{F,t}$ denotes the foreign consumer-price index.

The slope of the Phillips equation is denoted by ψ; for the open-economy expression slope of the aggregate supply, the equation is

$$\psi_1 \equiv \frac{\kappa n \omega_p}{1 + \omega_p \theta}.$$

If we shot off labor mobility, the Phillips curve reduces to

$$\hat{\pi}_t = \kappa \cdot \left[\frac{\omega \cdot n}{1 + \omega\theta} \cdot x_t + \frac{\omega \cdot (1-n)}{1 + \omega\theta} \cdot (\hat{Y}_t^F - \hat{Y}_t^N) + \frac{(1-n)}{n} \cdot \hat{q}_t \right. $$
$$\left. + \frac{(1-n)}{n} \cdot (\hat{q}_t - \hat{q}_{t-1}) + \beta \cdot E_t \left[\hat{\pi}_{t+1} - \frac{(1-n)}{n}(\hat{q}_{t+1} - \hat{q}_t) \right] \right],$$

where $\omega = \omega_p + \omega_w$ is the elasticity of marginal cost with respect to domestic output; it includes the expression

$$\omega_p = \frac{1 - \chi}{\chi},$$

the elasticity of the desired price with respect to output (for given wages). It is inversely related to the degree of returns to scale. It also includes the expression

$$\omega_w \equiv \frac{\phi}{\chi}.$$

This is the elasticity of demanded wage with respect to output (consisting of the labor-disutility elasticity and the labor-output elasticity). Because $\omega_w > 0$, we have $\omega > \omega_p$. Therefore, shutting off the migration channel (particularly outward migration) raises the slope of the aggregate supply curve. In this case, the slope of the Phillips curve is

$$\psi_2 \equiv \frac{\kappa n \omega}{1 + \omega\theta}.$$

Let us turn to the case of no labor mobility and no capital mobility. If the domestic economy is not integrated to the international financial market, then there is no possibility of consumption smoothing, and we have that the value of aggregate current spending equals the value of aggregate domestic output:

$$\hat{P}_{C,t}\hat{C}_t = \hat{P}_{Y,t}\hat{Y}_t \; ; \; \hat{P}_{C,t}\hat{C}_t^N = \hat{P}_{Y,t}\hat{Y}_t^N,$$

where $\hat{P}_{C,t}$ is the CPI-based price level, and $\hat{P}_{Y,t}$ is the GDP deflator. In this case, the aggregate supply curve is

$$\hat{\pi}_t = \kappa \cdot \left[\frac{(\omega \cdot n + \sigma)}{1 + \omega\theta} \cdot x_t + \frac{\omega \cdot (1-n)}{1 + \omega\theta} \cdot (\hat{Y}_t^F - \hat{Y}_t^N) + \frac{(1-n)}{n} \cdot \hat{q}_t \right. $$
$$\left. + \frac{(1-n)}{n} \cdot (\hat{q}_t - \hat{q}_{t-1}) + \beta \cdot E_t \left[\hat{\pi}_{t+1} - \frac{(1-n)}{n}(\hat{q}_{t+1} - \hat{q}_t) \right] \right].$$

The Phillips-curve slope is:

$$\psi \equiv \frac{\kappa(\omega n + \sigma)}{1 + \omega \theta}.$$

In the *closed-economy* case the aggregate supply equation (Phillips curve) reduces to

$$\hat{\pi}_t = \frac{\kappa}{1 + \omega \theta} \cdot (\omega + \sigma) \cdot x_t + \beta E_t \hat{\pi}_{t+1}.$$

In the case of the closed economy, the Phillips curve slope is

$$\psi_2 \equiv \frac{\kappa n \omega}{1 + \omega \theta} \geq \psi_3 \equiv \frac{\kappa(\omega + \sigma)}{1 + \omega \theta} \geq \psi_2 \equiv \frac{\kappa(\omega n + \sigma)}{1 + \omega \theta} \geq \psi_1 \equiv \frac{\kappa n \omega_p}{1 + \omega_p \theta}.$$

The Phillips curve is steeper in the closed-economy case, compared to openness regimes. The latter is steeper than the slope with perfect mobility of labor, capital, and goods.

Furthermore, changes in the foreign price pass through into domestic inflation in the open-economy case, but these effects are absent in the closed-economy case. This observation validates the proposition that globalization in the world of great moderation exerts inflation-moderating influences.

5   The 2008 Global Crisis and Israel-Economy Resilience

The global financial crisis generated the deepest and longest recession since the Great Depression of the 1930s. The defining event of the 2008 global financial crisis was a "hemorrhagic stroke": a paralytic implosion of the loanable funds markets. The post–September 15, 2008, emergency was caused by the terrifying realization that major financial institutions, especially those connected with hedge funds, could not cover their current obligations either with asset sales or short-term bank credit, because confidence in the value of their assets had been lost, and short-term lending suddenly ceased. People everywhere were panicked at the prospect of cascading financial bankruptcies, where the securities of failed companies contaminated the value of other assets, triggering margin calls, shuttered credit access, lost savings, bank runs, stock market crashes, liquidity crises, universal insolvency, economic collapse, and global ruination.

Economists had difficulty coping with the 2008 global financial crisis because prevailing analytic frameworks were not up to the task, mainly because the financial sector fragilities had not been addressed. They took inadequate account of four major factors:

(1) the destabilizing cumulative effects of financial deregulation, hedge funds, electronic trading, financial entrepreneurship such as subprime mortgages, derivatives, and mortgage-backed securities, moral hazard, regulatory laxness, regulatory hazard (such as "mark to market");

(2) one-way-street speculation which led to risk-shifting incentives, "too-big-to-fail" financial intermediaries, hard asset bubbles (real estate, commodities, energy);

(3) structural deficits with fiscal hidden liabilities, special interest transfers, global imbalances, and more;

(4) low inflation target leading to liquidity traps in the presence of financial shocks; and

(5) excessive world savings and low investment spending.

All these unrecognized pressures simmered without any policy response, perhaps because economists had come to believe that policy makers had learned how to tame the financial beast, decades after the Great Depression. With the advantage of hindsight, a decade after the global crisis, both the strengths and weaknesses of the pre-crisis economic consensus can be discerned anew. Strengths and weaknesses can be usefully appraised with an eye toward parsing future research.

Figure 5.1 illustrates how different the employment decline was under the Great Recession compared to all post–World War II downturns. The 2008 global financial crisis that erupted in the United States instantaneously swept across Europe.

A critical piece of the financial crisis and its perplexing aftermath is global imbalances, often called the global savings glut. This means that some nations (e.g., China) under-consume and over-export, while other nations, such as the United States, over-consume and over-import, devaluing their currency and pressuring the Federal Reserve to keep interest rates too high to adequately stimulate recovery. Asia's liquidity

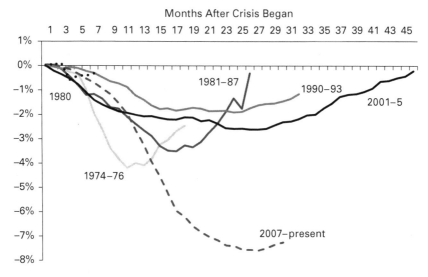

Figure 5.1
Employment declines in various U.S. crises. *Source*: Razin (2015).

glut flooded into the lightly regulated American shadow banking system (including mortgage institutions) and inundated many smaller countries (such as Iceland, Ireland, and Estonia), sparking speculation and asset bubbles that soon burst with dramatic adverse effects on risk perceptions in the world's short-term interbank loanable funds market. Burst asset price bubbles reduced banks' worldwide lending ability, a problem compounded by tightened loan requirements that limited access to emergency credit infusions.[1]

5.1 Comparing the Great Depression to the Great Recession

The recent global crisis had some similarities with the Great Depression. Both appear to have been triggered by a credit crunch following a sudden burst of asset-price and credit bubbles. Recovery of world industrial production started much earlier in the Great Recession than in the Great Depression. Periods of depressed output are significantly shorter in the former than in the latter, thanks to different policy reactions and improved financial and budget institutions. Figure 5.2 illustrates the similarity in terms of the initial financial shock suffered by

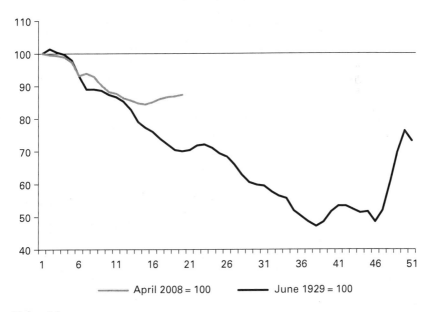

Figure 5.2
World industrial production in months after the crises peak. *Source:* FRED (economic database of the Federal Reserve Bank of St. Louis); Eichengreen and O'Rourke (2010).

world industrial production. It also indicates how the persistent decline in output was more severe in the Great Depression than in the Great Recession.

5.2 Fragility of Banks

Insights into the central role of the financial sector in contemporary macro-economies can be brought into sharp focus with four historical comparisons:

(a) credit implosion leading to a severe banking crisis in Japan;

(b) the meltdown of foreign reserves triggered by foreign hot-money flight from the frothy economies of developing Asian nations with fixed exchange rate regimes;

(c) the global financial crisis;

(d) the Eurozone crisis (see Razin [2015]).

Japan was lashed by a speculative tornado in 1986–1991. It was localized, brief, and devastating, with enduring paralytic consequences often described as the "lost decades" (1991–2013, before Abe economics). The phenomenon was a selective price bubble, disconnected from low and decelerating GDP inflation all the way to deflation. Economic growth was converging asymptotically toward zero.

Financial intermediary fragilities and credit frictions that periodically erupt into financial crises are rooted in coordination failures, incentive problems, asymmetric information, risk-shifting behavior, and excessive optimism among participants in collateralized debt markets. Each one of these forces is present in the global financial problems of the past few decades (see Goldstein and Razin [2015]).

Banks finance long-term assets with short-term deposits. The advantage of this arrangement is that it enables banks to provide risk sharing to investors who might face early liquidity needs. However, this also exposes the bank to the risk of a bank run, whereby many creditors decide to withdraw their money early. The key problem is that of a coordination failure, which stands at the root of the fragility of banking systems: when more depositors withdraw their money from a bank, the bank is more likely to fail, and so other depositors have a stronger incentive to withdraw.

A key policy question is how to avoid and/or mitigate the damages from coordination failures and runs in the financial system. While insurance has been effective, its implications for moral hazard merit careful consideration. There is room for more research on the optimal deposit insurance policy. Using recent developments in economic theory, global-games models enable analysis of the benefit of insurance in mitigating runs against the cost in generating moral hazard, leading to characterization of optimal insurance policy. The focus in these models is on the behavior of depositors or creditors of the banks. However, problems in the financial sector often arise from the other side of the balance sheet. The quality of loans provided by the banks is determined in equilibrium. Frictions, however, make banks curtail lending to protect assets.

While basic economic theory suggests that prices adjust so that supply equals demand and no rationing arises in equilibrium, recent models show that this will not occur in the credit market because of the endogeneity of the quality of the loan. The key frictions causing rationing are moral hazard and adverse selection. If a borrower has the ability to divert resources at the expense of the creditor, then creditors will be reluctant to lend to borrowers. Hence, for credit to flow efficiently from the creditor to the borrower, it is crucial that the borrower maintain "skin in the game"; that is, that he has enough at stake in the success of the project, and so does not have a strong incentive to divert resources. This creates a limit on credit, and it can be amplified when the economic conditions worsen, leading to a crisis.

5.3   Understanding Deflation Crises

Historical patterns of booms and busts typically exhibit frequent small recessions interrupted by rare but deep and long recessions. The traditional macroeconomic models, however, have not adequately captured these patterns. Thus, the traditional dynamic stochastic general equilibrium (DSGE) macroeconomic models, used often by central banks and many other policy-making institutions, are not capable of delivering crisis features in history: frequent small recessions punctuated by rare depressions. Financial intermediaries, who have largely been omitted from the traditional macroeconomic framework, were treated simply like a veil that exists between savers and investors, and not as a source of crisis by themselves. Financial frictions, however, have first-order effects on economic activity, both in the long and the short runs.

This does not mean that economists understand how to use fiscal policy and supplementary monetary instruments to recover optimally or prevent future reoccurrences, given the often-destabilizing expectations of the private sector due to conflicting incentives, finance fragility, and politically gridlocked governments. Rather, it means that complacency based on incomplete knowledge of how the system works is no longer tenable, and reassessment of past output, employment, and finance-stabilizing measures is in order.

Pre-crisis conventional wisdom held that business cycle oscillations were primarily caused by productivity shocks that lasted until price- and wage-setters disentangled real from nominal effects (Lucas 1975, 2000, 2003), or monetary shocks, in view of staggered wage and price adjustments. These real and monetary shocks sometimes generated inflation or deflation, which was best addressed with monetary policy. Accordingly, central bankers were tasked with the mission of maintaining slow and stable inflation. Zero inflation and deflation were shunned, because they purportedly were incompatible with full capacity and full employment (Phillips 1958; Phelps 1967; Friedman 1968) and well-managed monetary policy. Central bankers were supposed to be less concerned with real economic activity; many came to believe that full employment and 2 percent inflation could be sustained indefinitely by *divine coincidence*. The divine coincidence was said to be made all the better by the analytical discovery that the real economic performance could be regulated, in theory, with only a single monetary instrument, the short-term interest rate. Evidently, arbitrage across time meant that central banks could control economy-wide temporal interest rates, short and long, and arbitrage across asset classes implied that the Federal Reserve (the Fed) could similarly influence risk-adjusted rates for a diverse set of securities. Fiscal policy, which had "ruled the roost" under the influence of crude Keynesianism from 1950 to 1980, in this way was relegated to a subsidiary role of macroeconomic stabilization. This view was reinforced by macroeconomic theorists' beliefs in the empirical validity of friction-free Ricardian-equivalence arguments and skepticism about lags and political gridlocks, which makes discretionary fiscal policy as a stabilization tool practically irrelevant.

It is also true that little attention was paid to the financial sector in macroeconomic theory. The financial sector prudential policy was perceived as regulatory, only affecting structural performance but not business cycle performance. It was not treated as an aggregate demand management issue. The consensus view held that automatic stabilizers such as unemployment insurance should be retained in order to share privately uninsurable risks. Federal deposit insurance was preserved to deter bank runs, and commercial banks' credit and investments continued to be regulated to prevent moral hazard under the federal deposit insurance, but otherwise finance was lightly supervised, especially shadow banks, hedge funds, mortgages, and derivatives.

Two separate narratives have emerged in the wake of the 2008 global financial crisis. One interpretation speaks of the bubble-bursting role of private financial excess and the key role of the banking system in leveraging and deleveraging the economy. The other emphasizes the risk of inflation arising from the expansion of the central bank balance sheet, the public-sector debt over the private, and worries about the risks of lax fiscal policies. Most macroeconomic theorists now concede that the pre-crisis monetarist consensus was mistaken. Both narratives recognize that with the Fed funds rate near the zero lower bound, the burden for stimulating recovery and short-term growth falls to nonconventional monetary policies, such as quantitative and credit easing. However, the agreement stops here. From this point on, the profession has split into two contending camps.

The Ricardian faction contends that budget spending (in a ratio to GDP), in many large nations such as the United States will drive up interest rates, crowd out private investment, and have negative stimulatory impact. This could easily generate recession (depression) coupled with a bout of high inflation (deflation), due to excessive commercial bank liquidity. This is reminiscent of Friedrich Hayek warning that a surge of excessive liquidity can misdirect investments leading to a boom followed by a bust.

However, members of the other intellectual camp concerned about the non-Ricardian conditions, such as credit frictions, market freezes, liquidity traps, and deflation, have the opposite view. They insist that austerity policies and deflation are the danger under depressed markets (which via the Bernanke doctrine implies a great depression with rising real wages and excess savings; see Bernanke [1983]). They deduce that avoidance of disaster hinges on temporarily raising public spending to fill in the gap of shrinking private spending, continued central bank credit easing, and quantitative easing. They are aware that this could have inflationary ramifications, which is helpful to lower the real interest rate, but brush the soon-to-arrive inflation peril aside by claiming that speculators will absorb most of the idle cash balances governments are prepared to print, because, with zero interest rate, money and bonds are perfect substitutes. At the same time, inflationary expectations are to be replaced by deflationary expectations. Moreover, they contend that excess base money can be drained from the system, whenever banks decide to resume lending, but not fully, during a long period of deleveraging by households and firms. In addition, as the icing on the cake, they proclaim that large multiplier effects during depression-like situations will not only raise employment but also provide the wherewithal to repay the government debt. They also emphasize the longer-term implications of deep unemployment that create a segment of the labor force that may become unemployable (see Appendix 5C for a discussion of sovereign-debt issues).

Notwithstanding these disagreements, the bottom line, therefore, is that the pre-2008 faith in just one monetary lever ensuring stability and growth proved to be only dreaming. The dynamics of macro-aggregates depends on heterogeneous expectations, information, and contractual and credit frictions of erstwhile utility seekers under incomplete information, in morally hazardous and incomplete financial markets, subject to sundry shocks. Policy management is correspondingly complex, particularly in the presence of deleveraging and liquidity trap conditions; it is still more challenging in imperfect regulatory regimes where low inflation is targeted to ensure full employment and rapid economic growth, susceptible to moral hazard, adverse selection, coordination failures—the unavoidable characteristics of any financial intermediation. That is to say, we should not lose sight of the financial sector as a central pillar of the macroeconomic model. Fiscal policy also needs serious rethinking.

5.4   The EMU Crisis

The global financial crisis, which erupted in the United States, instantaneously swept across Europe and triggered the euro-zone crisis. Like the United States, the European Monetary Union was ripe for a crash. The EMU had its own real estate bubble (specifically in Ireland and Spain). EMU economies, which financially deregulated intermediaries, indulged in excessive deficit spending, and had rapidly expanded credit (partly through derivatives). Policy responses and recovery patterns for key European Union members, such as Germany, France (within the Eurozone), and the United Kingdom (outside the Eurozone), were similar.[2] However, after the bubble burst and the crisis began unfolding, it became clear that the Eurozone plight differed from America's in one fundamental respect. There was no exact counterpart of GIIPS (Greece, Ireland, Italy, Portugal, and Spain) in the United States. Some American states had over-borrowed, but the sovereign debt crisis did not place individual states at deflationary risk or threaten the viability of the federal union. Not so for some members within the Eurozone.[3]

Models of the balance of payment crisis, offered in Appendix 1A, are highly relevant to the current situation in the European Monetary Union. The international financial trilemma approach is particularly instructive. It stipulates that a country can choose only two of three policy goals: free international capital flows, monetary autonomy, or the stability of the exchange rate.[4] Countries in the Eurozone now realize that in their attempt to achieve the first and third goals they have given up on the second goal, and so have limited ability to absorb the shocks in economic activity and maintain their national debts, triggered by the global financial crisis. Coordination problems among investors and currency speculators aggravate this situation and may have an important effect on whether individual countries in Europe are forced to default and/or leave the monetary union.

5.5   Emerging Macroeconomics Paradigm

During a briefing by academics at the London School of Economics on the 2008 turmoil in the international markets, the British queen famously asked: "Why did nobody notice it?"

Indeed, macroeconomics had to reinvent itself. The key feature missing from the traditional macroeconomic model described above is the role of financial intermediaries. Clearly, the 2008 crisis has shown that financial intermediary capital has a crucial role in the economy, and losses incurred by financial intermediaries can have strong spillover effects on the rest of the economy. Recently, Gertler and Kiyotaki (2011) and Rampini and Viswanathan (2011) added a financial intermediary sector (albeit the global financial crisis is driven by panic, unlike Holmstrom and Tirole [1997]) and analyzed the dynamic interactions between this sector and the rest of the economy. Introducing this sector into macroeconomic models enables elaborate discussions on various policies conducted by governments during the recent crisis in the attempt to stimulate the economy via the financial intermediation sector. Such policies are discussed by Gertler and Kiyotaki (2011).

Eggertsson and Krugman (2013) provide a unique angle of the role played by credit frictions in the macroeconomics. They study a model with heterogeneous agents, where patient agents lend and impatient agents borrow, subject to a collateral constraint. If, for some reason, the collateral requirement becomes tighter, impatient agents will have to go into a process of deleveraging, reducing the aggregate demand. This excess saving leads to a reduction in the natural interest rate, which might become negative, and the nominal (policy) interest rate hits the zero bound, putting the economy into a liquidity trap. Then, traditional monetary policy becomes impossible, but fiscal policy regains some potency. In their model, unanticipated tightening in the credit market, manifested as a fall in borrowing limits, forces consumers to cut spending. The borrowing-limit shock triggers a vicious circle, whereby spending cuts lead to falling prices, which raise the real value of the consumer nominal debt. The ensuing debt overhang depresses consumption spending further; this leads to an additional fall in the price level and consumer spending, and so on. That is, the credit market shock leads to a transitional deleveraging period with depressed demand and a liquidity trap.[5]

5.6   Twin Gaps under Financial Depression

To understand the effects of monetary policy under financial depression we begin with the concept of the natural real interest rate. The issue is how the natural interest rate is affected by an economy-wide financial shock—essentially, the shock that tightens the borrowing limits. When a borrowing limit unexpectedly falls, borrowing consumers are forced to cut spending, in order to consume and pay back old debt. Through a standard general-equilibrium mechanism, this cut in spending lowers the natural interest rate. In a financially depressed economy, the (full-price flexibility) natural interest rate may become negative. However, the nominal interest is bounded by zero. When the nominal rate reaches its zero lower bound, by the Fisher equation the actual real rate must equal the rate of price deflation. A gap opens between the natural and the actual real rates.

Figure 5.3 illustrates how the real interest gap links to the output gap—the twin gaps. In the figure, the output gap is measured by the horizontal difference between the *actual* saving schedule and the *flexible-price* saving schedule.

Larry Summers (2014) put forward a conjecture about the longer-run implications of the negative real natural rate with an occasional liquidity trap. In his view, the world is demand short—that is, the real interest rates necessary to equate investment and saving at full employment are very low and may often be unattainable, given the bounds on nominal interest rate reductions. The result is very low long-term real rates and sluggish growth expectations.[6]

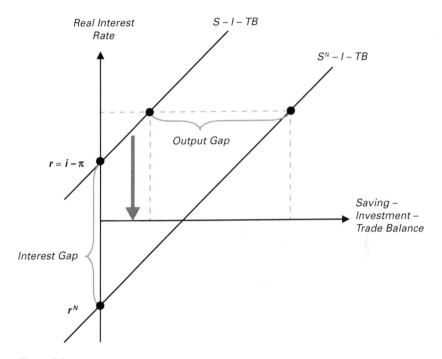

Figure 5.3
Twin gaps.
Note: The down-pointing arrow indicates that the real interest rate is driven down by the central bank, which lowers the nominal interest rate at a pace faster than the rate of decline in inflation. The assumption is that the inflation rate reaches zero when the arrow touches the horizontal coordinate, at the point where the nominal interest rate is set at its zero lower bound. *Source*: Razin (2015). See Appendix 5A.

The down-pointing arrow shows the central bank's policy-rate response to the output gap, while reducing the inflation rate. In the presence of inflation and slackness, financial depression forces are moving down the inflation rate, π. The nominal interest rate, i, is pushed down, until it reaches the zero lower bound. When the zero lower bound is reached, the central bank cannot push the policy rate down further to close output and real interest rate gaps. The central bank has to resort to unconventional, barely effective monetary policies. Fiscal expansion could effectively help the economy out of the liquidity trap, by shifting the S-I-TB schedule rightward.

Depression forces, such as they exist in Europe, or Japan, do not appear to hold in the case of Israel, and in emerging economies. The twin-gap diagram depicted in figure 5.3 represents the non-depression case of Israel. In this case, out of the zero lower bound, there is room to lower the rate of interest to stimulate the economy. That is, pushing down the interest rate, i, will shift down the upper line and shrink the twin gaps. In the depression case, the interest rate is at its zero lower bound, and there is no room for the conventional monetary policy. The economy is stuck with a negative natural interest rate (the real rate obtained under full-wage and price flexibility) and a positive actual real rate (if price deflation set in); only unconventional monetary easing, which is of limited effectiveness, can reduce the twin gaps.[7]

Israel, like many other emerging economies, did not have depression forces operating from within the domestic economic structure. Importantly, Israel's natural interest rate remained positive, thereby avoiding the slide into liquidity trap, shown in figure 5.3.

What are the potential spillovers from a depression situation in several advanced economies to a non-depression economy like Israel's? First, recall that the long-term arbitrage conditions for a financially integrated small economy whose natural real interest rate is positive implies a trend in real appreciation, provided that the world natural real interest is negative. Small country competitiveness weakens, thereby harming its export-led growth possibilities. Second, weakness in demand in the epicenter of the world's secular stagnation and a low inflation in the home economy generally lead to higher real exchange rates at home. This is due to the weaker demand for exports, which puts pressures on the central bank to lower rates to keep aggregate demand at pace with potential output.[8]

5.7   Israel's Resilience to Depression Pressures

Israel's resilience to the external financial shock during the global crisis was rooted in (a) the absence of a credit boom in the wake of the crisis, and (b) the relatively small commercial banks' exposure in terms of toxic assets that played a major role for the European countries.

The newly emerging macroeconomic paradigm spans the gamut from an analytical framework that features full capital-market arbitrage, smooth credit, Ricardian-equivalence properties, representative agents, and efficient monetary management, to a framework with multiple agents, incorporating debt frictions, liquidity traps, and relatively ineffective monetary management and providing a role for fiscal policy in aggregate demand management. The analytical framework based on the frictionless paradigm captures well the role of globalization forces and the reduction in inflation in the 1990s Great Moderation era. The multiple-agent, market-friction revised analytical framework captures some key features of the Great Recession that occurred in the aftermath of the 2008 global financial crisis. It gives insight about the macroeconomic effects of debt overhang on economic activity and inflation, when the monetary policy rate reaches its lower bound.

The concern at the time was that Israel, being well integrated into the world markets and the world finance, might suffer contagion that will be long lasting. At the end of the day, Israel suffered only a temporary trade shock because of the decline in world demand.

Hale, Razin, and Tong (2014) analyze the data for fifty-two developed and developing countries over the period 1980–2008. As a proxy for creditor protection, they use the creditor rights index (CRI) compiled by Djankov et al. (2007). This is a panel that covers 129 countries for 1978–2008. The CRI is constructed in the same way as in La Porta et al. (1998). It ranges from 0 to 4, with a higher number associated with better protection for creditors. Israel is among the "creditor rights index = 3" countries, grouped with Germany and Australia. Italy and Norway are among "creditor rights index = 2" countries. Hong Kong belongs to "creditor rights index = 4" countries. Hale, Razin, and Tong (2014) find support for the predictions of a Tobin-Q model of the stock market with credit frictions, as well as evidence consistent with the mechanism through which creditor protection affects stock market returns. Specifically, they find support for the three main testable implications of the model: higher frequency of crises, larger change in stock market returns during crises, and larger decline in investment during crises in countries with poor creditor rights protection. In addition, they demonstrate that, in both full and matched samples, the decline in investment growth rate during liquidity crises is small and not statistically significant in countries with strong creditor rights protection.[9] However, in countries with weak creditor rights protection, they find that the investment growth rate declines by a factor of two during crises, with a difference that is statistically significant in the full sample. This difference, however, is only borderline significant in the matched sample. In fact, investment growth during non-crisis periods is similar across subsamples, while investment growth during crisis periods is substantially lower in countries with weak creditor rights protection. Consistent with its strong creditor's protection laws and proper regulation, Israel did not have a significant credit boom in the wake of the 2008 crisis; see figure 5.4.

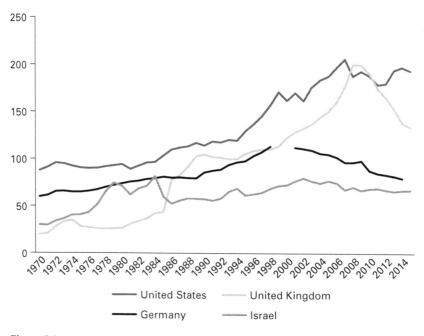

Figure 5.4
Domestic credit to private non-financial sector (% of GDP). *Note*: Domestic credit provided by the financial sector includes all credit to various sectors on a gross basis, with the exception of credit to the central government, which is net. The financial sector includes monetary authorities and deposit money banks, as well as other financial corporations where data are available (including corporations that do not accept transferable deposits but do incur such liabilities as time and savings deposits). Examples of other financial corporations are finance and leasing companies, moneylenders, insurance corporations, pension funds, and foreign exchange companies. *Source*: International Monetary Fund, International Financial Statistics, data files, and World Bank and OECD GDP estimates.

Because of lax regulation, however, the United States and the United Kingdom were vulnerable to a gigantic credit expansion; see figure 5.4.

Nevertheless, GDP growth in Israel has averaged 4 percent over the 2005–2010 period, compared with 0.7 percent on average for OECD countries. The overall living standards continue to improve gradually, with per capita real GDP growing more rapidly than in other OECD countries. The economy's resilience has been underpinned by solid economic fundamentals, including large foreign reserves, a dynamic high-tech export sector, and the absence of economy-wide deleveraging pressures leading to the downfall in economic activity. Israel did not have a credit bubble in the years preceding the global financial

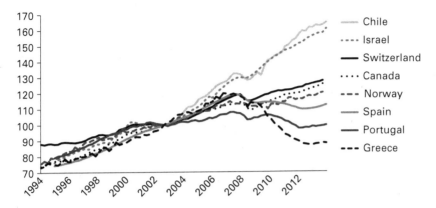

Figure 5.5
Real GDP, Israel and selected countries (January 2003 = 100). *Source*: FRED (economic database of the Federal Reserve Bank of St. Louis).

crash, unlike the other major advanced economies, where the bubble burst during the financial crisis.

Israel's growth performance during and after the global crisis was not unique, however. Figure 5.5 shows that among similar small open economies Israel's GDP grew over the recent twenty years, including the 2008–2010 period, at a similar cumulative rate as Chile, but at a much higher rate than Greece, Spain, and Portugal, which had a financial sector crash.

Furthermore, figure 5.6 depicts GNP levels for Israel, Turkey, Brazil, and Canada—economies that were spared a financial sector crash. Israel exhibits a more moderate drop of output than all these countries.

5.8   International Capital Flows

Capital flows provide another measure of the resilience of the Israeli economy to the shocks. In the aftermath of the global financial crisis, expansionary monetary policies in advanced economies, conventional or unconventional, that were conducted to boost up the economy, have affected emerging market economies and others, such as Israel, through three channels:

(1) reduced exports;

(2) exchange rate appreciation; and

(3) the effects of capital inflows on the domestic financial system.

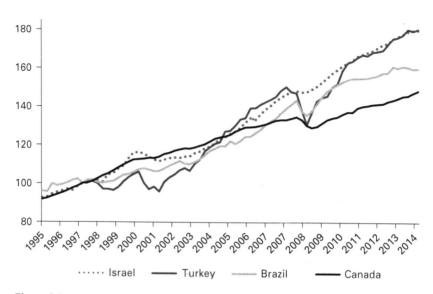

Figure 5.6
Real GNP, countries with no financial crisis (January 1998 = 100). *Source*: FRED (economic database of the Federal Reserve Bank of St. Louis).

A number of studies have found an effect of monetary policy on specific gross flows. Bruno and Shin (2015), for example, using a VAR methodology over the pre-crisis period (1995 Q4 to 2007 Q4), find an effect of the federal funds rate on cross-border bank-to-bank flows; however, the effect is barely significant. Fratzscher, Lo Duca, and Straub (2013), using daily data on portfolio equity and bond flows, find significant effects of different monetary policy announcements and actions since the beginning of the crisis. However, their results point to the complexity of the effects of apparently largely similar monetary measures. For example, they find QE1 announcements decreased bond flows to emerging markets (EM), while the US-Fed Quantitative Easing policy (QE2) announcements increased them. This suggests that, in each case, monetary policy worked partly through its effects on the risk premium. These studies cannot settle the further issue of whether or not total gross inflows increase with advanced economies monetary expansions. The increase in the inflows the researchers have identified may be offset by a decrease in other inflows.[10] However, studies of total inflows, or of the set of inflows adding up to total inflows, yield some mixed conclusions. A representative and careful paper, by Cerutti, Claessens, and Laeven (2015), using quarterly flows over the second quarter of 2001 to the second quarter of 2013, suggests two main conclusions. The most significant observable variable in explaining flows into emerging markets (EMs) is the VIX index:[11] an increase in the VIX leads to a decrease in inflows to EMs. The coefficients on the monetary policy variables, namely, the expected change in the policy rate and the slope of the yield curve, typically have the expected sign. Several studies found that movements in the VIX are strongly associated with global capital flows.[12]

It is worth looking now at capital inflows to EMs and Israel from the United States, the epicenter of the global financial crisis and the country that adapted, with virtually no lag, a brief expansionary fiscal policy and a persistent expansionary monetary policy.

Figure 5.7 describes the portfolio capital outflows from the United States to selected countries. Israel is in the middle of the pack of countries that enjoyed inflow of portfolio capital investments in the aftermath of the 2008 global financial crisis. These inflows put appreciation pressures on the exchange rates. Some central banks, including Bank of Israel, conducted a policy of a massive purchase of foreign currency

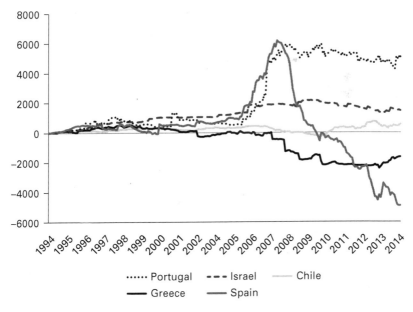

Figure 5.7
Portfolio flows, crisis economies (index, December 1994 = 100). *Source*: Anusha Chari.

denominated assets, to protect against the declining competitiveness in the world trade.

5.9   Exchange-Rate Policy Reaction

How did the Israeli policy makers react to the 2008 global financial depression and global trade-diminishing shocks? Policy makers' concern was threefold: First, banks' exposures to toxic assets such as mortgage-based securities and foreigners' debt obligations. Partly because Israel skipped the credit bubble, and bank regulations were relatively tight, Israel showed a sound resilience to the global financial shock. Second, Israel's export markets softened, and demand conditions deteriorated. Third, Israel's domestic currency got strengthened. Bank of Israel addressed the last two issues by a massive foreign exchange market intervention, to weaken the value of the domestic currency and stimulate exports.

In the aftermath of the global financial crisis, expansionary monetary policies in advanced economies, conventional or unconventional, that were conducted to boost up the economy have appreciated the currencies of the emerging market economies, including Israel. The question for these economies was whether an expansionary monetary policy, which tends to depreciate the currency and boost exports, requires a direct foreign exchange market intervention, or whether the latter can succeed without the former.[13]

Here's how covered interest parity works. Think of two ways to invest money, without risk, for a year. Option 1: buy a one-year Israeli bond. Option 2: Buy euros to purchase a one-year Euro bond, and enter a forward contract by which you get Israeli Shekels back for your euros one year from now, at a predetermined rate. Both are entirely risk free. They should therefore give exactly the same rate of return, by arbitrage. However, the covered interest rate parity relationship falls apart in a financial crisis. To take advantage of differential rates of return in favor of Euro bonds, one first has to borrow dollars, which are impossible for Israeli banks to lend in the midst of the financial crisis. Hence, the covered interest parity breaks down during financial distress conditions.

Israel's monetary authorities were concerned about the Great Recession downward pressures on the demand for Israel's exports and the strengthening of the Israeli currency as capital inflows rose. They engaged in an intensive (sterilized) intervention in the foreign exchange market to prevent the appreciation of the currency. However, there are evidently limits to how much such policy can stimulate the demand for Israel's output.

Sterilized intervention is ineffective when there is high private capital mobility to the extent that domestic and foreign securities viewed by a large group of investors are close substitutes. Conditions under which sterilized intervention is effective happen to exist for a crisis economy, however, when there is a probability of capital flow reversal, liquidity shortage, or major real trade shock, leading to financial-intermediaries collapse. (See Appendix 5B.) Under conditions where foreign and domestic assets are close substitutes, sterilized intervention is ineffective. Through a central-bank sale of domestic government debt assets, following a purchase of foreign currency in the foreign exchange market, the money supply fully adjusts to bring back the pre-intervention expected rates of return on domestic and foreign currency bonds into equilibrium (the standard interest parity). Therefore, sterilized intervention into the foreign exchange market by the monetary authorities, where the domestic money supply is unchanged, is incapable of pushing the exchange rate up or down. However, the proposition may change in the presence of imperfect asset substitutability, where domestic and foreign bonds command a different liquidity premium and risk premium. Changing the composition of central bank assets, between foreign and domestic assets (the case of sterilized foreign exchange rate market interventions), can then have real economic effects in the presence of credit market spreads and frictions. In this case, sterilized foreign exchange market intervention could effectively change the value of the foreign currency in terms of domestic currency. A sterilized purchase of foreign assets may change the liquidity premium that domestic bonds command, relative to foreign bonds, even though the money supply is left unchanged. A similar outcome may transpire when foreign exchange intervention changes market views of future foreign exchange market interventions. Similarly, liquidity-based imperfect asset substitution between domestic government and domestic private sector bonds during liquidity crises can be exploited by the central bank.[14] Israel's half-decade foreign exchange market episode started when credit frictions were relatively intensive following the Lehman moment in the United States on September 15, 2008. As Appendix 5B indicates, under these conditions the intervention aimed

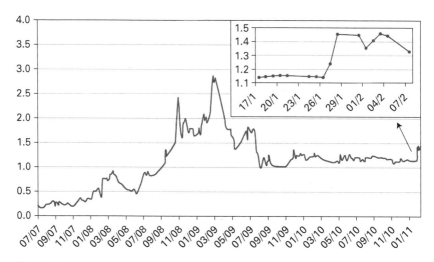

Figure 5.8
Five-year CDS spread for Israel, 07/2007–02/2011, percentage. *Source*: FRED, Bank of Israel.

at keeping the exchange rate overly depreciated is effective. But, over time, as credit conditions improved, the policy became potentially less and less effective, as Appendix 4A demonstrates.

Recall that a significant observable variable in explaining short-term flows into EMs is the VIX index: an increase in the VIX leads to a decrease in inflows to EMs. The VIX index is directly related to the risk-adjusted return on domestic government bonds in the periphery countries, like Israel. Specifically for Israel in the wake of the 2008 global crisis one can look at the credit default swap (CDS) spread to gauge the risk-liquidity premium market places on Israel's securities.[15] In Figure 5.8 we plot the five-year CDS spread, which shows a blip from 2008 to 2009.

A sterilized foreign-exchange market purchase of U.S. government bonds by the central bank is then capable of blocking exchange rate appreciation. This was the rationale for the Bank of Israel policy in the aftermath of the global financial crisis. However, the effectiveness of such a policy is short-lived. Once the VIX index falls, sterilized foreign exchange market intervention becomes ineffective. Excessively high foreign reserves also have fiscal medium term costs.

Figure 5.9 describes the changes in foreign exchange reserves for selected countries during the aftermath of the 2008 financial shock.

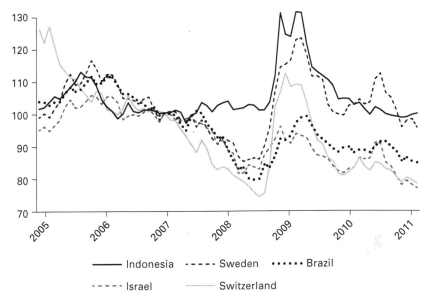

Figure 5.9
Nominal exchange rate of various countries that engaged in the currency war game: Israel, Switzerland, Sweden, Brazil, and Indonesia (2007 = 100). *Source*: FRED (economic database of the Federal Reserve Bank of St. Louis).

Israel's foreign exchange reserves grew significantly more than those of the advanced economies did, but not much differently from those among the non-OECD countries.[16]

Figure 5.9 describes the nominal exchange rate of various countries that engaged in the currency war: Israel, Sweden, Switzerland, Brazil, and Indonesia. Israel seems to have undervalued its currency the least among these countries, possibly because, thanks to its international financial integration and almost no capital controls, the effectiveness of sterilized intervention was weak (for an analytical framework see Appendix 5B). The effectiveness of foreign-exchange market intervention was short-lived in all the countries. In all cases, continuing with the policy when the credit conditions improved led to an over-buildup of the low-return international reserves. In comparing these countries, the policy effectiveness of Israel and Switzerland (both are with high private capital mobility) was relatively wobbly. The policy of Israel was less effective than those in Brazi and Indonesia—both with capital controls, hence the higher effectiveness and the ability to depreciate the currency more effectively. Sweden, with its high private capital mobility, was able to intervene more effectively than Israel for no straightforward reason.

5.10   Implications

Historical patterns of booms and busts typically exhibit frequent small recessions interrupted by rare but deep and long recessions. Traditional macroeconomic models, used often by central banks and many other policy-making institutions, do not capture the full features of crises: frequent small recessions punctuated by rare depressions. They do not illuminate how small open economies, like Israel, that are substantially integrated into the world economy perform when a global financial shock takes place, leading to recession as deep and persistent as the Great Recession. We discussed in this chapter the relatively robust performance of Israel (as well as some other advanced economies, like Canada) and major emerging markets in the aftermath of the 2008 global financial crisis. Factors contributing to this robustness are the absence of credit and real estate bubbles, and banks' tight regulation in the wake of the crisis, which precluded the deleveraging process following the crisis.

Appendix 5A: A General Equilibrium Model of Depression

This appendix details the effect of financial depression on the ability of monetary policy to stimulate the economy, and to reduce the twin gaps that are depicted in figure 5.3. Eggertsson and Krugman (2013) view depression (liquidity-trap) conditions as being the result of a deleveraging shock. They study a model with heterogeneous agents, where patient agents lend and impatient agents borrow, subject to a collateral constraint.[17] Collateral reduces the consequences of adverse selection because even if the borrower turns out not to be a good credit risk and defaults on a loan, the lender can sell the collateral and use the proceeds to make up for the losses on the loan. Collateral also reduces moral hazard by reducing the incentives for borrowers to take on too much risk. When a borrower has pledged collateral on her loan, she has more to lose if she cannot pay it back, and so she naturally is more reluctant to engage in risky activities that make it more likely she will default and lose the collateral. If, for some reason, the collateral requirement becomes tighter, impatient agents will have to go into a process of deleveraging, reducing the aggregate demand. This excess saving leads to a reduction in the natural interest rate that might become negative, and the nominal (policy) interest rate hits the zero bound, putting the economy into a liquidity trap. Then, traditional monetary policy becomes impossible, but fiscal policy regains some potency.

5A.1   Natural Rate of Interest, the Lower Bound, and the Output Gap

To understand monetary policy under economic depression, we begin the analysis with a technical issue: how the natural interest rate is affected by a decrease in borrowing limits. In a flexible-price endowments model, impatient agents borrow from patient agents, whereas the former are subject to a borrowing limit. When the debt limit unexpectedly falls, impatient consumers are forced to cut spending, which, through a standard general equilibrium mechanism, lowers the natural interest rate all the way to negative. The next step in developing the model allows the consumer debt to take the form of nominal obligations. In this case, the shock to the borrowing limit has a magnified effect on the natural interest rate, because the depressed demand that follows the shock lowers the price level, thereby raising the real value of debt overhang and lowering further consumer spending. Consequently, the nominal interest rate is pushed toward the zero lower bound. At this stage of developing the analytical framework into a full-fledged New Keynesian model, Eggertsson and Krugman (2013) introduce nominal price rigidity; consequently, output becomes variable.

5A.2   Natural Rate of Interest

To understand how severe tightening in the credit market causes a fall in the natural rate of interest, we start with a pure-endowment economy, a special case of the perfect price flexibility model.

Consider a continuum of households (with a mass equaling 1). Households are of two types: *patient*, with a low discount rate, denoted by s, and *impatient*, with a high discount rate, denoted by b. Each one of these two representative households gets a constant endowment $(1/2)Y$ each period. Borrowing and lending take the form of risk-free bonds denominated in the consumption good, as in an indexed bond case.

The utility function is

$$\sum_{t=0}^{\infty} \beta(i)^t \log c_t(i), \tag{5A.1}$$

where $i = s$ or b, and $\beta(s) = \beta > \beta(b)$.

The budget constraint of each individual household is

$$D_t(i) = (1 + r_{t-1})D_{t-1}(i) - \frac{1}{2}y + C_t(i),$$ (5A.2)

where D denotes debt, and $i = s$ or b.

A borrowing limit exists (inclusive of next-period interest rate payments), D^{high}, so that at any period-t debt,

$$(1 + r_t)\, D_t\,(i) \le D^{high} > 0.$$

We assume that this bound is at least strictly lower than the maximum repayment capacity, the present discounted value of output of each agent; that is, $D_{high} < (1/2)\,[\beta/(1-\beta)]Y$. Later, we will see that the equilibrium interest rate is equal to $(1 - \beta/\beta)$, which is used for the discounting operation.

Consumption of the saver satisfies a consumption Euler equation in each period:

$$\frac{1}{C_t^s} = (1 + r_t)\beta \frac{1}{C_{t+1}^s}.$$ (5A.4)

The impatient household borrows up to the borrowing limit:

$$C^b = \frac{1}{2}Y - \frac{r}{1+r}D^{high}.$$ (5A.5)

The goods-market clearing condition is

$$Y = C^s + C^b,$$ (5A.6)

implying

$$C^a = \frac{1}{2}Y + \frac{r}{1+r}D^{high}.$$ (5A.7).

Equations (5A.4), (5A.5), and (5A.6) imply that the non-stochastic, steady state real interest rate is determined by the discount factor of the *patient* consumer. That is, the equilibrium value of the natural interest rate is

$$r^N = (1 - \beta)/\beta.$$

Suppose that the debt limit falls unexpectedly (and discretely) from D^{high} to D^{low}.

5A.3   Borrowing Limit and the Natural Interest Rate

Eggertsson and Krugman (2013) at this stage assume that the transition to the new steady state, where borrowers have already fully adjusted their consumption decisions after the shock, takes only one period. Denote short-run variables with S and long-run variables with L. The next-period real interest rate remains

$$r^N = \frac{1-\beta}{\beta}.$$

In the new steady state, the equilibrium rate of interest depends on the saver's discount factor but not on the debt ceiling.

In the short run, as in steady state, we have for the borrower

$$C_L^b = \frac{1}{2}Y - \frac{r}{1+r}D^{low} = \frac{1}{2}Y - (1-\beta)D^{low}, \qquad (5A.8)$$

where, in equation (5A.8), we substituted for the long-run equilibrium real interest rate. In the short run, however, the borrower needs to deleverage to satisfy the new borrowing limit. Hence, his budget constraint in the short run is

$$D_S = D^{high} - \frac{1}{2}Y + C_S^b. \qquad (5A.9)$$

If before the shock the borrower's debt is always rolled over, period by period, now, after the shock, they are more severely constrained because they could borrow up to a lower borrowing limit. Therefore, in order to pay back old debt, the borrower consumption spending must fall during the entire deleveraging stage of the cycle. Because we made an assumption here that the borrower must deleverage to the new debt limit within a single period, so that

$$D_S = \frac{D^{low}}{1+r_S},$$

their short-run consumption falls to

$$C_S^b = \frac{1}{2}Y + \frac{D^{low}}{1+r_S} - D^{high}. \qquad (5A.10)$$

Short-run goods-market clearing implies

$$C_S^s + C_S^b = Y.$$

The long-run consumption of the saver is

$$C_L^S = \frac{1}{2}Y + \frac{r}{1+r}D^{low} = \frac{1}{2}Y + (1-\beta)D^{low}. \tag{5A.11}$$

Substituting for the consumption of the borrower, we get

$$C_S^S = \frac{1}{2}Y - \frac{D^{low}}{1+r_S} + D^{high}. \tag{5A.12}$$

Recall that the consumption decision of the saver satisfies the consumption Euler equation

$$C_L^S = (1+r_S)\beta C_S^S. \tag{5A.13}$$

Substitute the short- and long-run consumption of the saver into equation (5A.14), and, solving for $1+r_S$, we get

$$1+r_S = \frac{\frac{1}{2}Y + D^{low}}{\beta\frac{1}{2}Y + \beta D^{high}}. \tag{5A.14}$$

The deleveraging shock will cause the natural rate of interest r_S to become negative if

$$\frac{\frac{1}{2}Y + D^{low}}{\beta\frac{1}{2}Y + \beta D^{high}} < 1. \tag{5A.15}$$

Or,

$$\beta D^{high} - D^{low} > \frac{1}{2}\frac{1-\beta}{\beta}Y.$$

Naturally, we can define *debt overhang* by

$$\beta D^{high} - D^{low}.$$

The present value of the representative individual wealth is

$$\frac{1}{2}\frac{1-\beta}{\beta}Y.$$

This condition (5A.15) will apply if the debt overhang is larger than wealth.

The interpretation for the negative natural rate of interest is that the saver must be induced to make up for the reduction in consumption by the borrower; thereby raising the level of spending. For this to happen, the natural interest rate must fall, and, in the face of a large deleveraging shock, it must become negative to induce the saver to spend sufficiently more.

5A.4 Natural Rate of Interest and Zero-Bound Rate

To make the price level determinate, assume that nominal government debt is traded. This extension enables us to analyze the conditions where a borrowing-limit shock forces the nominal interest rate to attain the zero lower bound. As before, we assume that the long-run equilibrium, with market-clearing stable prices, is restored with a positive (nominal) interest rate after just one transition period.

In the transition period, the Euler equation, which has to be satisfied by the saver, becomes

$$\frac{1}{C_t^S} = (1 + i_t)\beta_t \frac{1}{C_{t+1}^S} \frac{P_t}{P_{t+1}}, \tag{5A.16}$$

where P_t is the price level, and i_t is the nominal interest rate. The saver behaves in accordance with the Fisher equation, which must prevail in the short run:

$$1 + r_S = (1 + i_S)\frac{P_S}{P*}.$$

We impose the zero bound

$$i_t \geq 0.$$

Solving for the price level, we get

$$\frac{P_S}{P*} = \frac{\frac{1}{2}Y + D^{low}}{\beta \frac{1}{2}Y + \beta D^{high}} < 1. \tag{5A.17}$$

That is, if a shock pushes the natural (real) rate of interest below zero, the price level must drop now by the amount of $P_S/P*$, so that it can rise into the future long-run equilibrium by the amount of $P*/P_S$, creating the inflation necessary to achieve a negative real interest rate.

This analysis has assumed, however, that the debt behind the dele-veraging shock is indexed (i.e., denominated in terms of the consumption good). However, suppose instead that the debt, B_t, is denominated in terms of money. In that case, short-run price-level fall will increase the real value of the preexisting debt. The debt limit is defined, however, in *real* terms, because the ability of the borrower to pay in the future out of his endowment is a real term. Therefore, the fall in the price level after the shock will increase the burden of deleveraging in real terms. Specifically, let debt be denominated in nominal terms, and the price level is P_S. Then, $D^{\text{high}} = B^{\text{high}} / P_S$.

In addition, in order to satisfy the debt limit, the indebted agent must make short-run repayments of

$$\frac{B^{\text{high}}}{P_S} - \frac{D^{\text{low}}}{1 + r_S}.$$

Then, the depression-period natural rate of interest becomes:

$$1 + r_S = \frac{\dfrac{1}{2}Y + D^{\text{low}}}{\beta \dfrac{1}{2}Y + \beta \dfrac{B^{\text{high}}}{P_S}} < 1. \tag{5A.18}$$

Hence, as the price level falls, the borrower must pay more, cutting on their consumption spending, and as a consequence the natural rate becomes more negative compared to the indexed debt case. The natural rate of interest is now endogenous.

To accommodate price rigidity and demand-determined output application, the model is transformed to the New Keynesian model. Consumption spending, C_t, is extended to a Dixit-Stiglitz aggregate of a continuum of goods giving the producer of each good market power with elasticity of demand given by θ. In addition, there is a continuum of firms, each of which produces one type of the varieties the consumers like.

Aggregate consumption is

$$c_t = \chi_S c_t^S + (1 - \chi_S) c_t^b,$$

where c_t is per capita consumption in the economy, c_t^S is per capita saver consumption, c_t^b is per capita borrower consumption, and χ_S denotes the share of savers.

The log-linearized Phillips curve (the relationship between inflation, π, and output gap) is of the following form:

$$\pi_t = \kappa \hat{Y}_t + E_{t-1}\pi_t,$$

where

$$\kappa \equiv \frac{\lambda}{1-\lambda}\xi, \ \hat{Y}_t \equiv \log\frac{Y_t}{Y}, \text{ and } \pi_t \equiv \log\frac{p_t}{p_{t-1}}.$$

Depression shock, $\hat{D} < 0$, is the driver of output depression and low inflation:

$$\hat{Y}_s = \Gamma - \frac{1-\chi_s}{\chi_s - (1-\chi_s)\kappa\gamma_D}\hat{D} < 0$$

$$\pi_s = \kappa\Gamma - \frac{(1-\chi_s)\kappa}{\chi_s - (1-\chi_s)\kappa\gamma_D}\hat{D} < 0.$$

See Razin (2015).

Appendix 5B: Foreign Exchange Market Intervention: Diagrammatic Presentation

By its very nature, a sterilized intervention is ultimately a swap of foreign currency for domestic government debt. Under the latter conditions, a sterilized purchase of foreign government bonds leaves the money supply unchanged but raises the risk-adjusted return that domestic government bonds must offer to offset the alternative return on foreign government bonds. Figure 5B.1 (see Krugman, Obstfeld, and Melitz [2015], 516) describes the shift in the return curve in the upper panel up and to the right. This is the consequence of the substitution of foreign government bonds for domestic government bonds in the asset side of the (domestic) central bank, which conducts the sterilized foreign exchange market intervention. That is, the stock of domestic bonds held by the private sector rises, and so does the risk premium.

Note that if the risk premium does not change the sterilized foreign exchange market intervention cannot affect the exchange rate. Figure 5B.1 demonstrates the effect of a sterilized central bank's purchase of foreign currency to depreciate the exchange rate, without changing the money supply. When the domestic and foreign treasuries are not perfect substitutes, a spread exists, indicated by ρ. The purchase of foreign exchange is sterilized through sale of domestic assets—a fall in A,

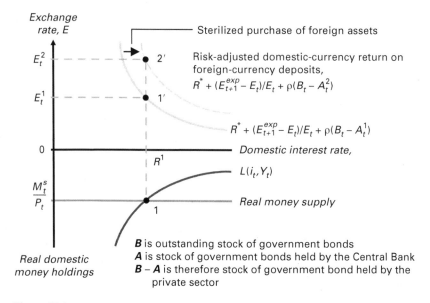

Figure 5B.1
Sterilized foreign exchange market intervention through the portfolio balance effect.
Note: A purchase of foreign assets coupled with a sale of domestic assets (that is, sterilized intervention) raises domestic asset risk premium and effects a depreciation of the domestic currency. In the absence of the portfolio balance effect, sterilized intervention cannot move the exchange rate. The effectiveness of the current foreign exchange market intervention depends also on the commitment of the central bank to do so in the future. Therefore, if E_{t+1}^{exp} is expected to be depreciated in the future, E_t will be more depreciated as well. *Source:* Krugman et al. (2015).

in terms of the figure symbols. The exchange rate is effectively pushed up. If, however, domestic assets are viewed by market participants as safe and liquid as foreign assets (e.g., domestic and foreign treasuries are perfect substitutes), $\rho = 0$, and sterilized intervention cannot affect the exchange rate at all.

Often a current foreign exchange market intervention, in which the central bank purchases foreign assets but sterilizes with the sale of domestic assets, may signal to market participants' future expansionary monetary policy. If the signal is credible, the future expected exchange rate will depreciate, thereby inducing the current spot rate to depreciate as well. The expectations mechanism is akin to "forward guidance," whereby the central bank announces credibly lowering the future path of the policy rate, causing a reduction in current long-term interest rates.

6   Israel's High Technology and Globalized Finance

Dovetailing with immigration in the 1990s, and the global information-technology surge, was the unprecedented growth of Israel's high-tech sector. Innovation requires scale, and scale requires trade. An isolated small economy cannot be a center of innovation. The incentives of entrepreneurs to invest effort and resources in generating valuable services are related to the ability to use the resulting knowledge repeatedly, on a large scale, over a long time. Foreign direct investment provides critical incentives to be able to use scale economies, so as to leap from the precarious innovation stage at the confines of a small economy to the execution stage, by utilizing the world markets. The globalization of an economy is crucial for its nascent high-tech industry to develop, and flourish.

The long-term benefits of the information and communications technology (ICT) surge were palpable.[1] At the same time, the wave of financial liberalization contributed heavily to the surge in development and global economic growth from 1985 to 2008. However, the deregulation turned out to be a two-way street. It spurred entrepreneurship, investment, and technological progress, but it also created a fertile environment for asset speculation and leveraging, sometimes with dire consequences. The 2008 global financial crisis followed.

Foreign direct investment (FDI) has been crucial for pushing Israel's high-tech sector into occupying an elite position in the world economy. Recall that FDI refers to investments in companies and production outside the realm of the stock market, and is generated by long-term considerations. Whenever a foreign company buys an Israeli high-tech startup, it is counted as FDI. Israel pulled in the fourth highest level of foreign direct investment in relation to the size of its economy in the 2010s. Israel brought in about 4 percent of GDP in FDI. The OECD average was just 1.4 percent. However, it fell short of Ireland's

16.1 percent and Chile's 7.4 percent. For Israel, of late, the OECD accounted for more than a quarter of FDI inflows. The lion's share came from the United States and the EU. Recently, China became an important source of FDI inflows.

6.1   Inward Foreign Direct Investment

Generally, a multinational firm that chooses to keep the production of an intermediate input within its boundaries can produce it at home or in a foreign country. When it keeps it at home, it engages in standard domestic vertical or horizontal integration. When it makes it abroad, it engages in foreign direct investment and intrafirm trade. A high-tech startup firm typically attempts to produce a product with two distinct characteristics. First, the success of the research and development is highly uncertain, needing venture capital financing because of the high risk. Second, the product is ultimately of multiple uses. That is, it is an input into increasing returns to scale technology, hence attractive to multinational firms. Deep-pocket international investment enterprises (such as CalPERS's pension fund) typically tend to allocate a small fraction of their investment portfolio to foreign high-tech startups in the form of venture capital.[2] The high-tech firm receiving the funds at the startup stage will have diminished transaction costs at a more mature stage.

The venture capital picture in Israel goes back to the early 1990s, with capital ebbing and flowing and with trends changing. It is highly correlated with inward FDI.[3]

6.2   Productivity-Induced FDI

Israel's inward FDI flows accelerated in the 1990s and the 2000s (see figure 6.1). Israel's venture capital development (data covers only the 2000s) exhibits a remarkable increase as a proportion of total inward FDI, demonstrating the sharp increase in funding to high-tech startups.

The dot-com bubble was a brief period of surging equity prices in the internet sector and related businesses in 1997–2000. Firms discovered that they could increase share prices merely by adding the prefix "e-" (e-Bay) or the suffix "com" (Amazon.com) to their corporate names. Purchasers of dot-com equities and derivatively hard assets gulled themselves into believing that normal standards of valuation could be set aside because dot-com ventures had unbounded profit horizons.

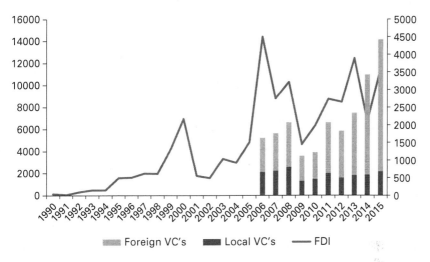

Figure 6.1
Israeli high-tech venture capital fund raising (right axis, million, current U.S. dollars) and inward foreign direct investments (left axis, million, current U.S. dollars). *Source:* IVC Research Center.

The mania had a direct impact on all countries with significant high-tech sectors, including Israel. The dot-com bubble not only increased the present discounted value of their capital stocks, it triggered large volumes of FDI to other economies, including the emerging high-tech sector in Israel, which had a beneficial effect on national income both during the bubble and after its burst. This started a steady rise in inward FDI into Israel.

The relatively high research and development (R&D) spending has not fully manifested itself in productivity. However, as figure 6.2 shows, Israel's labor productivity picked up moderately in the 2000s.

Israel recently pulled in the fourth highest level of foreign direct investment in relation to the size of its economy (OECD library, figures for 2013). The United States was the source of roughly 30 percent of global FDI outflows, followed by Japan, China, and Russia.

6.3 ICT Surge

In this section, we attempt to explore the short-run and long-run effects of the ICT surge on activity in Israel's high-tech sector.

We start with potential long-term effects of the global surge in ICT innovations, epicentered in the United States, on factor productivity in

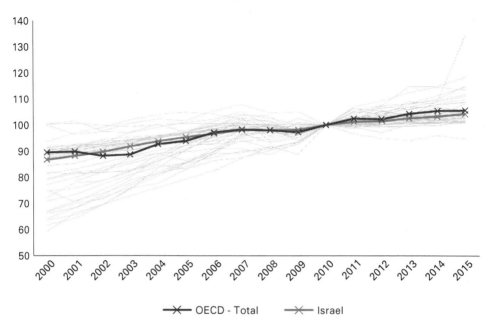

Figure 6.2
2000–2015 GDP per hour work (constant 2010 prices). *Source*: OECD Library.

a small advanced country. The spillover effects of technological innovations have strong implications for the issue that has recently been
debated; that is, whether per capita output levels of developing countries
converge to those of developed economies. As observed by Helpman
(1999), R&D expenditures, which have enormous rates of return, are
heavily concentrated within a small number of industrialized countries.
If R&D expenditures do not significantly spill over to developing countries, then R&D expenditures will tend to widen the cross-country
income gaps. Helpman (1999) raises the question of whether the benefits of R&D expenditures are as skewed as the expenditures themselves, or whether the substantial international spillover effects of R&D
expenditures cause the benefits to be more spread out internationally.
Such spillover can mitigate the cross-country income gaps. He brings
evidence for the conclusion that R&D spillover effects are important
and that there exist significant cross-country links driven by foreign
trade and FDI. Peri (2005) asserts that knowledge flows within and
across countries may have important consequences for both productivity and innovation. He uses data on 1.5 million patents and 4.5 million

citations to estimate knowledge flows at the frontier of technology across 147 subnational regions during 1975–1996, within the frame of a gravity-like equation. He estimates that only 20 percent of average knowledge is learned outside the average region of origin, and only 9 percent is learned outside the country of origin. However, knowledge in the computer sector flows substantially farther, as does knowledge generated by technological leaders. In comparison with trade flows, we see that knowledge flows reach much farther. External accessible R&D gained through these flows has a strong positive effect on innovative activity for a panel of 113 European and North American regions over 22 years.

6.4   R&D International Spillovers

Coe, Helpman, and Hoffmaister (2009) utilize an expanded data set for the purpose of this study. The new estimates confirm the key results reported in Coe and Helpman (1995) about the impact of domestic and foreign R&D capital stocks on total factor productivity (TFP). In addition, we show that domestic and foreign R&D capital stocks have measurable impacts on TFP even after controlling for the impact of human capital. Furthermore, we extend the analysis to include institutional variables. Our results suggest that institutional differences are important determinants of TFP and that they affect the degree of R&D spillovers. Countries where the ease of doing business and the quality of tertiary education systems are relatively high tend to benefit more from their own R&D efforts, from international R&D spillovers, and from human capital formation. Strong patent protection is associated with higher levels of total factor productivity, higher returns on domestic R&D, and larger international R&D spillovers. Finally, countries whose legal systems are based on French and, to a lesser extent, Scandinavian law benefit less from their own and foreign R&D capital than countries whose legal origins are based on English or German law.

Insightfully, de la Potterie and Lichtenberg (2006) investigate econometrically whether FDI transfers technology across borders. (The authors do not study R&D knowledge transmission mechanism through trade.) Data indicates that FDI transfers technology, but only in one direction: a country's productivity is increased if it invests in R&D-intensive foreign countries—particularly in recent years—but not if foreign R&D-intensive countries invest in it. Other findings are as follows:[4]

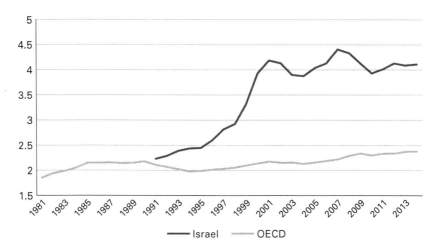

Figure 6.3
Gross domestic spending on R&D, total, percentage of GDP, 1981–2014: Israel and OECD average. *Source*: OECD Data.

Helpman (2003) examines the sources of the rise in TFP in Israel in the 1970s and 1980s and estimates that slightly more than half the rise in TFP can be attributed to R&D investment, and the rest to a rise in the level of education.

The ratio of foreign-R&D benefits conveyed by outward FDI to foreign R&D benefits conveyed by imports is higher for large countries than it is for small ones. The failure to account for international R&D spillovers leads to upwardly biased estimates of the output elasticity of the domestic R&D capital stock; and that are much larger transfers of technology from the United States to Japan than there are from Japan to the United States.[5]

Israel R&D spending received a boost after the ICT global surge. Figure 6.3 describes the extent to which Israel's domestic spending on R&D rose sharply to a higher plateau following the global ICT surge in the 1990s.[6] Israel moved up in OECD ranking. Israel's international ranking in domestic spending on R&D is truly exeptional.

6.5 R&D, FDI, and the Foreign Equity Markets

International trade, R&D spillovers, and TFP interact with each other in many different ways. Trade increases market size, reduces the duplication of R&D, increases knowledge spillovers, and increases specialization. All of which will increase R&D and hence TFP. On the other hand, trade increases competition and causes factor prices to change, which leads to a decline in TFP. In addition, trade does not necessarily imply an international convergence of income levels. If the R&D spillovers are international in scope, there will be convergence; however, if they are national in scope, there will be a divergence (see Helpman [2004]).

Capital flows of all types have increased over the past few decades, and, most recently, some of the biggest increases have occurred in foreign direct investment. This is especially true of rich countries, but is also increasingly true of developing nations too. Obstfeld and Taylor (2002) make a historical point: "A century ago, world income and productivity levels were far less divergent than they are today, so it is all the more remarkable that so much capital was directed to countries at or below the 20 percent and 40 percent income levels (relative to the United States). Today, a much larger fraction of the world's output and population is located in such low-productivity regions, but a smaller share of global foreign investment reaches them."

Foreign direct investment (FDI) occurs when an investor based in one country (the home country) acquires an asset in another country (the host country) with an intent to manage that asset. The management dimension is what distinguishes FDI from portfolio investment in foreign stocks, bonds, and other financial instruments. Inward FDI in the high-tech sector is driven by human capital and the fact that it is easy to do business in the host country. However, FDI flows, namely, the acquisition of the high-tech industry equity assets, provide strong incentive to innovate. Thus, FDI flows help to expand the high-tech sector activities. In other words, FDI flows are both driven by fundamentals, which drive the high-tech industry, and reinforcing its expansion. Israel's high-tech development in the last two and a half decades is a fascinating event study, flashing out the FDI-productivity interactions.[7]

Turning to the short-term aspects of FDI, we consider how they are related to the global stock market cycle. Capital flows in the form of FDI are important because it is believed that FDI has special benefits over other forms of capital flows. First, these flows are thought to be more stable, and do not leave the host country exposed to financial crises. Second, FDI if often supposed to be associated with technology transfer, which may have spillover benefits for the host country. Third, FDI is often attributed a special role in disciplining host country governments: the threat of moving business offshore limits the ability of host countries to extract taxes and introduce inefficient regulations. Offsetting this, FDI is also often associated with special domestic costs in cases where foreign ownership has caused domestic political unrest in the host country (this is often especially true in natural resource industries).[8]

Being equity investments, FDI flows are driven among other factors by credit availability and stock market performance. A central problem in the credit market is that lenders are reluctant to make loans because they cannot easily determine whether a prospective borrower has resources to repay the loan. If the loan is made, the lender is concerned about whether the borrower will engage in risky behavior that could lower the probability that the loan will be repaid. Collateral reduces this information asymmetry problem because high-quality collateral (that is, assets that are easily valued and easy to take control of) significantly decreases the losses to the lender if the borrower defaults on the loan. High-quality collateral also reduces the moral hazard problem because the borrower is reluctant to engage in excessively risky behavior since now they have something to lose. Creditor protection enhances the ability of the lender to take control of the collateral in case of default and thereby alleviate credit constraints. Thus, creditor rights regulation helps to mitigate the problems of information asymmetry and moral hazard between creditors and borrowers. Hale, Razin, and Tong (2014) developed a model predicting two channels through which creditor protection enhances the performance of stock prices: the probability of a liquidity crisis leading to a binding investment-finance constraint falls with a strong protection of creditors; the stock prices under the investment-constrained regime increase with better protection of creditors. They find strong empirical support for both predictions, using data on stock market performance for fifty-two countries over the period 1980–2008. In particular, they demonstrate that better creditor protection is correlated across countries with lower average stock market volatility; crises are more frequent in countries with poor creditor protection. Using propensity score matching they demonstrate that, during crises, stock market return investments fall by more in countries with poor creditor protection.[9] Israel has had international high ranking in credit protection. It also became an attractive place for foreign direct investment at the time the high-tech industry, capitalizing on Israel's human capital, emerged into the world economy.

6.6   High-Tech Israel and Inward FDI

Israel's high-tech industry benefitted from a surge in inward FDI.[10] Figure 6.4 describes the time pattern of FDI inflows in Israel, compared with the ones in other developed economies.

In figure 6.4, we interpret FDI flows (in percentage of gross domestic product) as reflecting the intense interactions of the FDI flows with the high-tech investment in Israel. Three features are noteworthy:

(1) The sharp rise in inward FDI during the dot-com equity bubble;

(2) The effect of the dot-com equity in the early 2000s that triggered a temporary fall in inward FDI flows. Inward FDI underwent a sharp rise in the late 1990s. The upturn happened when the nascent high-tech industry in Israel emerged on the global stage, and with the upside-down V-shaped fall when the early 2000s dot-com equity collapse took place;

(3) The effect of the boom and bust of the equity markets around the 2008 crisis when Israel's high-tech industry gained strength in global high-tech sectors.

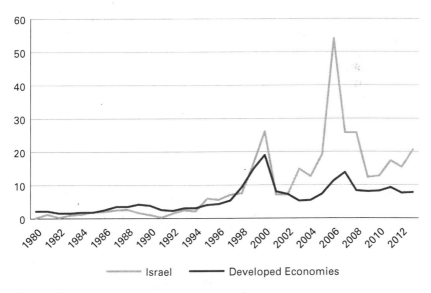

Figure 6.4
Foreign direct investment: inward flows, annual, 1980–2013 (percentage of GDP). *Source*: United Nations Conference on Trade and Development database.

Helpman (2003) observes that over the last decades Israel's economy grew faster than average, but not exceptionally fast. Compared with countries at a similar level of development, Israel is not outstanding. Seven-tenths of the rise in its GDP can be explained by the increase in labor input (measured by hours worked) and investment in machinery, structures, and equipment. Nonetheless, the investment is made possible by the increase in productivity, which in turn was fed by improved levels of schooling, investment in R&D, and knowledge spillovers from other countries.

6.7 Trends and Cycles

Israel's economy is the most tech dependent in the world, with 13 percent of the country's GDP and 31 percent of all exports originating in the high-tech sector; thus, the global high-tech slowdown has hit Israel harder than other advanced economies.

Friedmann (2016) analyzes the implications for labor productivity of the three groups of external shocks that have hit the industry since the early to mid-1990s, before the birth of the dot-com bubble:

(1) early 2000s, after the burst of the dotcom bubble;

(2) before and during the early stages of the 2008 global crisis, which triggered the global stock market crash and the sharp decline in world trade;

(3) the Great Recession that followed the global crisis.

Table 6.1 exhibits the high productivity increase of the private and the ICT sectors around the global ICT surge in the 1990s; the low productivity increase in the early 2000s in the sectors following the burst of the dot-com bubble; and the return to a state of medium-to-high productivity before the 2008 global stock market crash.

There is an intriguing positive correlation between high-tech industry productivity (shown in table 6.5) and FDI flow cycles (shown in figure 6.1). The clustering of high-tech industries and startups primarily in Tel-Aviv, Israel's center of commerce and economic activities, is another productivity-enhancing development. In general, productivity-boosting mechanisms arising from the clustering of high-tech and university centers is complementary to the productivity-enhancing effects of industrial agglomeration. These have attracted great attention in policy circles. Empirical evidence suggests that region-level productiv-

Table 6.1
Israel's Labor Productivity (annual percentage changes)

	1991–1995	1996–2000	1996–2010	2006–2010
Private Sector: Total	1.5	3.5	1.5	1.2
	(1,399)	(1,559)		(2,057)
Information Technology Sector	1.1	10.2	3.4	1.7
	(71)	(126)		(176)
Information Technology (excluding electronics)	3.1	11.6	6.0	3.3
	(35)	(38)		(38)
IT Services	–3.6	5.7	1.7	–0.4
	(26)	(71)		(112)

Note: In parentheses is the number of employees (in thousands).
Source: Friedmann (2016).

ity rises 3–8 percent when market size is doubled (World Bank [2009]). A recent study employed plant product-level data from Japanese manufacturing to assess the effects of urban agglomeration on product quality (Saito and Matsuura [2016]). Their findings suggest that state and municipal tax breaks and other public efforts to attract enterprises enhance economic competitiveness by improving product quality along with productivity. Productivity gains traditionally used to project agglomeration benefits underestimate the benefits by ignoring the quality incentives accompanying a productivity shock.

Appendix 6A: Venture Capital Investment vs. Portfolio Investment[11]

Consider a small economy faced by a continuum [0, 1] of foreign investors. Each foreign investor has an opportunity to invest in one project, as in B-to-B transactions (FDI). Foreign investment can occur in one of two forms: either as a direct venture capital, where the direct investor effectively acts like a manager, or as a portfolio investment, where the investor does not manage the project.

There are three periods: 0, 1, and 2. In period 0, each investor decides whether to make a direct investment or a portfolio investment. In period 2, the project matures. The net cash flow from the startup project is given by

$$R(K,\varepsilon) = (1+\varepsilon)K - \left(\frac{1}{2}\right)AK^2, \tag{6A.1}$$

where ε is an idiosyncratic random productivity factor, which is independently realized for each project in period 1, R is the payoff of the project, and K is the level of capital input invested in the project in period 1, after the realization of ε. The parameter A reflects production costs. The productivity shock ε is distributed between -1 and 1 with mean 0 with the cumulative distribution function $\Phi(\cdot)$, and the density function is $f(\cdot) = \Phi'(\cdot)$. Investors choose the form of investment that maximizes (ex ante) expected payoff.

In period 1, after the realization of the productivity shock, the manager of the project observes ε. Thus, if the investor owns the project as a direct investment, they observe ε, and choose K, so as to maximize the net cash flow: $K^d(\varepsilon) = (1 + \varepsilon)/A$.

Therefore, the ex ante expected net cash flow from a direct investment, if held until maturity, is

$$EV_d = \frac{E[(1 + \varepsilon)^2]}{2A}, \tag{6A.2}$$

where E denotes expectation operator and V denotes the present value of a mature project. In the case of a portfolio investment, the owner has an arm's-length relationship with the manager, and thus they cannot observe ε. In this case, the owner maximizes the expected return, absent any information on the realization of ε, and decisions are based on the ex ante zero mean. Thus, the manager will be instructed to choose $K^p = K^d(0) = (1/A)$. Then, the ex ante expected payoff from a portfolio investment, if held until maturity, is

$$EV_p = 1/(2A). \tag{6A.3}$$

Comparing (6A.2) with (6A.3), we see that if the project is held until maturity, it yields a higher payoff as a direct investment than as a portfolio investment. This reflects the efficiency that results from a hands-on management style in the case of a direct investment.

There are also costs for FDI investment, however. First, an FDI investor has to incur a fixed cost in order to acquire the expertise to manage the project directly. We denote this cost, which is exogenously given in the model, by C. Second, there is an endogenous cost arising from the possibility of liquidity shocks occurring in period 1. There is a discount when selling a project managed as direct investment, due to information asymmetries, as demonstrated below.

In period 1, before the value of ε is observed, the owner of the project might get a liquidity shock. With the realization of a liquidity shock, the investor is forced to sell the project in period 1. This feature of the model is similar to the preference-shock assumption made by Diamond and Dybvig (1983): an investor who is subject to a liquidity shock derives their utility only from period 1 consumption. If, however, they are not subject to a liquidity shock, they derive their utility from period 2 consumption. We denote by λ the probability of a liquidity shock. We assume that there are two types of foreign investors. In particular, half of the investors will need to sell with probability λ_H and half with probability λ_L, such that $1 > \lambda_H > (1/2) > \lambda_L > 0$, and $\lambda_H + \lambda_L = 1$.

Investors know ex ante whether they are of a λ_H type or a λ_L type, and this is their private information. In addition to liquidity-based sales, there is a possibility that an investor will liquidate a project in period 1 if they observe a low realization of ε. Then the price that buyers are willing to pay for a direct investment that is being sold in period 1 is

$$P_D = \frac{1}{2A} \frac{(1 - \lambda_D) \int_{-1}^{\varepsilon_D} (1 + \varepsilon)^2 f(\varepsilon) d\varepsilon + \lambda_D}{(1 - \lambda_D) \Phi(\underline{\varepsilon}_D) + \lambda_D}. \tag{6A.4}$$

Here, ε_D is a threshold level of ε, set by the direct investor, below which the direct investor is selling the project without being forced to do so by a liquidity shock; λ_D is the probability, as perceived by the market, that an FDI investor gets a liquidity shock. In equation (6A.4) it is assumed that if the project is sold because of a liquidity shock, that is, before the initial owner observes ε, the value of ε is not recorded by the firms before the sale. Therefore, the buyer does not know the value of ε. However, if the project is sold for low-profitability reasons, the new owner will know the value of ε after the sale. The threshold ε_D is determined in equilibrium. The initial owner sets the threshold level ε_D, such that, given the price P_D, when observing ε_D, an investor is indifferent between selling and not selling the project in absence of a liquidity shock. Thus,

$$P_D = \frac{\left(1 + \underline{\varepsilon}_D\right)^2}{2A}. \tag{6A.5}$$

Equations (6A.4) and (6A.5) together determine P_D and ε_D as functions of the *market-perceived* probability of sale due to the liquidity shock (λ_D). We denote these functions as $\varepsilon_D(\lambda_D)$ and $P_D(\lambda_D)$.

When a portfolio investor sells the projects in period 1, everybody knows they do it because of a liquidity shock. Thus, the price of the project is given by

$$P_p = \frac{1}{2A}.$$ (6A.6)

Comparing the price of FDI, which is determined by equations (6A.4) and (6A.5), with the price of FPI, which is determined by equation (6A.6), we see that the resale price of a direct investment in period 1 is always lower than the resale price of a portfolio investment in that period. The intuition is that if a direct investor prematurely sells the investment project, the market price must reflect the possibility that the sale originates from inside information on low prospects of this investment project. This constitutes the second (liquidity) cost of FDI.

Based on our analysis, we can write the ex ante expected net cash flow from FDI:

$$EV_D(\lambda_i, \lambda_D, A, C) = \left\{ (1 - \lambda_i) \left(\begin{array}{c} \left[1 + \underline{\varepsilon}_D(\lambda_D)\right]^2 \Phi\left[\underline{\varepsilon}_D(\lambda_D)\right] \\ + \int\limits_{\underline{\varepsilon}_D(\lambda_D)}^{1} \frac{(1+\varepsilon)^2}{2A} f(\varepsilon) d\varepsilon \end{array} \right) \right.$$

$$\left. + \lambda_i \frac{\left[1 + \underline{\varepsilon}_D(\lambda_D)\right]^2}{2A} \right\} - C.$$ (6A.7)

The ex ante expected net cash flow from FPI is simply

$$EV_p(A) = \frac{1}{2}A.$$ (6A.8)

Then, the difference between the expected value of FDI and the expected value of FPI is

$$\text{Diff}(\lambda_1, \lambda_D, A, C) \equiv EV_D(\lambda_1, \lambda_D, A, C) - EV_p(A).$$ (6A.9)

Clearly, investors will choose FDI (FPI) when $\text{Diff}(\lambda_1, \lambda_D, A, C) > 0$ (<0) and will be indifferent between the two (i.e., may choose either FDI or FPI) when $\text{Diff}(\lambda_1, \lambda_D, A, C) = 0$.

To complete the description of the equilibrium, it remains to be specified how λ_D, the market-perceived probability that an FDI investor will get a liquidity shock, is determined. Assuming that rational expectations hold in equilibrium, λ_D has to be consistent with the equilibrium choice of the two types of investors between FDI and FPI, such that

$$\lambda_D = (\lambda_H \lambda_{H,FDI} + \lambda_L \lambda_{L,FDI}) / (\lambda_{H,FDI} + \lambda_{L,FDI}), \qquad (6A.10)$$

where $\lambda_{H,FDI}$ is the proportion of λ_H investors (H investors) who choose FDI in equilibrium, and $\lambda_{L,FDI}$ is the proportion of λ_L investors (L investors) who choose FDI in equilibrium.

Five possible cases can potentially be observed in equilibrium. Case 1: all investors choose FDI. Case 2: L investors choose FDI; H investors split between FDI and FPI. Case 3: L investors choose FDI; H investors choose FPI. Case 4: λ_L investors split between FDI and FPI; H investors choose FPI. Case 5: all investors choose FPI. Equilibrium outcomes depend on production cost A and liquidity preferences (λ_L, λ_H).

As the production cost A increases, we are more likely to observe FPI and less likely to observe FDI in equilibrium. As the difference in liquidity needs of the two types of investors widens, we are more likely to see a separating equilibrium, where different types of investors choose different forms of investment.

Appendix 6B: A Brief on FDI Literature

Studies of FDI divide into two main categories: micro-level (industrial organization and international trade) studies and macro-finance studies. Initially, the literature that explained FDI in microeconomics terms focused on market imperfections, and on the desire of multinational enterprises to expand their market power; see, for instance, Caves (1971). Subsequent literature centered more on firm-specific advantages, owing to product superiority or cost advantages, stemming from economies of scale, multi-plants economies and advanced technologies, or superior marketing and distribution.

6B.1   Trade-Based Studies

A multinational may find it cheaper to expand directly in a foreign country, rather than through trade, in cases where its advantages stem from internal, indivisible assets associated with knowledge and technology.[12]

We refer to the latter form of FDI as horizontal FDI. Note therefore that horizontal FDI is a substitute for exports. Brainard (1997) employs a differentiated product framework to provide an empirical support for this hypothesis. Helpman, Melitz, and Yeaple (2004) incorporate intra-industry heterogeneity to conclude, among other things, that FDI plays lesser role in substituting for exports in industries with large productivity dispersion.

However, horizontal FDI is not the only form of FDI. Multinational corporations account for a very significant fraction of world trade flows, with trade in intermediate inputs between divisions of the same firm constituting an important portion of these flows; see, for instance, Hanson, Mataloni, and Slaughter (2001). This is referred to as vertical FDI. See, for instance, Helpman, Melitz, and Yeaple (2004) for an empirical investigation of the scope of vertical FDI.

One of the key determinants of vertical FDI is the abundance of human capital; see Antras (2004) for a comprehensive theoretical and empirical treatise of the various forms of FDI. In a recent survey, Helpman (2006) observes that between 1990 and 2001 sales by foreign affiliates of multinational corporations expanded much faster than exports of goods and nonfactor services. He also points out that fast-growing trade in inputs has accompanied the fast expansion of trade in services. Furthermore, "the growth of input trade has taken place both within and across the boundaries of the firm, i.e., as intra-firm and arm's-length trade." In light of these developments, Helpman argues, "the traditional classification of FDI into vertical and horizontal forms has become less meaningful in practice." Indeed, his survey includes some new applications of the theory of the organization of the firm to analyze the patterns of exports, FDI, outsourcing, and so on.

Razin and Sadka (2007) emphasize that FDI is distinct from FPI investment with respect to the quality of monitoring management. Foreign direct investors, by definition, acquire some significant control over the firm they invest in, whereas portfolio investors, plagued by free-rider problems, have no control. Consequently, foreign direct investors can apply hands-on management (or micro-management) standards that would enable them to react in real time to changing economic environments. This feature may stem from "intangible capital" accumulated through a specialization by the foreign direct investors in a certain niche.[13] Indeed, there is some micro evidence in support of this hypothesis. For example, Djankov and Hoekman (2000) report that foreign direct investors pick the high-productivity firms in transition economies. Similarly, Griffith and Simpson (2003) find that foreign-owned manufacturing establishments in Britain, over the period

1980–1996, have significantly higher labor productivity than those that remain under domestic ownership.

In addition, labor productivity improves faster over time and faster with age in foreign-owned establishments. Other studies found that this phenomenon is accounted for by the greater capital intensity of multinationals. For an overview, see Lipsey (2000).

6B.2 Macro-Finance Studies

FDI combines not only aspects of international trade in goods and services but also aspects of international financial flows. The macro-finance literature attempts to analyze the composition of aggregate international flows into FDI, FPI, and bank loans, as well as the breakdown of the aggregate flow of FDI according to either modes of entry or modes of finance. As with respect to the modes of entry, FDI can be made either at the greenfield stage or in the form of purchasing ongoing firms (M&A). U.N. (2005) observes, "The choice of mode is influenced by industry—specific factors. For example, green field investment is more likely be as a mode of entry in industries in which technological skills and production technology are key. The choice may also be influenced by institutional, cultural and transaction cost factors, in particular, the attitude towards takeovers, conditions in capital markets, liberalization policies, privatization, regional integration, currency risks and the role played by intermediaries (e.g. investment bankers) actively seeking acquisition opportunities and taking initiatives in making deals."[14]

As for the modes of finance, there is a distinction between equity capital, intra-company loans, and reinvestment of retained earnings. Figure 6B.1 describes the relative share of these three modes of finance over the last decade. The lion's share of FDI is financed through equity capital, 60–70 percent. The share of intra-firm loans has risen in the 1990s but has declined sharply in the 2000s. This decline is due mainly to repatriation of such loans by multinationals in developed economies. The third mode of finance, reinvestment of retained earnings, seems to exhibit a mirror-image pattern to the intra-firms loans.

The macro-finance literature on FDI started with studies examining the effects of exchange rates on FDI. These studies focused on the positive effects of the exchange rate depreciation in the host country on FDI inflows. A real exchange rate depreciation lowers the cost of production and investment in the host country, thereby raising the profitability of foreign direct investment.[15] See, for instance, Blonigen (1997). The

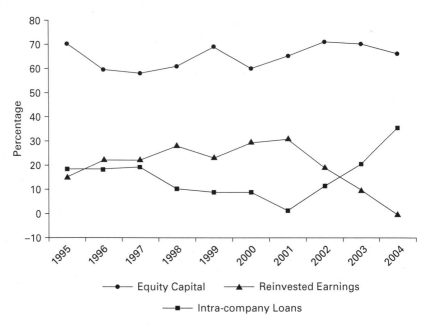

Figure 6B2.1
Share of different financing components in world FDI inflows, 1995–2004, percentage.
Note: Based on data only for countries for which all three components of FDI inflows
were available. This number ranges from 66 to 110 economies and accounts for an aver-
age of 87 percent of total FDI inflows. This is figure 1.4 of U.N. (2005). *Source*: Razin and
Sadka (2007).

wealth effect is another channel through which a depreciation of the
real exchange rate could raise FDI. By raising the relative wealth of
foreign firms, a depreciation of the real exchange rate could make it
easier for these firms to use the retained earnings to finance investment abroad, or to post a collateral in borrowing from domestic lenders in the host country capital market; see, for instance, Froot and Stein
(1991).

Later macroeconomic studies emphasize the effect of FDI on long-
run economic growth and cyclical fluctuations. A comprehensive study
by Bosworth and Collins (1999) provides evidence on the effect of
capital inflows on domestic investment for fifty-eight developing countries during 1978–1995.

Note that foreign investment per se is not one-to-one mapped to
domestic investment. As noted by Froot and Stein (1991) for the case
of FDI, it actually requires neither capital flows nor investment in
capacity. Conceptually, FDI is an extension of corporate control over

international boundaries: "When Japanese-owned Bridgestone takes control over the US firm Firestone, capital need not flow into the US. US domestic lenders can largely finance the equity purchase. Any borrowing by Bridgestone from foreign-based third parties also does not qualify as FDI (although it would count as an inflow of portfolio capital into US). And, of course, in such acquisition there is no investment expenditure; merely an international transfer in the title of corporate assets."

Alfaro et al. (2004) find that education level, development of local financial markets, and other local conditions play an important role in allowing the positive effect of FDI to materialize.[16] Similarly, Razin (2004) finds strong evidence for the dominant positive effect of FDI (relative to other forms of foreign investments) on domestic investment and growth.

The macroeconomic finance literature also notes that foreign direct investment has proved to be resilient during financial crises. For instance, in East Asian countries, such investment was remarkably stable during the global financial crises of 1997–1998. In sharp contrast, other forms of private capital flows—portfolio equity and debt flows, and particularly short-term flows—were subject to large reversals during the same period; see Dadush, Dasgupta, and Ratha (2000), Lipsey (2000), Loungani and Razin (2001), and Razin and Sadka (2003). The resilience of FDI during financial crisis was also evident during the Mexican crisis of 1994–1995 and the Latin American debt crisis of the 1980s. The role of the financial institutions is the focus of Hale, Razin, and Tong (2014). They define a liquidity crisis as a union of two sets of events: a sharp decline in bank credit to the private sector and a sharp increase in the real interest rate. In both cases they define observations in the top 10 percent tail of annual changes in the underlying variable as crises. These correspond to the annual decline of credit to the private sector by 10 percent and to an increase in the real interest rate of over 4.3 percentage points in one year. Thus, the liquidity crisis variable measures domestic liquidity crises and proxies for periods when credit constraints are likely to be binding. Analyzing the data for fifty-two developed and developing countries over the period 1980–2008, they find support for the predictions of the model as well as evidence consistent with the mechanism through which creditor protection affects stock market returns. Specifically, they find support for the three main testable implications of the model: higher frequency of crises, larger change in stock market returns during crises, and larger decline in investment during crises in countries with poor creditor rights protection.

Furthermore, the flow of FDI may even intensify during financial crises. Krugman (2000) argues that in financial crises foreigners can take advantage of fire sales of assets by liquidity-constrained domestic investors. Razin, Rubinstein, and Sadka (2004) provide a selection-bias empirical application. They develop a model in which foreign direct investors are better equipped to skim domestic projects than their domestic direct and portfolio counterparts, due to rich experience in the skimming of "good" firms. Employing this advantage, foreign direct investors are able to outbid direct domestic and portfolio investors for the good firms. Better hands-on management standards, which characterize FDI investors, entail a cutting-edge advantage over portfolio investors in reacting in real time to a changing business environment. Evidently, this feature is highly pronounced in high-productivity firms, resulting in the acquisition of high-productivity firms by FDI investors. This mechanism applies both to mergers and acquisitions and to greenfield investments. The productivity signal, however, is likely to be coarser in the latter, conveying less information about the true productivity. Thus, the advantage of the FDI investors over their domestic direct investor counterparts is even more highly pronounced in the case of greenfield investments than in mergers and acquisition.

III   Trending Developments

This part includes four topics: the rerouting of Israel export to East Asia, brain drain, fertility spike and diminishing skill acquisition, and economic effects of the cascade of Palestinian uprisings.

China has become the second-largest economy in the world, after the United States, if measured on the purchasing power parity (PPP) scale. Essentially a closed economy since the days of Mao Zedong, the Communist State of China experienced a transition from a planned economy to a market economy when Deng Xiaoping came to power in 1978. Since then, China has seen a more than twentyfold increase in its GDP (gross domestic product) from that year. For Israel, East Asia is becoming the third-largest export market.

Israel's economy shields itself from the cyclical effects of the ongoing military conflicts, such as the cascade of wars with Hamas-led Gaza and Hezbollah-led Lebanon. An important reason for such robustness is that Israel is well integrated into the world economy through trade and financial links. This served Israel as a way to buffer cyclical external shocks.

7 Israel and East Asia

The global economy was jolted in the mid-1980s by China's and Vietnam's decision to abandon autarky in favor of export-led growth and to embrace "market communism." Socialist India and Muslim Indonesia liberalized and emulated their neighbors' trade participation strategy soon thereafter.[1] Suddenly, and with little warning, more than a third of the world's population joined the postwar globalization parade, powerfully effecting global demand everywhere, including Israel.

Liberalization, globalization, outsourcing, and technology transfer were the key drivers, not domestic rates of economic growth. China claimed double-digit GDP growth from 1950 to 1976 during the Maoist epoch, but its trade participation, outsourcing, and inflowing foreign direct investment were negligible, as was its contribution to global economic vitality.[2]

7.1 China Transforms

Beijing began distancing itself from autarky in the1980s when Deng Xiaoping introduced special economic zones (SEZ) in Shenzhen, Zhuhai, Shantou, and Xiamen, and designated the entire province of Hainan as a special economic zone. In 1984, China further opened fourteen coastal cities to overseas investment: Dalian, Qinhuangdao, Tianjin, Yantai, Qingdao, Lianyungang, Nantong, Shanghai, Ningbo, Wenzhou, Fuzhou, Guangzhou, Zhanjiang, and Beihai.

China leveraged the opportunities for outsourcing and technology transfer afforded by SEZs by liberalizing its domestic economy. This involved a rapid sequence of market-oriented reforms that circumvented communist ideological prohibitions against private ownership by allowing entrepreneurs and state companies to lease assets while preserving the party's monopoly on freehold property. The first reform, called Gaige Kaifang (literally, reforms and openness), lasted more than a decade, from 1976 until shortly after the Tiananmen Square massacre, June 5, 1989. The idea at its core was the gradual reversal of the three ideological pillars of command economy: criminalization of private property, criminalization of private business, and criminalization of entrepreneurship.

The centerpiece of the post-Mao system was the "household-responsibility system" (allowing peasant family households to operate their plots independently of team and communal influences), which made it possible for them to prosper by increasing productivity and selling above quota output in collective farm markets and household (cottage) industries in 1980. The principle soon thereafter was applied nationwide. The household-responsibility system was coupled with the "town village enterprise" (TVE) movement, an effort to transform the separate profit-seeking activities of individual households into a coordinated agro-industrial communal business. TVEs were flexible, and enjoyed considerable discretion in choosing and implementing agro-industrial activities. As time passed, many TVEs began operating as private enterprises, despite their cooperative form,[3] and prospered in part due to the absence of freehold property-owning competitors[4] and to the newly decentralized state finance.[5]

The second phase of Deng Xiaoping's march to partial consumer sovereign markets (as distinct from market-assisted command) can be conveniently dated at 1992, when he undertook his famous southern tour to Shenzhen. During the trip, Deng characterized China's emerging productive order as a "socialist market economy,"[6] and asserted that "if China does not practice socialism, does not carry on with 'reform and opening' and economic development, does not improve the people's standard of living, then no matter what direction we go, it will be a dead end." This clarion call to reinvigorate the marketization process in the aftermath of the Communist Party's post-Tiananmen Square retrenchment was successful.

Deng's team promptly transformed red directors into managers of market-competitive state-owned enterprises (SOEs), and then ultimately into managers of private companies, by expanding and codifying their powers in "The Regulations on Transforming the Management Mechanism of State-Owned Industrial Enterprises," issued July 1992. The document granted managers fourteen control rights over (1) production, (2) pricing, (3) sales, (4) procurement, (5) foreign trade, (6) investment, (7) use of retained funds, (8) disposal of assets, (9) mergers and acquisitions, (10) labor, (11) personnel management, (12) wages, (13) bonuses, and (14) internal organization, and refusal to pay unauthorized charges by the government.

These developments have been accompanied by parallel stock market and banking reforms, allowing SOEs to increase equity (shares) sales to outsiders, and banks to tighten credit discipline over profligate SOEs. They also facilitated market-driven reshuffles of corporate structure through mergers and acquisitions. China joined the WTO in 2002. Vietnam followed a nearly identical path to liberalization and globalization under the banner of *doi moi* (renewal) and joined the WTO in 2007.[7]

7.2   India Transforms

India and Indonesia were never communist nations and did not have to undo the trammels of command economies, but both markets were severely over-controlled. While details of their liberalization and globalization differed, the thrust to laissez-faire was the same.

The reform process in India sought to accelerate economic growth and the eradication of poverty. The process of economic liberalization began in the late 1970s and picked up momentum in July 1991, with a systemic shift to a more open economy, greater reliance upon market forces, and a larger role for the private sector, including foreign investment. Subsequent reforms have gone a long way in decontrolling the domestic economy,[8] emphasizing, like China, gradual transition rather than shock therapy.

The changes initiated in 1991 eliminated the dominance of the public sector in the industrial activity, discretionary controls over private industrial investment, trade and exchange controls, tight restrictions on direct foreign investment, and the overregulation of the financial sector. The reforms unleashed powerful entrepreneurial forces. Since 1991, successive governments across political parties have successfully carried forward the country's economic reform agenda. Most of the central government industrial controls were dismantled. Massive deregulation of the industrial sector was done in order to bring in the element of competition and increase efficiency. The list of industries reserved solely for the public sector—which used to cover eighteen industries, including iron and steel, heavy plant and machinery, telecommunications and telecom equipment, minerals, oil, mining, air transport services, and electricity generation and distribution—was drastically

reduced to three: defense aircrafts and warships, atomic energy generation, and railway transport. Further, restrictions that existed on the
import of foreign technology were withdrawn.

Before the reforms, trade policy was characterized by high tariffs
and pervasive import restrictions. Imports of manufactured consumer
goods were completely banned. For capital goods, raw materials, and
intermediates, certain lists of goods were freely importable, but for
most items where domestic substitutes were being produced, imports
were only possible with import licenses. The criteria for issue of licenses
were nontransparent; delays were endemic and corruption unavoidable. The economic reforms phased out import licensing and reduced
import duties.

7.3   East Asia Opens to Israel

In the last decade the Arab boycott on Israeli international trade, which
was in force for trade with China, India, Indonesia, and several other
East Asian countries, became effectively nonbinding. Markets in East
Asia are growing in importance for trading nations like Israel. If we look
at shares of global gross domestic product at market prices, China's
share jumped from 4 percent in 2000 to 15 percent in 2016. The share
of Asia (including Japan) is 31 percent. Meanwhile, the United States
and the EU together account for 47 percent of global GDP. Similarly,
despite growing rapidly, China's share in global imports was only
12 percent in 2015, while that of Asia was 36 percent. The United States
and EU (excluding intra-EU trade) still accounted for 31 percent of
world imports.

7.4   Exports Rerouted

Israel went through major trade liberalization, entering important
FTAs in the 1970s and 1980s (with the EEC and United States, respectively), and a substantial cut of tariffs and removal of non-tariff barriers
(NTBs) in the 1990s. These had important effects on income redistribution
and probably contributed to Israel's orientation toward exports. More
than two-thirds of Israel's trade was in the early period with the EU
and the United States.

Israel's exports to Asia grew substantially throughout the years,
relative to all other export destinations. Figure 7.1 shows Israel's exports
shares by destination region.

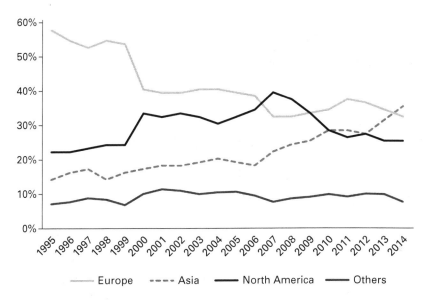

Figure 7.1
Israel's export shares by regional destination. *Source*: The Observatory of Economic Complexity, MIT.

Financial reforms that emphasized liberalization, including the interest rate and reserve requirements, have made India's financial industry globally competitive. The financial system has been deregulated and opened to international financial markets, and it employs derivatives and other modern innovations.

Recently, Israeli exports to Asia have surged, and they have stayed stable with the United States, but exports to most of Europe sharply declined. The "gravity" model helps explain these trends.

As the force between two objects in physics depends on the product of their masses and the distance between them, so trade between two countries is thought to depend on their economic mass (GDP) and all frictions affecting trade, including transport costs and policy variables. The theoretical and empirical foundations of the gravity model have been solidified in recent years by Eaton and Kortum (2002), Anderson and van Wincoop (2003), and Helpman, Melitz and Rubinstein (2008).[9] The shifts in trade between Israel and East Asia are likely to be a direct consequence of the policy transformations in China and India that can be captured via the gravity effect: the increasing economic "mass" (GDP) in southern East Asia coupled with the tearing down of the border restrictions (as indicated above).[10]

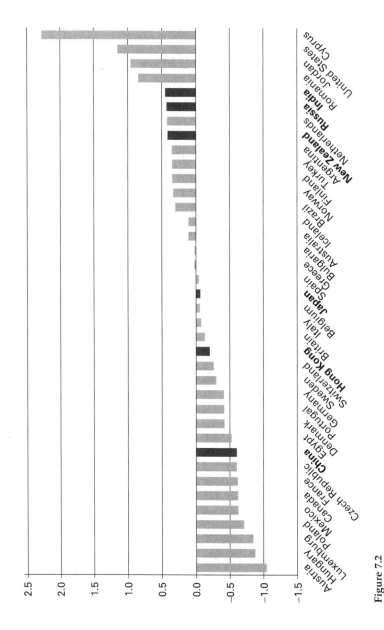

Figure 7.2
Differences between the gravity model predictions and the actual share of Israeli exports in trading partners' imports*
(percentages). *Source:* Mohar (2009).
*Countries without a trade agreement with Israel are emphasized.

Mohar (2009) studied the share of Israel's goods exports in the total imports of the destination country, by using a nonstructural gravity model. The main explanatory variables in the destination country are GDP (representing the market size), GDP per capita (representing the buying power of the average individual), distance, and a dummy variable representing whether or not there are trade agreements between Israel and the destination country. The sample period is 2001–2008.

Figure 7.2 describes the excessive/deficient shares, above or below what is predicted by the gravity model. Exports to China are underpredicted, while exports to the United States are over-predicted. The gaps predominantly reflect missing variables such as lagged exports (the gravity model is static), measurement errors associated the date and scope of bilateral trade agreements, and the heterogeneity of the good composition of the destination-country imports.[11]

Summing up, the global economy has been changed since China decided to abandon autarky in favor of export-led growth, India liberalized its trade, and both lifted the Arab League boycott on trade with Israel.[12] Israel, like other export nations, is pivoting toward emerging markets in East Asia.

The gravity models (pioneered by Tinbergen [1962]) have been a workhorse in analyzing the determinants of bilateral trade. A nonstructural model applied to the trade between Israel, Europe, and the United States (Israel's traditional trading partners), as well as East Asia (Israel's emerging trading partner), indicates the importance of East Asia to the export-led growth of the Israeli economy. Furthermore, it guarantees a more sustainable growth in the decades to come.

8 Brain Drain from Israel and Skill-Biased Global Immigration Policy

We know from basic economic principles that high-skill immigration enriches the workforce, allowing for a more finely graded specialization that raises average productivity and living standards. Diverse workforces are likely to be more productive, especially in industries where success depends on specific knowledge, such as computing, health care, and finance. By easing labor bottlenecks, low-skilled migrants help to keep down prices of goods and services. This is the main factor behind skill-based immigration policies. The other side is that international migration of skilled workers (the so-called brain drain) deprives the origin country from its scarce resource—human capital.

8.1 Immigrants' Skill Composition

Scientists, technology professionals, engineers, and mathematicians (STEM workers) are fundamental inputs in scientific innovation and technological adoption, the main drivers of productivity growth in the United States. Peri, Shih, and Sparber (2014) identify the effect of STEM worker growth on the wages and employment of college- and non-college-educated native workers in 219 U.S. cities from 1990 to 2010. In order to identify a supply-driven and heterogeneous increase in science, technology, engineering, and mathematics (STEM) workers across U.S. cities, Peri, Shih, and Sparber and use the distribution of foreign-born STEM workers in 1980 and exploit the introduction and variation of the H-1B visa program granting entry to foreign-born college-educated (mainly STEM) workers. We find that H-1B–driven increases in STEM workers in a city were associated with significant increases in wages paid to college-educated natives. Wage increases for non-college-educated natives are smaller but still significant. We do not find significant effects on employment. We also find that STEM workers increased

Table 8.1
Skill Composition of Immigration

Country of immigration	Low education as % of total immigration in 2000	High education as % of total immigration in 2000
Austria	47.5	12.7
Belgium	65.7	18.3
Denmark	44.8	17.3
Finland	48.7	23.8
France	74.6	16.4
Germany	65.9	21.8
Greece	44.5	15
Ireland	13.6	41.1
Italy	52.9	15.4
Netherlands	50.2	22
Norway	22	28.7
Portugal	59.7	18.6
Spain	28.7	18.5
Sweden	34.1	25.7
Switzerland	54.9	18.6
UK	34.1	34.9
Average EUROPE	*46.37*	*21.8*
Australia	35.3	40.3
Canada	29.6	58.8
USA	37.9	42.7
Average AUS, CAN & US	*34.27*	*47.27*

Source: Docquier, Lohest, and Marfouk (2005).

housing rents for college graduates, which eroded part of their wage gains. Together, these results imply a significant effect of foreign STEM workers on total factor productivity growth in the average U.S. city between 1990 and 2010.

The skill composition of immigrants to OECD countries other than the United States, Australia, Canada, and Ireland is skewed toward the low education group, thanks to the less rigorous screening of immigrants. See table 8.1.

8.2   Understanding Immigration Policy

How does the size of the welfare state affect the skill composition of immigration? A more generous welfare state is more attractive to low-skilled immigrants; this is known as the magnet effect (Borjas 1999). This is a supply-side explanation for the different composition of immigrants in the United States and Europe. Europe, with its generous welfare states, is an attractive destination for low-skilled immigrants, but far less so for high-skilled immigrants, who are likely to be net fiscal contributors. However, the demand for immigrants goes in the opposite direction. A more generous welfare state (particularly with an aging population) has financing needs that immigrants could fill. With high-skilled immigrants more likely to pay in rather than draw on the welfare state, more generous welfare states are more inclined to try to attract high-skilled immigrants.[1]

To highlight the demand-side forces, this subsection present a minimalist model that features two migration regimes: free and policy-controlled migration regimes. In summary, the policy-controlled migration regime leads to a positive effect of the welfare benefits on the skill composition of migration rates, because voters will internalize the fact that skilled migrants will be net contributors to the system (i.e., the fiscal burden effect), whereas unskilled migrants will be net beneficiaries (i.e., the social magnet effect). Under the free-migration regime, unskilled migrants will gravitate to a generous welfare state, while skilled migrants will be deterred.

We assume a Cobb-Douglas production function, with two labor inputs, skilled and unskilled:[2]

$$Y = AL_e^{\alpha}L_u^{1-\alpha}, \; 0 < \alpha < 1. \tag{8.1}$$

Here, Y is the GDP, A denotes a Hicks-neutral productivity parameter, and L_i denotes the input of labor of skill level i, where $i = e,u$ for skilled and unskilled, respectively. Wages, w_i, are competitive and equal to the marginal productivity of L_i.

Aggregate labor supply, for skilled and unskilled workers, respectively, is given by

$$L_e = (e + \sigma\mu)l_e \tag{8.2}$$

and

$$L_u = [1 - e + (1 - \sigma)\mu]l_u. \tag{8.3}$$

Here, l_i denotes the individual labor supply, e denotes the share of native-born skilled workers in the total native-born labor supply,

σ denotes the share of skilled migrants in the total number of migrants, μ denotes the total number of migrants, and is μ,

the labor supply of an individual with skill level i. The total population (N) is comprised of native-born workers (which is normalized to 1) and migrants (μ).

We specify a simple welfare-state system, which levies a proportional labor income tax at the rate τ, with the revenues redistributed equally to all residents, N, as social benefit per capita, b. The social benefit captures not only a cash transfer but also outlays on public services, such as education, health, and other provisions that benefit all workers, regardless of their contribution to the tax revenues.

The government budget constraint is therefore

$$Nb = \tau Y. \tag{8.4}$$

Assume that the utility function for skill type i, $i \in \{e,u\}$, is

$$u_i = c_i - \frac{\varepsilon}{1+\varepsilon} l_i^{(1+\varepsilon)/\varepsilon}, \tag{8.5}$$

where c_i denotes consumption of an individual with skill level i, l_i denotes the individual labor supply, and $\varepsilon > 0$. The budget constraint of an individual with skill level i is

$$c_i = b + (1 - \tau) l_i w_i. \tag{8.6}$$

Individual utility-maximization yields the following labor-supply equation:

$$l_i = [(1 - \tau) w_i]^\varepsilon. \tag{8.7}$$

The general equilibrium wages for skilled and unskilled workers are

$$w_e = A(\alpha \delta^\varepsilon \theta^{1-\alpha})^{1/(1+\varepsilon)}, \tag{8.8}$$

$$w_u = A[(1-\alpha)\delta^\varepsilon \theta^{-\alpha}]^{1/(1+\varepsilon)}, \tag{8.9}$$

where

$$\delta \equiv \alpha^\alpha (1-\alpha)^{1-\alpha}$$

and

$$\theta \equiv [1 - e + (1 - \sigma)\mu] / (e + \sigma\mu).$$

8.2.1 Immigration Policy

The host-country migration policy is to be determined by the median voter in the host country. Let us assume that the policy decisions on the tax rate τ and the total volume of migration μ are exogenous. We do this in order to focus the analysis on a single endogenous policy variable, which is the skill composition of migrants (i.e., σ). Note that once σ, μ, and τ are determined, then the social benefit per capita, b, is given by the government budget constraint. Thus, we denote the social benefit per capita, b, as $b(\sigma;\tau)$, where the exogenous variable μ is suppressed. The indirect utility of an individual with skill level i is given by

$$V_i(\sigma;\tau) = b(\sigma;\tau) + \frac{1}{1+\varepsilon}\left[(1-\tau)w_i(\sigma;\tau)\right]^{1+\varepsilon}. \tag{8.10}$$

Differentiating the equation with respect to σ, and employing the envelope theorem, yields

$$\frac{dV_i(\sigma;\tau)}{d\sigma} = \frac{db(\sigma;\tau)}{d\sigma} + (1-\tau)l_i\left[w_i(\sigma;\tau)\right]\frac{dw_i(\sigma;\tau)}{d\sigma}. \tag{8.11}$$

Thus, a policy-induced change in the share of skilled migrants in the total number of migrants, σ, affects the utility level through two channels. First, an increase in σ raises average labor productivity and thereby tax revenues. This, in turn, raises the social benefit per capita, b. Second, an increase in σ, which raises the supply of skilled labor relative to the supply of unskilled labor, depresses the skill premium in the labor market. If the decisive voter is unskilled, both of the above effects increase his utility. Thus, an unskilled voter would like to set the skill composition of migrants at the maximal limit, $\sigma = 1$. This means that the share of skilled migrants preferred by the decisive skilled voter is typically lower than that preferred by the decisive unskilled voter. The decisive skilled voter would like to set σ below 1 (which is equivalent to assuming that the first-order condition is met before σ reaches 1).

Let superscript i denote the choice of the skill mix of immigrants by a decisive voter i; $i = u, e$. Define σ^i as the share of skilled immigrants most preferred by an individual with skill level $i = e, u$ in the host country, we obtain

$$\sigma^e < \sigma^u = 1$$

Recall that the purpose is to find the effect of the change in the generosity of the welfare state on the migration policy concerning σ. The generosity of the welfare state, captured by the magnitude of the social benefit per capita, b, depends positively on the tax rate, τ (we assume that the economy is on the "correct side" of the Laffer curve). Thus, we examine the effect of an increase in τ on the change in the skill composition of the migrants, σ. It can be shown that

$$\frac{d\sigma^M}{d\tau} = 0; \frac{d\sigma^M}{d\tau} > 0. \tag{8.12}$$

$$\frac{d\sigma^u}{dA} = 0, sign\frac{d\sigma^e}{dA} = ?.$$

This means that, if the decisive voter were an unskilled worker, an increase in the tax rate τ would leave the skill-migration policy unchanged, because it is always set at the maximum possible limit. However, if the decisive voter is a skilled worker, an increase in the tax rate τ will change the policy concerning the skill composition of migrants in the direction toward a larger share of skilled migrants. The reason for this is that when the tax rate is higher, the redistribution burden upon a skilled decisive voter increases. Allowing an additional skilled migrant can ease this rise in the fiscal burden. Note also that the result applies to the skill mix of migration rates.

Under native-born skill control, the effect of domestic productivity increase on the skill mix of immigration is to improve the mix, $sign\frac{d\sigma^e}{dA} = ?$. On the one hand, the increase in the wage premium also raises tax revenues and eases the fiscal burden. This force makes unskilled migrants less burdensome to the *Fisc*. At the same time, the increase in productivity also raises the efficiency gains (thereby mitigating the skill-labor wage), which makes the influx of skilled migrants desirable.

8.3   Controlling Skill Composition of Immigration by Advanced Economies

While immigration from poor countries often invokes images of large masses of unskilled laborers, in reality it has been quite skill intensive. Immigration into high-income countries, even if from countries with lower income per person, tends to be more concentrated among highly educated than among less educated, relative to the population of the country of destination (see Peri [2016]).

The explanation for the concentration of rich-country immigrants among the highly educated is the screening and selection migration policies by the destination countries. In this context, Razin and Wahba (2015) researched two hypotheses associated with migration skill mix: the fiscal burden hypothesis and the magnet hypothesis. The former asserts that under host-country migration policies the rise in the generosity of the welfare state will skew the skill mix toward skilled migrants because they can ease fiscal burden. The latter hypothesis asserts that under free migration would-be low-skilled migrants will be more attracted to the welfare state, so that a more generous welfare state will have its skill mix skewed toward the low-skilled migrants. Accordingly, they investigate the effect of welfare state generosity on the difference between skilled and unskilled migration rates, and the role of mobility restriction in shaping this effect. They utilize the free labor movement within the European Union plus Norway and Switzerland (henceforth referred to as EUROPE) and the restricted movement from outside EUROPE in order to compare the free-migration regime to the controlled-migration regime. Using bilateral migration movements, and splitting the sample among flows within EUROPE and flows from outside EUROPE, they identify the migration regime effect. In table 8.1 the dependent variable is the share of skilled migrants in the migrant population, and the main explanatory variable is "benefits per capita"—a measure of the generosity of the welfare state. The hypothesis is that under free migration the coefficient of this variable is negative, whereas under controlled migration the coefficient of "benefits per capita multiplied by R" is positive. The indicator X is a dummy variable: $R = 1$ if migration is controlled, whereas $R = 0$ if migration is free. Recall that the bilateral migration flows within EUROPE are referred to as free migration, whereas bilateral migration flows where the source is outside and the destination is inside EUROPE are referred to as controlled migration. Appendix 8A includes some robustness tests of the model.

In the regression analysis (see also Appendix 8A) Razin and Wahba (2015) control for differences in educational quality and returns to skills in source and host countries, and for endogeneity bias (by using instrumental variables). Overall, the fiscal burden and the magnet hypotheses, tested with the coefficient of social benefit in the regressions, are statistically significant.[3] Therefore, regression findings yield support for the magnet hypothesis under the free-migration regime and for the fiscal burden hypothesis under the restricted-migration regime.

Table 8.2
Skill Composition of Immigration: OLS Estimates (Dependent variable: skill difference in migration rates in 2000)

	EUR & DC to EUR			EUR & LDC to EUR		
Welfare generosity						
Benefits per capita (logs) 1974–1990 (host)	-0.110 (0.057)*	-0.112 (0.056)**	-0.116 (0.047)**	-0.115 (0.056)**	-0.136 (0.053)**	-0.131 (0.047)***
Benefits per capita (logs) 1974–1990 (host) X R	0.113 (0.053)**	0.137 (0.064)**	0.132 (0.055)**	0.102 (0.065)	0.101 (0.079)	0.110 (0.066)*
Lagged migration rates						
Low-skilled migration rate 1990	-0.719 (0.133)***	-0.719 (0.129)***	-0.710 (0.140)***	-0.612 (0.128)***	-0.611 (0.129)***	-0.609 (0.137)***
Low-skilled migration rate 1990 x R	1.723 (0.173)***	1.751 (0.169)***	1.723 (0.171)***	0.278 (0.196)	0.560 (0.234)**	0.552 (0.226)**
High-skilled migration rate 1990	1.062 (0.150)***	1.061 (0.147)***	1.049 (0.155)***	0.963 (0.145)***	0.959 (0.146)***	0.957 (0.153)***
High-skilled migration rate 1990 x R	-0.725 (0.149)***	-0.726 (0.144)***	-0.712 (0.151)***	-0.481 (0.157)***	-0.627 (0.170)***	-0.623 (0.173)***
Returns to skills						
High-low labor ratio in 1990 (host)	-0.484 (0.237)**			0.309 (0.326)		
High-low labor ratio in 1990 (host) X F	0.309 (0.500)			0.019 (0.656)		

	(1)	(2)	(3)	(4)	(5)	(6)
High-low wage diff. in 1995 (host)				0.003 (0.002)		0.001 (0.003)
High-low wage diff. in 1995 (host) X F				-0.007 (0.003)**		-0.005 (0.003)*
Gini in 1990 (source)		0.012 (0.004)***		0.013 (0.004)***	0.011 (0.004)**	0.011 (0.005)**
Gini in 1990 (source) X R		-0.012 (0.005)***		-0.014 (0.005)***	-0.010 (0.005)**	-0.010 (0.005)*
High-low unemp. rate diff. in 1990 (host)		0.002 (0.002)		0.001 (0.002)	0.003 (0.002)	0.006 (0.002)
High-low unemp. rate diff. in 1990 (host) X F		-0.002 (0.004)		-0.004 (0.004)	-0.005 (0.005)	-0.008 (0.005)*
Immigration policies						
Total migrant stock in 1990	-0.001 (0.001)	-0.001 (0.001)	-0.002 (0.001)***	-0.001 (0.001)	-0.002 (0.001)**	-0.002 (0.001)**
Share of refugees in 1990	-2.079 (2.803)	-1.023 (3.237)	-0.238 (2.145)	-3.904 (3.403)	-1.945 (2.477)	-1.297 (3.007)
Observations	384	384	601	360	570	534
R-squared	0.864	0.870	0.832	0.874	0.809	0.814

Notes: F = free migration; R = restricted migration. Regressions include log distance, dummy for same language in host and source, strong dummy between host and source, and real GDP per capita in host and in source countries. Robust standard errors in parentheses; * significant at 10%; ** significant at 5%; *** significant at 1%.

8.4 Brain Drain

Schooling gaps are closely related to the average level of schooling among native-born workers: poor countries exhibit higher schooling gaps. Bilateral schooling gaps vary across destination countries; hence, destination choices affect the intensity of the brain drain. With other things equal, the brain drain is stronger in small and poor countries, which send most of their emigrants to selective countries (i.e., host countries with quality-based immigration policies). Ceteris paribus, the brain drain is stronger in poor countries where the average level of schooling is relatively low.

In setting up a migration policy, one is certainly concerned by the skill composition of immigrants as a crucial factor. Naturally, highly skilled immigrants are more attractive to the destination countries than low-skilled immigrants, for a variety of reasons. For instance, highly skilled immigrants are expected to pay more in taxes to the *Fisc* in excess of what the *Fisc* provides them with. In addition, these immigrants are also expected to boost the technological edge of their destination countries. In contrast, low-skilled immigrants tend to depress the wages of the low-skilled native-born workers, and they are deemed to impose a burden on the fiscal system. However, if a migration policy that favors the highly skilled is coupled with a generous family-unification policy, then an influx of low-skilled migration takes place too. The 1990 U.S. Immigration Act increased the number of temporary visas to highly skilled workers. In addition, during those decades, the U.S. universities and research centers—funded, significantly, by the U.S. federal and state governments, directly and indirectly—attracted talented researchers from all over the world. Many of them remained in the United States after completing their original term of education, training, or research. Many became citizens. By the mid-1990s, 30 percent of documented immigrants to the United States were highly skilled.[4]

Gould and Moav (2007) focus on twenty-eight countries that represent the largest exporters of immigrants to the United States. The sample includes mostly advanced economies. Table 8.2 shows that the average index of emigration, that is, the number of émigrés per 10,000 residents, is 33.36, with the index for Israel being nearly three times as high: 95.51. Only two countries have a higher index—Ireland (143.9) and Portugal (99.21). When examining the index for educated émigrés, that is, those with a college degree, the average index is 12.41, and Israel's index is more than three times higher, 41.45. When we use this index, Israel is now higher than Portugal, and the gap between Israel and Ireland (49.09) narrows considerably (see table 8.2).

Table 8.3 presents international selective indicators of emigration to the United States by education attainment. Israel is ranked at the very top for college graduate émigrés to the United States per 10,000 residents, with number of about 41. Only Ireland with 49 is ranked above Israel. South Korea, also suffering from brain drain, has only about 25 college graduate émigrés per 10,000 residents.

8.5   Israel's Top-Talent Drain

Kerr et al. (2016) observe that the number of migrants with a tertiary degree rose by nearly 130 percent from 1990 to 2010, while low-skill (primary school–educated) migrants increased by only 40 percent during that time. High-skilled migrants are departing from a broader range of countries and heading to a narrower range of countries—in particular, to the United States, the United Kingdom, Canada, and Australia.[5] At the policy level, they compare the points-based skilled migration regimes, as historically implemented by Canada and Australia, with the employment-based policies used in the United States through visa-control mechanisms, like the H-1B visa program. Because of the links of global migration flows to employment and higher education opportunities, firms and universities also act as important conduits, making employment and admission decisions that deeply affect the patterns of high-skilled mobility.

Today, Israel ranks third in the world in the number of university graduates per capita, after the United States and the Netherlands. It possesses the highest per capita number of scientists in the world, with 135 for every 10,000 citizens (compared to 85 per 10,000 in the United States), and publishes the highest number of scientific papers per capita—6. According to one recent survey, almost 81 percent of Israelis own cell phones, placing it sixth in the world. Another survey found that 54 percent of Israelis own personal computers, in comparison to only 42 percent of U.S. respondents.

As for the brain drain in academia, Ben-David (2008) demonstrates how differences between universities are inducing a massive academic migration from Israel to the United States. The magnitude of this scholarly brain drain is unparalleled in the western world. (See figures 8.1 and 8.2.) The European Commission (2003) reported that 73 percent of the 15,000 Europeans who studied for their PhD in the United States

Table 8.3
Indicators of Emigration to the US by Education Attainment

Country of origin	Number of 30- to 50-year-old émigrés	Percentage college graduates	Number of college graduates	Population of country of origin	Émigrés per 10,000 residents	College graduate émigrés per 10,000 residents
Denmark	10,275	52	5,329	5,368,854	19.14	9.93
Finland	8,170	55	4,487	5,172,033	15.80	8.68
Norway	9,030	55	4,943	5,183,545	17.42	9.54
Sweden	17,174	56	9,584	8,876,744	19.35	10.80
Great Britain*	307,694	42	128,600	59,778,002	51.47	21.51
Ireland	55,877	34	19,061	3,883,159	143.90	49.09
Belgium	12,034	53	6,397	10,274,595	11.71	6.23
France	89,213	47	42,323	59,765,983	14.93	7.08
Netherlands	34,318	49	16,691	16,067,754	21.36	30.39
Switzerland	17,295	60	10,300	7,301,994	23.69	14.11
Greece	70,825	27	19,366	10,645,343	66.53	18.19
Italy	147,789	27	39,532	57,715,625	25.61	6.85
Portugal	100,044	10	9,700	10,084,245	99.21	9.62
Spain	46,564	39	18,020	40,077,100	11.61	4.50
Austria	15,936	43	6,877	8,169,929	19.51	8.42
Czechoslovakia	19,990	41	8,230	10,256,760	19.49	8.02
Germany	429,158	34	145,130	83,251,851	51.55	17.43
Hungary	20,498	39	7,969	10,075,034	20.35	7.91
Poland	176,737	27	47,587	38,625,478	45.76	12.32
Romania	48,294	43	20,877	22,317,730	21.64	9.35
USSR/Russia	271,364	53	143,202	144,978,573	18.72	9.88
China	709,415	55	387,900	1,284,303,705	5.52	3.02
Japan	225,484	48	108,981	126,974,628	17.76	8.58
South Korea	388,783	45	173,128	70,548,195	55.11	24.54
Thailand	57,733	35	19,987	62,354,402	9.27	3.21
India	667,434	65	432,037	1,045,845,226	6.38	4.13
Israel/Palestine	57,589	43	24,994	6,029,529	95.51	41.45
Turkey	39,649	45	17,974	67,308,928	5.89	2.67

*England, Scotland, and Wales.
Source: Gould and Moav (2007).

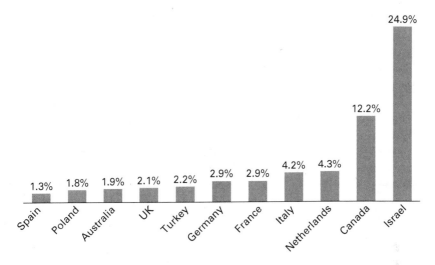

Figure 8.1
Foreign scholars in U.S. universities, as percent of scholars in home country, 2003–2004.
Source: Ben-David (2008).

between 1991 and 2000 planned to remain in America. If Europeans are concerned about the migration of their academics to the States, then Israelis should be nothing less than alarmed.

The United States serves as a magnet for top scientific immigrants. Immigrants hold a disproportionate share of jobs in science, technology, engineering, and math in the United States (see Hanson and Slaughter [2016]). Top-talent drain from Israel is disproportionately high among the highly educated immigrants.

In general, the number of foreign scholars in America as a percentage of scholars in the home country ranged from 1.3 percent in Spain to 4.3 percent in the Netherlands (see figure 8.1). At 12.2 percent, Canada was an outlier, though this is much more of a two-way street than in any of the other cases. While Canada is an outlier, Israeli scholars in America are in a class by themselves. Israeli academics residing in the States in 2003–2004 represented 24.9 percent of the entire senior staff in Israel's academic institutions that year—twice the Canadian percentage and over five times the percentage of the other developed countries.

Figure 8.1 describes the percentage of home-country scholars who have academic position in U.S. universities. Figure 8.2 similarly describes Israeli scholars (in percentage of Israel universities' senior faculty) in the top U.S. universities.

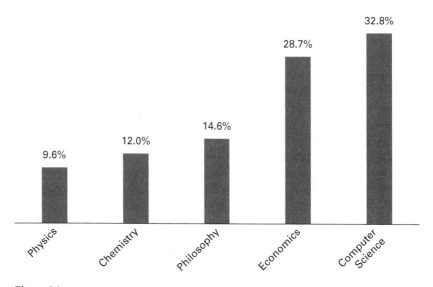

Figure 8.2
Israelis in top American departments, 2007, as percent of senior faculty in Israel, by field
Source: Ben-David (2007).

The figures demonstrate that Israel stands out internationally in terms of the size and quality of the brain drain.

Top-talent drain is therefore an issue of concern in Israel, because, despite Israel's current technological and scientific prowess, it has been trending upward.

Appendix 8A: Robustness Tests

Tables 8A.1–8A.3 describe the skill mix-benefit correlations under various econometric specifications. Overall, the fiscal burden and the magnet hypotheses, tested with the coefficient of social benefit in the regressions, are statistically significant. Therefore, regression findings yield support for the magnet hypothesis under the free-migration regime, and to the fiscal burden hypothesis, under the restricted-migration regime. In the regression analysis, Razin and Wahba (2015) control for differences in educational quality and returns to skills in source and host countries, and for endogeneity bias (by using instrumental variables).

Table 8A.1
OLS Estimates Using Migration Rates Adjusted by Relative Educational Quality (Dependent variable: skill difference in migration [REQ] rates in 2000)

Welfare generosity	EUR & DC to EUR			EUR & LDC to EUR		
Benefits per capita (logs) 1974–1990 (host)	-0.105 (0.052)**	-0.115 (0.049)**	-0.109 (0.042)**	-0.111 (0.051)**	-0.116 (0.054)**	-0.138 (0.054)**
Benefits per capita (logs) 1974–1990 (host) X R	0.115 (0.053)**	0.139 (0.062)**	0.135 (0.054)**	0.104 (0.059)*	0.111 (0.070)	0.132 (0.062)**
Lagged migration rates						
Low-skilled migration rate (REQ) 1990	-0.697 (0.151)***	-0.695 (0.149)***	-0.686 (0.160)***	-0.681 (0.156)***	-0.595 (0.143)***	-0.578 (0.150)***
Low-skilled migration rate (REQ) 1990 x R	1.711 (0.175)***	1.738 (0.172)***	1.713 (0.174)***	0.715 (0.295)**	0.576 (0.217)***	0.314 (0.208)
High-skilled migration rate (REQ) 1990	1.037 (0.169)***	1.033 (0.168)***	1.022 (0.176)***	1.011 (0.175)***	0.937 (0.162)***	0.920 (0.167)***
High-skilled migration rate (REQ) 1990 x R	-0.702 (0.167)***	-0.702 (0.164)***	-0.688 (0.171)***	-0.584 (0.194)***	-0.637 (0.175)***	-0.468 (0.178)***
Returns to skills						
High-low labor ratio in 1990 (host)	-0.482 (0.234)**			0.205 (0.302)		
High-low labor ratio in 1990 (host) X R	0.325 (0.482)			0.043 (0.571)		

(continued)

Table 8A.1 (continued)

Returns to skills	EUR & DC to EUR			EUR & LDC to EUR		
High-low wage diff. in 1995 (host)	0.002 (0.002)			0.003 (0.003)		
High-low wage diff. in 1995 (host) X R	-0.007 (0.003)**			-0.006 (0.003)*		
Gini in 1990 (source)		0.013 (0.004)***	0.014 (0.004)***		0.011 (0.004)***	0.013 (0.005)***
Gini in 1990 (source) X R		-0.013 (0.005)***	-0.014 (0.005)***		-0.011 (0.005)**	-0.011 (0.005)**
High-low unemp. rate diff. in 1990 (host)			0.001 (0.002)		0.001 (0.002)	0.006 (0.004)
High-low unemp. rate diff. in 1990 (host) X R			-0.004 (0.004)		-0.005 (0.004)	-0.009 (0.005)*
Immigration policies						
Total migrant stock in 1990	-0.001 (0.001)	-0.001 (0.001)	-0.001 (0.001)	-0.001 (0.001)	-0.002 (0.001)***	-0.002 (0.001)**
Share of refugees in 1990	-1.907 (2.547)	-1.168 (3.230)	-3.680 (3.298)	-0.672 (1.983)	-2.954 (2.509)	-1.497 (3.081)
Observations	384	384	360	569	569	533
R-squared	0.861	0.867	0.871	0.842	0.816	0.835

Notes: All the migration rates are adjusted for the quality of education by the relative education quality in source to host country; that is, $REQ = (EQ_s/EQ_h)$; F = free migration; R = restricted migration. Regressions include log distance, dummy for same language in host and source, strong dummy between host and source, and real GDP per capita in host and in source countries.

Robust standard errors in parentheses; * significant at 10%; ** significant at 5%; *** significant at 1%.

Table 8A.2
IV Estimates with Lagged Dependent Variable (Dependent variable: skill difference in migration rates in 2000)

Welfare generosity	EUR & DC to EUR			EUR & LDC to EUR		
Fitted benefits per capita (logs) 1974–1990 (host)	-0.157 (0.081)*	-0.217 (0.097)**	-0.118 (0.063)*	-0.181 (0.080)**	-0.180 (0.089)**	-0.154 (0.070)**
Fitted benefits per capita (logs) 1974–1990 (host) X R	0.270 (0.089)***	0.261 (0.099)***	0.207 (0.078)***	0.198 (0.088)**	0.209 (0.103)**	0.161 (0.083)*
Lagged migration rates						
Low-skilled migration rate 1990	-0.711 (0.130)***	-0.711 (0.125)***	-0.706 (0.135)***	-0.592 (0.131)***	-0.581 (0.131)***	-0.581 (0.137)***
Low-skilled migration rate 1990 x R	1.774 (0.171)***	1.775 (0.166)***	1.752 (0.169)***	0.563 (0.229)**	0.556 (0.229)**	0.562 (0.221)**
High-skilled migration rate 1990	1.055 (0.147)***	1.052 (0.142)***	1.046 (0.150)***	0.944 (0.148)***	0.931 (0.148)***	0.933 (0.152)***
High-skilled migration rate 1990 x R	-0.726 (0.147)***	-0.722 (0.141)***	-0.713 (0.148)***	-0.627 (0.166)***	-0.611 (0.168)***	-0.618 (0.168)***
Returns to skills						
High-low labor ratio in 1990 (host)		-1.455 (0.541)***			0.060 (0.458)	
High-low labor ratio in 1990 (host) X R		0.794 (0.548)			0.522 (0.690)	
High-low wage diff. in 1995 (host)			0.003 (0.002)			0.003 (0.003)

(continued)

Table 8A.2 (continued)

Returns to skills	EUR & DC to EUR			EUR & LDC to EUR		
High-low wage diff. in 1995 (host) X R			-0.008 (0.003)***			-0.006 (0.003)*
Gini in 1990 (source)		0.012 (0.004)***	0.012 (0.004)***		0.011 (0.004)***	0.011 (0.004)**
Gini in 1990 (source) X R		-0.013 (0.005)***	-0.015 (0.005)***		-0.010 (0.005)**	-0.010 (0.005)**
High-low unemp. rate diff. 1990 (host)		0.011 (0.005)	0.000 (0.002)		0.005 (0.003)	0.005 (0.004)
High-low unemp. rate diff. 1990 (host) X R		-0.005 (0.005)	-0.005 (0.004)		-0.008 (0.006)	-0.008 (0.005)*
Immigration policies						
Total migrant stock in 1990	-0.001 (0.001)	-0.001 (0.001)	-0.001 (0.001)	-0.002 (0.001)***	-0.003 (0.001)***	-0.003 (0.001)**
Share of refugees in 1990	-2.470 (3.174)		-4.835 (3.670)	-1.590 (2.603)	-2.990 (2.827)	-2.261 (3.266)
Cragg-Donald F- statistics	49.46	54.34	103.01	86.23	98.44	159.12
Observations	384	384	360	538	538	504
R-squared	0.865	0.871	0.875	0.811	0.815	0.821

Notes: F = free migration; R = restricted migration. Instrumented using legal origin dummies, and the interaction of legal origin dummies and R. Regressions include real GDP per capita growth rate in host, log distance, dummy for same language in host and source, strong dummy between host and source, and real GDP per capita in host and in source countries. Robust standard errors in parentheses; * significant at 10%; ** significant at 5%; *** significant at 1%.

Table 8A.3

Estimates with Lagged Dependent Variable and Adjusted by Relative Educational Quality (REQ) (Dependent variable: skill difference in migration rates [REQ] in 2000)

Welfare generosity	EUR & DC to EUR			EUR & LDC to EUR		
Fitted benefits per capita (logs) 1974–1990 (host)	-0.159 (0.075)**	-0.207 (0.087)**	-0.170 (0.070)**	-0.175 (0.076)**	-0.179 (0.079)**	-0.178 (0.064)***
Fitted benefits per capita (logs) 1974–1990 (host) X R	0.269 (0.089)***	0.268 (0.098)***	0.207 (0.077)***	0.207 (0.083)**	0.218 (0.102)**	0.194 (0.080)**
Lagged migration rates						
low-skilled migration rate (REQ) 1990	-0.686 (0.148)***	-0.685 (0.145)***	-0.678 (0.155)***	-0.602 (0.144)***	-0.665 (0.154)***	-0.666 (0.164)***
low-skilled migration rate (REQ) 1990 x R	1.753 (0.172)***	1.765 (0.170)***	1.732 (0.174)***	0.553 (0.212)***	0.694 (0.290)**	0.686 (0.292)**
high-skilled migration rate (REQ) 1990	1.026 (0.166)***	1.022 (0.163)***	1.014 (0.171)***	0.941 (0.163)***	0.991 (0.173)***	0.989 (0.180)***
high-skilled migration rate (REQ) 1990 x R	-0.698 (0.164)***	-0.693 (0.162)***	-0.684 (0.168)***	-0.632 (0.173)***	-0.566 (0.193)***	-0.564 (0.198)***
Returns to skills						
high-low labor ratio in 1990 (host)	-1.192 (0.358)***				0.075 (0.386)	
high-low labor ratio in 1990 (host) X R	0.833 (0.534)				0.027 (0.574)	

(continued)

Table 8A.3 (continued)

Returns to skills	EUR & DC to EUR		EUR & LDC to EUR	
high-low wage diff. in 1995 (host)		0.004 (0.002)*		0.003 (0.002)
high-low wage diff. in 1995 (host) X R		-0.007 (0.003)**		-0.007 (0.005)**
Gini in 1990 (source)	0.012 (0.004)***	0.013 (0.004)***	0.012 (0.004)***	0.013 (0.005)***
Gini in 1990 (source) X R	-0.013 (0.005)***	-0.015 (0.005)***	-0.012 (0.004)***	-0.012 (0.004)***
High-low unemp. rate diff. in 1990 (host)	0.008 (0.003)**	0.002 (0.003)	0.003 (0.003)	0.006 (0.004)
High-low unemp. rate diff. in 1990 (host) X R	-0.005 (0.005)	-0.005 (0.004)	-0.008 (0.005)	-0.012 (0.004)***
Immigration policies				
Total migrant stock in 1990	-0.001 (0.001)	-0.001 (0.001)	-0.002 (0.001)**	-0.001 (0.001)
Share of refugees in 1990	-2.592 (3.245)	-2.809 (3.548)	-1.768 (2.476)	-1.315 (2.919)
Cragg-Donald F-statistics	51.69	62.65	86.45	169.49
Observations	384	360	538	533
R-squared	0.863	0.871	0.805	0.835

Notes: All the migration rates are adjusted for the quality of education by relative quality in source to host, i.e., $REQ = (EQ_s / EQ_h)$, $F =$ free migration; $R =$ restricted migration. Instrumented using legal origin dummies, and the interaction of legal origin dummies and R. Regressions include real GDP per capita growth rate in host, log distance, dummy for same language in host and source, strong dummy between host and source, and real GDP per capita in host and in source countries. Robust standard errors in parentheses; * significant at 10%; ** significant at 5%; *** significant at 1%.

9 High Fertility and Anemic Skill Acquisition

The Israeli fertility rate of nearly three births per woman exceeds the industrial nations' norm by a wide margin.

Europe and East Asia have fertility rates below the replacement rate, which leads to stagnant population. East Asia shows the sharpest decline in the fertility rates[1] (see figure 9.1).

Furthermore, Israel's fertility rate stands out among all the OECD countries (see figure 9.2).

At the same time, levels of skills of Israel's labor force ranked high, indicating the relatively large stock of human capital in Israel (see figure 9.3).

Unlike many Western countries that need a young workforce to supplement their aging societies, Israel has an unusually young population. The relatively low skill level of a large portion of this local population could have reduced the demand for additional workers from abroad who are similarly poorly educated, to the extent that the low-skill native-born workers participate in the labor market. However, the latter have very low participation rate. Therefore, the demand for foreign workers is strong in certain industries, like construction, agriculture, and household aid. And, large numbers of foreign workers continue to receive work permits in the country.

9.1 Schooling Gaps

Even though the overall education attainment level of Israel's (native-born) labor force is highly ranked currently, schooling gaps emerge. Israel has below average school gaps among advanced economies—a test score of 4.686, compared to the group average of 4.939. See table 9.1.

The main reason for Israel's exceptionally high average fertility rates are the even higher rates among the Jewish ultra-Orthodox and the

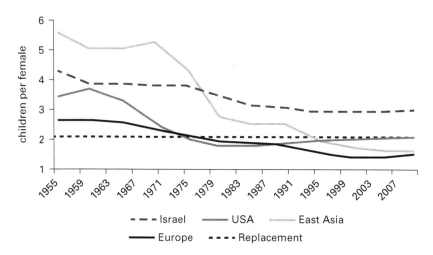

Figure 9.1
Total fertility rates: Israel and selected industrial countries. *Source*: Goldman (2013).

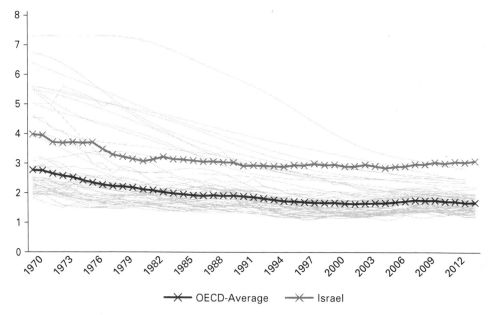

Figure 9.2
Fertility rates among OECD countries. *Source*: OECD Library.

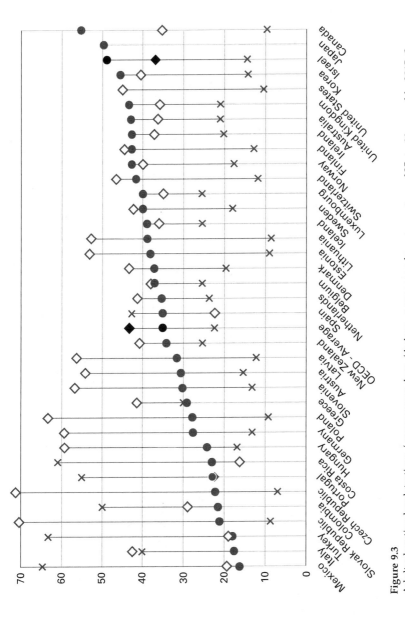

Figure 9.3
Adult education level: tertiary / upper secondary / below upper secondary, percentage of 25- to 64-year-olds, 2015. *Source: OECD Education at a Glance: Educational Attainment and Labor-Force Status.*

Table 9.1
Test Scores

EUR		DC		LDC	
Country	EQ	Country	EQ	Country	EQ
Austria	5.089	Australia	5.094	Argentina	3.920
Belgium	5.041	Canada	5.038	Brazil	3.638
Switzerland	5.142	Hong Kong	5.195	Chile	4.049
Denmark	4.962	Israel	4.686	China	4.939
Spain	4.829	Japan	5.310	Colombia	4.152
Finland	5.126	Korea, Rep.	5.338	Egypt	4.030
France	5.040	New Zealand	4.978	Indonesia	3.880
United Kingdom	4.950	Singapore	5.330	India	4.281
Germany	4.956	Taiwan (Chinese Taipei)	5.452	Iran	4.219
Greece	4.608	United States	4.903	Jordan	4.264
Ireland	4.995			Lebanon	3.950
Italy	4.758			Morocco	3.327
Netherlands	5.115			Mexico	3.998
Norway	4.830			Malaysia	4.838
Portugal	4.564			Nigeria	4.154
Sweden	5.013			Peru	3.125
				Philippines	3.647
				Thailand	4.565
				Tunisia	3.795
				Turkey	4.128
				South Africa	3.089
Group Averages	*4.939*		*5.132*		*3.999*

Israeli Arabs. Their share of the population is therefore on a path to a steady increse. However, their skill endowments are small. Consequently, Israel's dependency ratio is also likely to be rising over time, and its competitiveness is expected to erode.

9.2 Private and Social Incentives

Most ultra-Orthodox Jews[2] lack the skills to work in a modern economy, having studied little or no math and science beyond primary school (their curriculum focuses almost entirely on religious texts such as the Torah and Talmud). As a result, more than 60 percent live below the poverty line, compared with 12 percent among non-Haredi

Jews. Most also opt out of military service, which is compulsory for other Israelis. The net effect: as the Haredi community expands, the burden of both taxation and conscription falls on fewer and fewer Israelis.[3]

Manski and Mayshar (2003) computed (smoothed) completed-fertility rates by year of marriage, for each of the four subgroups of Israeli Jews whose parents were not born in Israel. During 1945–1950, the Mizrahi-ethnic women were bearing about three times as many children as Ashkenazi-ethnic women. Thirty years later, during 1975–1980, completed fertility again separates the population into two groups, but now the relevant dimension is religiosity rather than ethnicity, with ultra-Orthodox women bearing about twice as many children as non-ultra-Orthodox Jewish women.

Manski and Mayshar (2003) explore how private and social incentives for fertility may have combined to produce the complex fertility pattern observed in Israel, where over decades fertility declined within some ethnic-religious groups but increased among the ultra-Orthodox Jewish population. The latter experienced a *reversed fertility transition*.[4] They identify the contribution of child allowances and the related public welfare program for the reverse transition.[5] The identification technique they adapted helps to disentangle the child allowance effects from the socioeconomic and religious effects that are at play. In general, the different rates of completed fertility observed in different ethnic or religious groups at different times could be generated by

(1) cross-sectional and time series variations in the woman-specific utility parameters;

(2) cross-sectional and time series variations in the child allowance policy; and

(3) social interactions within and across groups.

Using these rigorous techniques, Mansky and Mayshar (2003) find evidence for the effects of both private and social incentives on the fertility rates of the ultra-Orthodox.

However, the question arises about the mechanism behind the assumed social incentives. Berman (2000) interpreted the trends toward increased fertility, decreased labor force participation, and increased supply of time to religious studies in the ultra-Orthodox community in terms of the behavior of a "club" that has strengthened its norms of religious stringency in an attempt to brace for exclusion.

Razin and Sadka (1995, chapter 4) provide an insight to the puzzle. The economic self-preservation of the "club" is akin to the old-age security motive for having children, where children are a means for parents during their income-generating years to prepare (through income, child allowances, and other government subsidies) for their old-age unproductive years. To minimize "defection" from the community, the parents choose not to endow the children with labor-market skills.

The mechanism works like the human-capital accumulation in the twentieth-century kibbutz community in Israel. Through narrowing the selection of topics in children's schooling, the Kibbutz parents tend to endow their children with good skills to help maintain the kibbutz economy, but relatively poor skills for the labor markets outside of the club. The kibbutz system excluded itself from the primary and secondary national education system and did not support tertiary education. Abramitzky (2011) gives strong evidence in support of a related hypothesis: that, for the kibbutz equality system to be maintained, the cost of exiting the community has to be raised.

Abramitzky and Lavy (2014) use an unusual pay reform during the kibbutz privatization era to test the responsiveness of investment in schooling to changes in the redistribution scheme and whether it increases the market rate of return to education. Their identification strategy exploits an episode where different Israeli kibbutzim shifted from equal sharing to productivity-based wages in different years and finds that students in kibbutzim that reformed earlier invested more in high school education and, in the long run, also in post-secondary schooling.

Parents' hopes that their children will live with them are complicated by the fact that the community cannot directly control whether the children exit, and what a child finds optimal may deviate from what the parents and the community would prefer. This creates an incentive problem between the parents, their children, and the community. While the parents and the community cannot directly influence children's decisions, parents do control the number of children and the amount of schooling they provide for their children, and thus may be able to limit their children's potential future benefits from migration out of the community.

China's one-child policy has a reversed effect on fertility and investment in education.[6] Can one extrapolate from the Chinese one-child state-imposed policy (which reduced the fertility rate) to the social norms and social pressures among the ultra-Orthodox, which help explain the high fertility rate?

Choukhmane, Coeurdacier, and Jun (2016) explore the effects of the one-child policy on fertility rates, savings, and investment in human capital. They provide evidence that the dramatic fall in fertility rates raised aggregate personal saving and led to rapid accumulation of human capital of the one-child generation. Is it relevant for the reversed effects on fertility rates among the ultra-Orthodox Jewish? The similarity between these apparently two different episodes is that in both cases the fertility rates are influenced by the state (in the case of China) or by the community (in the case of Israel). The difference between the two is that the state is not a club. The state can force the fertility rate down but has no control over the savings and human capital investment of the individual household. Choukhmane, Coeurdacier, and Jun (2016) find that a drop in fertility rates creates incentives to increase savings and parents' investment in the human capital of their children in order to support the parents in old age. Acquired skills help the children function better in the job market, and raise their labor supply. However, the Jewish ultra-Orthodox community puts pressures on the individual household to maximize the number of children, and to prevent children from acquiring job-market skills. Poor job-market skills ensure little defection from the ultra-Orthodox club.

9.3   Fertility Rates: The Israeli Arabs

The Arab population in Israel, particularly the Muslim, ranks far lower on the socioeconomic scale than the Israeli Jews.[7] This gap had not changed much during the half century since the foundation of Israel as a state, but has started to close in the last decade. The major factor behind this wide socioeconomic gap is the differential opportunity structure between the Jewish and the Arab populations, particularly Muslims, and the social norms concerning women. There are large differences not only in human capital between Jews and Arabs, but, even for those Arabs whose educational status is relatively high, entrance into higher-status employment is difficult. This differential opportunity structure results in reduced motivations for the attainment of higher educational levels among Arabs.

Muslim Arabs' lifetime-completed fertility rate was about 7.5–8.0 at the beginning of the 1940s, and reached a record 9.3 in the 1960s.

However, it subsequently started to decline and reached 4.6 in the mid-1980s, remaining at that level through the year 2000. The Christian Arab population, which has been at a higher stage of socioeconomic modernization since the 1930s, has experienced major fertility declines—from a total fertility rate of 7.5 in the 1940s, to 3.6 in the early 1970s, and to 2.5 in the year 2000 (see Friedlander [2009]).

Labor-force participation rate among Israeli Arabs is relatively low. Those who do participate have difficulty finding suitable jobs and suffer from high unemployment. Most workers concentrate in a narrow range of low-paying occupations (see Yashiv and Kasir [2014]). As for educational attainment, Yashiv and Kasir (2011, 2014) observe that Israeli Arabs have low educational levels, relative to the Jewish population. The evidence is from international tests (according to OECD data), from national feedback tests in primary education, and from the tests that determine school efficiency and growth indicators (*meitzav*). Dropout rates from the educational system are higher in the Arab sector—21 percent in grades 9–11, in comparison to about 11 percent in the Jewish sector. Arabs' share of the university student population in Israel is only half their share of the population—in 2011/2012 Arabs accounted for only 10.8 percent of all university and college students in Israel. The rate goes down the higher the academic degree, and in PhD studies Arabs make up only 4.4 percent of all students.

These trends seem to be reversing, as Arab women have recently begun to take advantage of the Israeli higher educational system. Furthermore, the participation of Arab women in the labor force is steadily rising.

9.4   Long-Term Implications

Currently, the rankings of Israel in terms of the population growth rates and skill of the labor force are high. However, the high fertility rate among the Jewish ultra-Orthodox and Israeli Arabs, and the lack of proper investment in children to prepare them to the labor market, are bound to raise the dependency ratio. These trends, if they are not reversed, could severely lower future GDP growth and weaken international competitiveness. The trend is akin to *productivity regress*.

10 Rising Cost of Occupation

Since May 14, 1948, Independence Day, Israel has fought six wars, continuous terrorism threats, an Arab-League inspired economic boycott, and, as a result, bears high defense burden. Israel now has peace treaties with two neighboring countries (Jordan and Egypt—Egypt being the pillar of the Arab world). However, Israel is still in a state of war with two of its immediate neighbors (Syria and Lebanon), and in a transitional stage toward some economic interactions with the other Arab countries (Saudi Arabia and the Gulf states); but there is no formal peace yet.

All along, Israel's economy had to bear the costs of regional hostilities, instabilities, and a never-ending arms race. Consequently, Israel had to cope with the long-lasting social and economic cost of a heavy defense burden. At the height of its defense spending in 1976–1977, Israel's military expenditures totaled more than 13 percent of its GNP. In comparison, the United States spent 5.7 percent, the United Kingdom 4.9 percent, and France 3.85 percent for the same period. A quarter-century later, despite peace agreements with Egypt and Jordan and massive reductions in defense outlays, Israel's defense budget as a percentage of GDP remains three times higher than that of the United States or European countries, at a current rate of around 7 percent of GDP (see Sharaby [2002]). The hostile surroundings also have some dire domestic implications in terms of a political polarization.

The costs of the conflicts include the high defense budget, but also additional costs that are not part of that budget. A major cost is the loss of human capital due to conscription and reserves' service, as young people are drafted to serve three (for men) or two (for women) years. When serving as a draftee, one does not receive the market-equivalent salary for their labor. Thus, the cash outlays underestimate the true economic costs. However, the economic cost of conscription (and, to some extent, the cost of the military reserves) is not limited to the loss of labor by the draftees during their military service; it includes the loss of human capital throughout the worker's lifetime in the job market. Human capital tends to rise over a person's lifetime career due to acquisition of education, on-the-job training, and experience. Conscription delays this human capital accumulation by three or two years, thus increasing the loss of human capital.[1]

Since 1967, when the West Bank and Gaza Strip occupation began, there have been increasingly taxing socioeconomic effects on Israel. There are about 2.6 million Palestinians in the West Bank, besides the 313,000 in East Jerusalem.[2] The Palestinian uprising covered three defining moments: the relatively mild "stone-throwing" (first) Palestinian intifada (1989–1990), the "suicide-bomb" (second) Palestinian intifada (2000–2005), and the "knife-intifada" (third) Palestinian intifada (2015–2017).[3] Since the second intifada, the Palestinian political split into Fatah and Hamas brought about the ongoing military clashes between Israel and the Hamas-dominated Gaza.[4]

10.1   Economic Parable

The economic relationship between Israel and the West Bank and Gaza is a classic parable of a large open economy trading with a small closed economy. Economic theory suggests that, in such a case, the small open economy, with relatively high mobility of goods, services, capital, and labor, being trade-locked away from the rest of the world, becomes very dependent on the large economy. Moreover, the benefits from the integration skew toward the small economy.[5] Most of the links of the emerging Palestinian economy to the world economy were indirect. The channels through which the Palestinian economy traded with the rest of the world advanced economies went through (almost exclusively) Israel's links with these economies. When the large economy has access to the world economy (see Israel's globalization trends, in 10.2), any military conflict between the small economy and the large economy would unavoidably hit hard the economic integration between these two asymmetric economies. The harmful military conflict hits primarily the small economy, which has indirect links to the world economy only through the customs union with the large economy.

Globalization provides a big cushion for the large economy. Given Israel's weak direct trade linkages to the region, regional tensions mainly affect Israel through security, through investor and consumer confidence, through the public finances, and so on. The latter turned out to be very short-lived; globalization proved to be a shield against the Palestinian-Israeli military conflicts and regional trade obstacles for the Israeli economy.

10.2   Cascade of Uprisings

General MacArthur famously wrote to the U.S. congress less than two years after the occupation of Japan begun: "History points out the unmistakable lesson that military occupations serve their purpose at best for only a limited time, after which a deterioration rapidly set in." The occupying power under MacArthur attempted to impose new political, economic, and social institutions on the occupied Japan territory, with no intent on the part of the occupier to have more than temporary occupation. The occupation lasted for seven years, and the new Japan was a prime success story.[6]

Although at the beginning of Israel's occupation of the West Bank and Gaza new political, economic, and social institutions were erected and the territories' economy made unmistakable progress, there was no end game. The occupying power was struggling to reach the ultimate decision if and when to leave, and the territories' indigenous population was poorly coordinated. It had an ongoing struggle whether to compromise or to expand the sovereignty into Israel's own territories.

The first uprising broke out in December of 1987 in the West Bank (which has been occupied by Israel since the Six-Day War in 1967) and the Gaza Strip (occupied from the 1967 war until the mid-2000s). It all came unexpectedly, following a fatal collision between an Israeli truck and a bus carrying Palestinians from Gaza who worked in Israel as part of a large Palestinian work force employed in Israel. The employment in Israel provided a big boost to the Palestinian economy at the time. Riots crystalized a new local Palestinian leadership; the old guards of the PLO were expelled to Tunis after the first Lebanon-Israel war. The uprising had dramatically transformed the nature of the Palestinian-Israeli conflict into a continuous political struggle against the Israeli administration in the West Bank and Gaza, punctuated by a short period of political reconciliation during the Oslo agreement. The second uprising broke out after the collapse of the Oslo agreements, in early 2002. The Israeli economy was hit twice. It was first hit by the dot-com crash in the United States, and again by the 2000–2005 second intifada.

This had drastic effects on the Palestinian economy, which shortly after split into two political units (the West bank, controlled by the Palestinian Authority, and the Gaza Strip, controlled by Hamas); the Gaza strip economy got down to the level of humanitarian crisis.[7] The crisis became deep following the ongoing skirmishes punctuated only by short ceasefire breaks.

The Oslo Accord divided the West Bank into three administrative divisions: the Areas A, B, and C. The distinct areas were given a different status, according to their governance pending a final status accord: Area A is exclusively administered by the Palestinian Authority, Area B is administered by both the Palestinian Authority and Israel, and Area C, which contains the Israeli settlements is administered by Israel. The West Bank economy bears the heavy cost of being under such transitional arrangement.[8]

10.3   Short-Term Implications for Israel's Economy

Figure 10.1 demonstrates that the early 2000s' shock had a relatively small effect on the long-term trajectory of Israel's real GDP. The effect on the Israeli economy of the second intifada shock was mild, and short-lived.

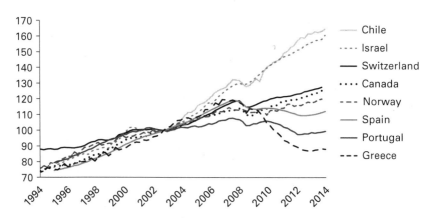

Figure 10.1
Real GDP, Israel and small open OECD economies (January 2003 = 100). *Source*: OECD Library; FRED (economic database of the Federal Reserve Bank of St. Louis).

10.4   Israel's Global Reach as a Shield

Returning to the small-large economy narrative, the large economy globalization feature provides a cushion. Given Israel's weak direct trade linkages to the region, regional tensions mainly affect Israel through security, investor and consumer confidence, and the public finances. The latter proved to be short-lived. That is, globalization proved to be a shield against the Palestinian-Israeli military conflicts and regional trade obstacles for the Israeli economy. This means, however, that the Israeli economy is exposed to alarming long-run risks. If, and when, the Palestinian-Israeli conflict and the long occupation of the West Bank territory trigger political conflicts between Israel and its trade and finance partners, this shield, provided by Israel's high level of integration with the global economy, may break down.

Appendix 10A: Matrix of Control

Following Israel's war of independence, after the ceasefire in 1949, the Green Line divided Israel from Jordan. Israel has been building a separating barrier since the second *intifada* of 1967. The barrier runs mostly along the Green Line, but in several places makes deep incursions into the West Bank. The Oslo Accord divided the West Bank into three administrative divisions: Areas A, B, and C. The distinct areas were given different status according to their governance, pending a final status accord: the Palestinian Authority (PA) exclusively administers Area A, Area B is administered by both the PA and Israel, and Area C, which contains the Israeli Settlements, is administered by Israel. The PA controls now only 40 percent of the West Bank, containing 90 percent of the Palestinian population. The other 60 percent, plus East Jerusalem, is land that remains under transitional arrangements. Area C comprises 61 percent of the entire West Bank. It is home to almost 380,000 Israelis, but only around 150,000 Palestinians. In addition, roughly 200,000 Israelis live in East Jerusalem (annexed in 1967 by Israel).

In 2005, Israel withdrew from Gaza. Hamas, a radical Islamist group, took over. Hamas does not recognize Israel's right to exist and has never signed to the Oslo agreements. Border crossings between Area C and Israel and between Gaza and Israel are a prime opportunities, not taken, to strengthen economic integration, but they pose major security issues. Although the PA is supposed to control security inside the Oslo-defined "Area A" (comprising the main West Bank cities), Israeli forces routinely enter them to grab suspected terrorists, including Hamas operatives.

The poorly managed PA is wholly dependent on Israel. Most of its revenues come from customs duties, collected by Israel since Israel controls the seaports, airports, and land crossings through which goods destined for the West Bank must travel. Israel can cut those off at any time, and has done so in the past. At least 100,000 Palestinians commute daily from the West Bank to work in Israel, half with permits, the rest smuggled in. Another 50,000 or so work in Israel's 130 Israeli settlements. With a 26 percent unemployment rate and an employed workforce that numbers not much above 1 million, the dependency on Israeli employers is acute.

The "matrix of control" is the occupation structure which allows Israel to control key aspects of Palestinian life in the West Bank through an interlocking series of mechanisms, only a few of which require physical occupation of territory. Together, however, these mechanisms virtually create barriers to mobility and trade across the entire territory. Most facets of the matrix rely upon subtle involvements, largely bureaucratic and legal. Nevertheless, these are backed by overwhelming military force, which Israel reserves for itself the right to employ. Occupation imposes a heavy burden for the Israel Defense Forces' regular troops. A survey conducted by the chief of staff and the Knesset Foreign Affairs and Defense Committee in March 2016 states: "At this stage, the IDF operates 65 percent of its regular army, most of the regular troops, in the West Bank." Most important for the long term, sovereign and contiguous territory is a prerequisite for a viable Palestinian state, when a two-state solution would have been put in place.

IV   Early Literature

Israel adopted from its very beginning as an independent state a rule-based, as opposed to deal-based, capitalism, which has progressed over time with the strengthening of institutions such as free media, independent tax authorities, and the like.[1] This is the social-political-legal construction within which Israel was able to become as rich as the average OECD member state in a relatively short time. Indeed, Israel's development as a market economy is the main topic of the earlier surveys. The development of the market economy is a common theme.

11 Israel Surveyed

The earliest book exploring Israel's economy, Don Patinkin's *The Israel Economy: The First Decade*, was written in the late 1950s, and the most recent volume, *The Israeli Economy, 1985–1998: From Government Intervention to Market Economics* (edited by Avi Ben-Bassat), was published in 2002.[1] Patinkin (1959) is the pioneering text on the economy of the then-nascent state. To absorb massive immigration and at the same time form a robust defense posture (against threats from the seven Arab countries that were defeated during the war of independence), it established fiscal, financial, and monetary institutions. With the fast increase in population through the massive immigration waves, pervasive price controls and rationing and strict capital controls were put in place temporarily. Government spending at this time was largely financed by a monetary expansion.[2] Because of this, the money supply grew at an annual rate of 36 percent during this period (Patinkin [1959], 108). The price controls, coupled with the monetary expansion, led to widespread shortages, the development of a black market, and, ultimately, a crisis that began in the autumn of 1951. From the perspective of the late 1950s, the crisis of 1951 appeared as a watershed to Don Patinkin.

A somewhat different opinion than that of Patinkin that gives less weight to efficiency gains and more to labor and capital accumulation during the first phase of development is presented by Syrquin (1985). He attributes about 40 percent of the growth in output to total factor productivity growth over the period 1950–1970. But he also notes that "the relatively low contribution of increases in efficiency to output growth conceals the magnitude of the achievement of having incorporated into the productive process the vast increase in inputs while improving their efficiency" (Syrquin [1985], p. 49). As Syrquin suggests, the "Israel miracle" continued to be the context for the Israeli economy when Nadav Halevi and Ruth Klinov-Malul wrote *The Economic Development of Israel*, which was published in 1968.

Although each one of the surveyed books considers the Israeli economy at a different stage of its development,[3] six common themes are as follows:

(1) the relevant comparison group for considering the Israeli economy;

(2) the challenges of immigration, integration, and inequality;

(3) the appropriate roles of the government and markets;

(4) openness and dependence;

(5) inflation, crisis, and stabilization; and

(6) growth.

Overall, the chronology of economic views presented in these books corresponds to an increasing acceptance of the role of markets and an increasing desire for open trade in goods and assets. It is often remarked upon that the State of Israel, during its short existence, has been severely challenged by its engagement in numerous wars and military conflicts. Less often cited, but also important, is the fact that the State has also had more than its share of economic crises since its founding. These crises have helped forge the country's economic system, as suggested in the subtitle of the book edited by Ben-Porath (1986), *Maturing through Crises*. Ben-Porath's point on the importance of a political commitment to stabilization is supported by the postmortem of the 1985 heterodox plan by Razin and Sadka (1993). Razin and Sadka write that, in 1985, "the active and authoritative role played by Shimon Peres was a remarkable contrast to the passive, unenthusiastic role played by Prime Minister Menachem Begin in 1983" (p. 30n). They underscore Peres's efforts to build support for the plan among various constituencies, including "the pillars of the political economic system: the government, the Histadrut, and the Private Employers Association" (p. 23). They also note that public support for this program that emerged "as soon as it was implemented, clearly played a role in its success" (p. 30). The importance of this support, and the political backing of the program, is stressed by Razin and Sadka because they believe that a cause of the crisis was "a weak government, which lacked resolve and had at best a poor understanding and awareness of the real seriousness of these problems" (p. 26). Razin and Sadka also discussed the recession that occurred in the wake of the stabilization plan, beginning in the second half of 1987.

They see this recession as "the inevitable outcome of the economic policy of 1986–1988" (p. 49). They note that a similar post-stabilization recession took place in Latin American countries. More specifically, they view the fixed exchange rate component of the policy as tying the hands of the central bank in a way that caused adverse upswings and downswings in the real exchange rate and real interest rates. They state that "in the spring of 1988, well before the general elections held in November, it became evident that the stubborn policy of freezing the exchange rate, in effect since January of 1987, inflicted a heavy toll on the economy" (p. 99). The use of the exchange rate as a nominal anchor, and the subsequent appreciation of the real exchange rate, is, however, a common feature of stabilization programs, as pointed out by Fischer and Orsmond in their contribution to the Ben-Bassat (2002) volume. Another survey book on the Israeli economy, edited by Leiderman (1999), focuses on monetary policies related to inflation and disinflation. The main theme there is the ways Israel's central bank adopted the inflation target policy.

As can be gathered from this brief survey, currently there is a gap of a decade and a half in book-size research-oriented surveys of the fast-developing Israeli economy. Futhermore, no previously published book put Israel's globalization at the center. The present book attempts to fill part of the gap.

Epilogue

Some of the powerful forces of globalization—responsible for many inflection points in the history of the economy of Israel—that this book analyzes are immigration waves; inflation-reduction spillovers from the advanced economies during the Great Moderation; foreign direct investment in technology and spillovers from the global information technology revolution; the effects of the large influx of skilled immigrants from the former Soviet Union; the rise in income inequality; the opening to East Asian large markets; and the rising cost of occupation.

These critical driving forces explain how Israel, in a relatively short period, transformed from developing to developed economy and gained entry in 2010 into the OECD—the thirty-five-member group of world advanced economies.

Israel's fast development, although unique, is not unknown elsewhere. Ireland somewhat parallels Israel in greatly benefitting from globalization. Ireland entered the 1950s as a very poor postcolonial society. However, it realized major successes by its integration into the EU, and by reaching an elite hi-tech status. Ireland was able to attract from the rest of the world (other than the EU) massive FDI, thanks to its being a tax-sheltered gate to the EU massive markets. However, Ireland regulated its banking sector poorly and allowed the credit bubble to flourish in the wake of the 2008 global financial crash. Its overexposed banking sector collapsed during the financial crisis. Ireland has continued to be burdened by the Eurozone's nearly secular stagnation.[1] Israel's robust performance during the crisis is partly attributable to not being a member of a single currency area.

However, going forward, fundamental challenges are acute. High fertility and low skill acquisition among the increasing share in the population of ultra-Orthodox, peripheral towns, and Arab communities drive down the average productivity and participation rate in the

working-age population of the labor force. Immense political uncertainty concerns the Palestinian-Israeli conflict. The uncertainty centers
on the slide toward the politically combustive one-state solution. All
these are major tests that Israel's economy faces.

The high fertility, low labor force participation, and excessive supply
of school time to religious non-core studies in the ultra-Orthodox community can be explained in terms of the behavior of a "club" that has
strengthened its norms of religious stringency, in an attempt to stay
excluded from the outside world. That is, the isolation from the outside
society forces the community to be redistributive and develop its own
social insurance. Parents tend to endow their children with good skills
to help maintain the survival of the club, but poor skills for the labor
market outside of the club. Societal transformations that can reverse
this trend are hard to come by. The high fertility rate and the low labor-
market participation rate among the Jewish ultra-Orthodox, and to a
lesser extent the Israeli Arabs, could raise the dependency on the welfare state, which will have fewer revenue sources and more transfer to
hand out. Furthermore, among the high-fertility groups, the lack of
proper investment in education to prepare their children for the labor
market, could create economy-wide productivity regress, which would
negatively affect Israel's competitiveness in the global economy. Brain
drain may reinforce the productivity-regress process. Overcoming such
backwardness-driving forces that would weaken Israel's competitive
power in the world economy is a big task ahead.

The almost intractable Israeli-Palestinian conflict leads to increased
level of uncertainty about the entire future political and economic
arrangements. A concern for Israel lies both from heightening internal
conflicts and from external injurious affairs—the danger of international
political/economic isolation. There are a number of parallels of political/
economic isolation, although none are perfect. The Latin American
countries were more or less forcibly isolated economically by the Great
Depression and World War II.[2] The Israel-Palestinian conflict creates
enormous uncertainty as to whether the two-state solution is slipping
away for good. The standing of Israel in the global politics is uncertain.
Putting things in real estate terms, 40 percent of the West Bank, containing 90 percent of the Palestinian population, was ceded to the Palestinian Authority in the Oslo-based peace negotiations. The other 60 percent,
plus East Jerusalem, is the land that remains disputed, with the divergence among sides only growing. The two-state issue has been side-
lined partly by the political fecklessness of a divided Palestinian

camp, by international concern over migration and refugees, by the destabilizing fallout from the conflicts in Syria and Iraq, and by the renewed confidence and support within the country of the Greater Israel political parties within a combustible political polarization environment. There are many reasons to be concerned. Severing economic links with, say, the EU, resulting from potential political pressures, can be devastating to Israel's economy. The reader can be reminded of the following quote from the international economist Rudi Dornbusch: "The crisis takes a much longer time coming than you think, and then it happens much faster than you would have thought."

Foreign direct investment is about 4 percent of GDP. The OECD average was just 1.4 percent. For Israel, the OECD accounted for the lion's share of FDI inflows. Israel's exports of goods and services is about 30 percent of GDP, and imports of goods and services is about 30 percent. For Israel, the OECD accounted also for the lion's share of its trade in goods and services. Israel's exports are reoriented toward East Asia opening markets. Pointedly, Israel is among the economies that are included in the Chinese "Belt and Road" infrastructure initiative. However, the uncertainty about the future Israeli economic and financial links to the global economy arises precisely from the potential of Israel being sanctioned by the international community, and thereby becoming politically and economically isolated from some world markets, because of future regional crises. Both sides of the Palestinian-Israeli conflict are on increasingly more extreme polarizing trajectories.

Notes

1. In answering repeated threats of reimposing of tariffs, the Chinese Leader, Xi Jinping, said: "Pursuing protectionism is just like locking oneself in a dark room. While wind and rain may be kept outside, so are light and air."

2. See Appendix 3A.

Chapter 1

1. Obviously, the way capitalistic system works is more complicated. Organized sectoral lobbying efforts for export subsidies and importable industry protection, government cronyism, and excessive influence of big business are common across all variants of capitalistic systems; but they are more pronounced under deal-based market economies.

2. Calvo and Vegh (2001) observe that in many high-inflation stabilization programs around the world inflation failed to converge to world averages. Real economic activity expanded in the early years of the stabilization program. Later in the program, a recession set in. Unlike Israel's stabilization program, in many developing economies the program later collapsed.

3. Dornbusch and Edwards (1989) address macroeconomic populism in Latin America, which they roughly define as policies that are favored by a substantial part of the voting population but that ultimately harm the majority of the population. They found that populism surfaces when the economy has endured a period of external shocks and domestic upheavals, and "a highly uneven income distribution usually presents a serious political and economic problem, providing the appeal for a radically different economic program." In the first phase after their policies are enacted, the populists are vindicated. Growth and wages indeed rise, as a combination of profligate spending and intrusive government control does expand the economy. The surging government spending and mandated wage hikes tend to produce a temporary "sugar high," followed by a crash. Populist policies, because they are unsustainable, cause people to shift spending from uncertain future to the present, when the economy is temporarily booming. Beneath the surface, however, the country's economic potential is deteriorating. Financial disorders appear. Rather than make the hard choice of returning to principled economic oversight, the populist leader recommits to harmful policies and steers the country toward decline, capital flight, and sometimes debt crises. In all cases, write Dornbusch and Edwards, "there

were disastrous effects for those groups who were supposed to be the beneficiaries of the policies."

4. The trilemma as a situation in which someone faces a choice among three options, each of which comes with some inevitable problems. In international finance it is cast in terms of economic regime choices. The international finance trilemma goes back to the classic works of Fleming (1962) and Mundell (1963). See Mankiw (2010) for blog interpretation. For a balance-of-payments crisis model in the trilemma regime-switch framework, see Appendix 1A.

5. See Appendix 1A.

6. Schneider and Tornell (2004) provide a model of boom-bust episodes in middle-income countries that may explain the logic of the boom-bust episodes that followed the stabilization program. It is based on sectoral differences in corporate finance: the non-tradable sector (e.g., real estate and financial services) is special in that it faces a contract enforceability problem and enjoys bailout guarantees (e.g., bailing out mortgages). As a result, currency mismatch in the balance sheet arises endogenously in that sector. This sectoral asymmetry allows the model to replicate the main features of observed boom-bust episodes. In particular, episodes begin with a lending boom and a real appreciation, peak in a self-fulfilling crisis during which a real depreciation coincides with widespread bankruptcies, and end in a recession and credit crunch. Israel's economy fully recovered in the late 1980s and early 1990s, a time when there was a new wave of immigrants from the former Soviet Union (see chapter 2). For detailed account of the stabilization policy, see Razin and Sadka (1993).

7. The U.S. government provided also a one $1.5 billion cushion. See Cukierman (1988b) for a comprehensive analysis of the stabilization policy.

8. Over a third of government outlays targeted by the program came from subsidies.

9. Persson and Tabelini (1990) point out that incentives to surprise the private sector by deviating from preannounced policy rule arise if conflicts exist between private individuals and policy makers. Having a broad-based coalition reduces these conflicts, and policy credibility is enhanced.

10. Necessary condition for maximization of seigniorage revenue across a steady state is that the inflation rate is equal to one over the semi-elasticity of demand for money. This Laffer point is significantly below the rates in high inflation episodes.

11. Seigniorage is calculated instantaneously as the monthly change in base money, deflated by mid-month CPI (Consumer Price Index).

12. See Kydland and Prescott (1977) and Calvo (1978).

13. See Calvo (1992).

14. Israel's expectations-changing episode is akin to the Volcker-policy effect on inflationary expectations in the United States; see Sargent (1999).

15. For details, see the "first generation" model of a balance-of-payments crisis, driven by budget deficits, in Appendix 1A.

16. See more on balance-of-payments crises in Appendix 1A.

17. This is the first variant of the first-generation models. For discussion of the second and third generations of crises, see chapter 5.

18. See Appendix 1A for details of the "first generation" modeling.

19. Krugman (2000) explains the crisis-prone possibility by an appeal that the contractionary balance-sheet effects of currency depreciation will outweigh the expansionary pro-competitive effects of such depreciation. But suppose that the traded share of output increases? Another channel through which globalization might reduce the risk of crisis is foreign direct investment. Local subsidiaries of multinational firms will not be subject to the same adverse balance-sheet effects of depreciation as domestic firms.

20. In a radical exchange-rate–based, anti-inflation program in the late 1990s, Argentina moved to hard-currency peg—the Convertibility Plan. Budget deficits and extensive foreign borrowing triggered a triple megacrisis in 2001, as the domestic currency slid to free fall, banks failed, and public debt became unpayable. A decade-long stagnation and inaccess to the world capital market followed in crushing forces.

21. See Razin (2015).

22. See a comprehensive analytical survey of second-generation and third-generation models in Razin (2015).

Chapter 2

1. Benhabib and Jovanovich (2012) consider world-welfare perspective. Our analysis focuses on an individual state.

2. See Razin and Sadka (1993)

3. After World War I the League of Nations granted Great Britain a mandate over the whole of Palestine. It ended in May 1948, when Israel gained its independence.

4. The first hint came in the enterprise reform law of January 1988, which allowed state enterprise managers to use company funds at their discretion instead of complying strictly with central plans (*tekhpromfinplans*). Soon thereafter, central plans ceased being obligatory. The stated intention of the enterprise reform law was to give managers more latitude in dealing with day-to-day operations, but the opportunity to divert funds from operations and investment to personal consumption and roundabout insider privatization was not missed (*kleptostroika*).

5. Narodnoe Khoziastvo (1990).

6. Sachs (2012).

7. Rosefielde and Hedlund (2009).

8. See Razin (1995).

9. Although the table alludes to simple correlation between migration and growth, the migration-wave shocks are considered to be an exogenous variable, a migration-push factor triggered by forces in the origin country. See Neuman (1999).

Chapter 3

1. See Appendix 3A.

2. See Sachs (2017) for an illuminating discussion of international migration regimes.

3. See Gornick and Jäntti (2014) for a comprehensive report on income inequality and redistribution among rich countries. Krugman (2006) argues that to the extent that globalization explains rising income inequality in the United States, it is through the effect of international trade on the "skill premium"—the gap between the incomes of college-educated workers and those without a college degree. What we know, however, is that rising inequality is not mainly about the rising skill premium. Only around a third of the rise in U.S. inequality over the past generation is associated with a rising premium for education. Economic estimates indicate that the widening of the skill premium itself is more a result of "skill-biased technological change"—a growing demand for highly educated workers due to the rising importance of information technology—than a result of globalization.

4. Yashiv and Kassir (2011) write:

The most prominent phenomenon among Arab women is the high level of variation in the rate of participation. Its source apparently lies in the differences between 'modern' and 'traditional' women from the point of view of education, family status, number of children and proficiency in various skills (such as knowledge of English and the use of a computer). There appears to be a dichotomy or some type of dual market, in which 'traditional' women almost never participate. This can explain the low rate of participation in comparison to other countries. 'Modern' women have quite a high rate of participation, which also explains the simultaneous increase in participation and levels of education over time, together with additional cultural changes. The finding that participation rates among Arab women are very different from those observed in Western countries and among Jewish women in Israel, though not significantly different from rates in Moslem countries.

5. Dahan (2007) explores the main factors behind the steep decline in the participation rate of Israeli men. He observes four factors responsible for the decline in participation rate between 1980 and 2001: increases in the population of students (21 percent), the ultra-Orthodox (21 percent), the disabled (32 percent), and discouraged workers (25 percent).

6. About the voting right franchise in the United States in the 1930s, Meltzer and Richard (1981) conclude: "In recent years, the proportion of voters receiving social security has increased, raising the number of voters favoring taxes on wage and salary income to finance redistribution. In our analysis the increase in social security recipients has an effect similar to an extension of the franchise."

7. Social expenditures temporarily increased during the migration wave, thanks to one-shot absorption expenditures on new immigrants. They declined at the beginning of the 2000s.

8. The model is based on Razin, Sadka, and Swagel (2002a, b).

9. Note that this specification assumes that capital does not depreciate at all.

10. In an unpublished version, Razin and Sadka extended the tax to apply to capital income as well.

11. Such a framework is akin to a steady state in a dynamic model with rational expectations.

12. One may wonder why there is no tax on the initial endowment (E). However, in a dynamic setting, which we mimic in a static framework, E represents accumulated savings, and taxing it will be distortive. Furthermore, because all native-born individuals possess the same initial endowment, taxing it in our static model does not distribute

income across native-born income groups; but taxing E amounts to transferring income from the native-born individuals to the migrants static model; such a tax is not distortive.

13. In addition, equation (3.1) defines I_S^N as a function of c.

14. For numerical simulation, see Appendix 3B.

Chapter 4

1. Bentolila, Dolado, and Jimeno (2007) have recently addressed the impact of the Spanish immigration boom on the Phillips curve.

2. Rogoff's prediction has proven to be correct. Global inflation moved sideways also after 2003 and then fell sharply asymptotically, approaching zero after 2008, despite massive monetary and credit expansion in the United States and the European Union.

3. See a simple formula in Appendix 4A.

4. Similarly, Mishkin (2007a, b) writes about the U.S. inflation-output tradeoff: "The finding that inflation is less responsive to the unemployment gap, suggests that fluctuations in resource utilization will have smaller implications for inflation than used to be the case. From the point of view of policy makers, this development is a two-edged sword: On the plus side, it implies that an overheating economy will tend to generate a smaller increase in inflation. On the negative side, however, a flatter Phillips curve also implies that a given increase in inflation will be more costly to wring out of the system."

5. See Binyamini and Razin (2008). See also Gali (2008) for a comprehensive treatise of the open-economy New Keynesian model. Borio and Filardo (2007) present cross-country evidence in support of their contention that global factors have recently become empirically more relevant for domestic inflation determination. But Ihrig et al. (2007) have shown that their result is very specific to the econometric method used. Based on cross-country analysis, Badinger (2007) finds that globalization is also correlated with more aggressive policy toward inflation. Tetlow and Ironside (2007), although not dealing with globalization, find that for the United States the slope of the Phillips curve has—largely and continuously—lessened during recent years. ·

6. See chapter 1.

7. The expectations-based framework whereby a change in monetary and fiscal regime helps conquest inflation is in Sargent (1999).

See more discussion of the inflation crisis in chapter 12.

8. Oil-consuming developed economies hit by the oil price shock like Israel were able to crush the nascent inflation pressures. Other developing countries experienced similar hyperinflation episodes. Many Latin American countries, particularly Argentina in 2002, went through similar processes. The 1997 Asian crisis also had similar features, except that a more disciplined fiscal policy had been maintained before the crisis erupted.

9. Globalization also affected the conduct of central banks. Inflation targeting was born in New Zealand in 1990. Admired for its transparency and accountability, it achieved success there, and soon also in Canada, Australia, the UK, Sweden, and Israel. It subsequently became popular as well in Latin America (Brazil, Chile, Mexico, Colombia, and Peru)

and in other developing countries (South Africa, South Korea, Indonesia, Thailand, and Turkey, among others).

10. Leiderman (1999) comprehensively analyzed Israel's disinflation with a focus on monetary policies related to inflation and disinflation. He especially focused on inflation targeting as an instrument of disinflation.

11. Recall that by the Fisher equation

$$1 + r_t^{US} = (1 + i_{US}^t) \frac{P_{US,t}}{P_{US,t+1}}. \text{ That is, } (1 + r_t^i) \frac{q_{i/US,t+1}}{q_{i/US,t}} = (1 + i_i^t) \frac{P_{i,t}}{P_{i,t+1}} \frac{q_{i/US,t+1}}{q_{i/US,t}}.$$

12. See also chapter 2 for the development in the disposable income inequality governed by the changed redistribution policies.

13. See also Razin (2015), chapter 11.

Chapter 5

1. For spillovers of the global financial crisis to the single-currency area in Europe, see Appendix 5A.

2. Real estate bubbles are often irrational. Miller (1977) points out that the housing market is not an efficient market in which divergent views cannot produce bubbles. Efficient markets require the possibility of selling short. As Shiller (2015) observes, in the stock market (for example) with short selling, people who think the market is overpriced and headed for a fall can borrow shares and sell the borrowed shares at the current high price. If share prices do indeed fall, they can buy the shares back at a lower price and repay the loan, with a profit. Short selling helps to prevent bubbles from forming. However, such negative bets cannot easily occur in the housing market. You cannot routinely borrow a house and sell it, promising to buy back the same house later to repay the loan. Markets without the possibility of making these negative bets will be inefficient. That is because if it is not possible to short sell, the smart money can do no more than avoid holding an overpriced asset. Canny traders are forced to sit on the sidelines, and watch in futility as prices decline as they expected. Without short sellers, there is nothing to stop a group of ignorant investors—who get some ill-conceived idea that a certain investment is just terrific—from bidding up prices to extravagant levels. In the housing market, that poses an enormous problem.

3. For the sovereign-debt issue in the Eurozone, see Appendix 4A.

4. See Razin (2015).

5. See Appendix 5A.

6. Ben Bernanke (2016) recently analyzed the main reasons for the U.S. FOMC's (Federal Open Market Committee) change of view concerning current interest policy. He advances three reasons: (1) projections of potential output growth, (2) projections of the natural rate of unemployment, and (3) projections of the natural (real) interest rate. Projections of all three long-term variables have been reduced significantly. These projections are not inconsistent with the secular stagnation hypothesis.

7. See Appendix 5A for a stylized twin-gap model, which can serve to provide an analytical background to figure 5.3.

8. See also Eggertsson, Mehrotra, and Summers (2016).

9. See Appendix 5C.

10. See Blanchard (2016), who surveyed the literature about the aftermath of the 2008 crisis in advanced economies and emerging economies that were hit to different degrees. To a large extent, the emerging markets escaped the brunt of the crisis. Israel evidently belongs to the second group.

11. The VIX is the Chicago Board Options Exchange Market Volatility Index. It is a measure of the implied volatility of S&P 500 index options. The VIX rises when put option buying increases and falls when call buying activity is more robust. (Note: A put option gives the purchaser the right—but not the obligation—to sell a security for a specified price at a certain time. A call option is a right to buy the same.)

12. See Rey (2015).

13. In the presence of trending capital exports, the central bank cannot persistently appreciate the domestic currency by selling foreign exchange denominated assets in the foreign exchange market, because depleted international reserves could quickly reach their lower bound. However, in the presence of trending financial capital imports, the central bank can persistently depreciate the domestic currency by purchasing foreign exchange denominated assets in the foreign exchange market through money issue. This is why the foreign exchange market intervention is referred to as a "half instrument" in the hands of the central bank.

14. See Krugman, Obstfeld, and Melitz (2015).

15. A CDS is a financial swap agreement that the seller of the CDS will compensate the buyer (the creditor of the reference loan) in the event of a loan default. That is, the seller of the CDS insures the buyer against loan defaulting. The buyer of the CDS makes a series of payments (the "spread") to the seller and, in exchange, receives a payoff if the loan defaults.

16. The phenomenon of a group of countries intervening to retain undervalued exchange rate is often referred to as a "currency war."

17. Collateral is a crucial tool to help the financial system in general, and financial intermediaries like banks in particular, to minimize the asymmetric information problems of adverse selection and moral hazard. As Mishkin (2007a) puts it, "Collateral also reduces moral hazard by reducing the incentives for borrowers to take on too much risk. When a borrower has pledged collateral on her loan, she has more to lose if she cannot pay it back and so she naturally is more reluctant to engage in risky activities that make it more likely she will default and lose the collateral."

Chapter 6

1. However, Robert Gordon (2016), using standard productivity residual methods, found that the impact of internet-driven inventions on productivity growth of GDP was less than counterpart nineteenth-century inventions.

2. For a theory of how foreign investor liquidity determines its venture capital and portfolio investment, see Razin (2015).

3. For a brief on FDI literature see Appendix 6A.

4. For a brief on the FDI literature see Appendix 6B.

5. Bransfetter (2006) introduces a framework for measuring international knowledge spillovers at the *firm* level. He uses this framework to directly test the hypothesis that FDI is a channel of knowledge spillovers for Japanese multinationals undertaking direct investments in the United States. Using an original firm-level panel data set on Japanese firms' FDI and innovative activity, he finds evidence that FDI increases the flow of knowledge spillovers both from and to the investing Japanese firms.

6. Another factor that explains the Israel-OECD gap is the expansion of OECD membership, with some of the new member countries (e.g., Mexico) having low R&D spending.

7. Not all countries follow the 10 percent mark for the definition of FDI. Most countries do indeed report long-term intra-firm loans, but not all countries report short-term loans. Most countries report reinvestment of retained earning only with a considerable lag. One implication of these measurement problems is that FDI inflows do not contemporaneously match FDI outflows. The UN (2005) annual report on world investment documents how countries are becoming more receptive to FDI. In the years 1991–2004 the vast majority of changes in laws and regulations pertaining to investment were more favorable to FDI. An exception is developing countries, which introduced some laws and regulations intended to protect some natural resources (especially in the energy field) against "foreign intruders." The report also indicates that countries are cooperating with each other in designing pro-FDI bilateral policies: "The number of bilateral investment treaties (BITs) and double taxation treaties (DTTs) reached 2,392 and 2,559 respectively, in 2004, with developing countries concluding more such treaties with other developing countries." Razin and Sadka (2007) provide a comprehensive survey of theory and empirical applications of FDI.

8. See also Feenstra (1999).

9. The reason is that creditor rights protection affects the probability of the crisis. Hale, Razin, and Tong (2014) estimate PROBIT regressions of stock market crashes. They construct the propensity score and match crisis observations (treatment group) to non-crisis observations (control group), by using the Epanechnikov-kernel matching technique. Having done this, they then compute the average treatment effect on treated (ATT), using the matched sample, for stock-market return and volatility. They find that the stock market average return is only half as high during the crisis, and that in a matched sample the stock return volatility is substantially and significantly higher during crisis.

10. Globalization in the shape of a drop-off of capital controls typically leads to foreign direct investment in the form of mergers and acquisition (M&A), but not in the form of greenfield investment. The latter are typically encouraged in the political-economy setups, even under a regime of capital-inflow restrictions, provided that the profits from the investments are allowed to be repatriated. Greenfield FDI surges are primarily driven by high return projects such as high-tech startups.

11. Based on Goldstein and Razin (2006).

12. For a comprehensive treatise of the role of multinationals in international trade see Markusen (2002) and Bransfetter (2006).

13. See Gopinath (2004) for a different application of a search model for a study of FDI flows into developing economies.

14. Antras (2015) provides a rigorous theory survey.

15. Foreign portfolio investment is different from FDI in that it lacks the element of lasting interest and control. Foreign portfolio investment also includes lending in the form of tradable bonds. The third type of foreign investment is loans, primarily bank loans. Among these types of foreign investment flows, FDI stands out. The world flows of FDI rose about sevenfold in current U.S. dollars over the 1990s. Other forms of foreign investment, such as debt, also increased dramatically, especially to non-OECD countries. Furthermore, the vast majority of these flows are among OECD countries. FDI flows from OECD to non-OECD countries are also significant.

Among non-OECD countries, China, with $72 billion, is by far the largest recipient of FDI in 2005, surpassed only by the United Kingdom and the United States.

16. The sample covers nearly all of Latin America and Asia, as well as many countries in Africa. They find that an increase of one dollar in the volume of capital inflows is associated with an increase in domestic investment of about fifty cents. (In the regression, both capital inflows and domestic investment are expressed as percentages of GDP.) This result, however, masks significant differences among different types of inflows. FDI appears to bring about a one-for-one increase in domestic investment; there is virtually no discernible relationship between portfolio inflows and investment; and the impact of loans falls between those of the other two. These results hold for both the sample of fifty-eight countries and for a subset of eighteen emerging markets. Borensztein, De Gregorio, and Lee (1998) find that FDI increases economic growth when the level of education in the host country—a measure of its absorptive capacity—is high.

Chapter 7

1. Biru Pashka and Das (2012).

2. Rosefielde and Dallago (2016).

3. Wong (1988).

4. Kung and Lin (2007).

5. Oi (1992).

6. The possibility of market socialism was debated in the nineteenth century, but rejected by most communists in 1929, when Stalin forcibly collectivized the Soviet Union. The idea was resurrected in the West by Oscar Lange in 1936–1937, and has been influential ever after. See Lange and Taylor (1938). Stalin was impressed by Lange's theory. He summoned him to Moscow for consultations, and Lange lobbied Franklin Roosevelt on Stalin's behalf regarding the government of postwar Poland. From 1961 to 1965 Lange served as one of four acting chairmen of the Polish State Council (head of state).

7. China's long-lasting fixed exchange rate policy, put together with capital controls, enabled the Chinese authorities to encourage export-led growth (with the renminbi being frequently undervalued) while using monetary policy to control domestic inflation. But, China is likely to have to let the renminbi exchange rate float freely sometime over the next decade. It might seem odd that a country running a huge trade surplus ($600 billion in 2015) would be worried about currency weakness. But a combination of factors, including slowing economic growth, and a gradual relaxation of restrictions on investing abroad, has unleashed a torrent of capital outflows.

8. Indian federal government embraced free-market policies in 1991 and at the same time devolved the power of the states, including authority over taxes. But only recently, Indian

lawmakers cleared the way for India to become a single economic zone, by introducing the federal goods-and-services tax (a value-added tax), which can abolish the overlapping federal and state taxes. This new law is in the process of being put in place after a long series of legislative steps and the approval of the constitutional amendment by the upper house of the parliament.

9. While economists have been estimating gravity equations on bilateral trade data, the theoretical foundations of these equations had been sketchy, and only recent work has provided satisfactory formulations. See the recent survey by Head and Mayer (2016).

10. For gravity-based analysis of China's trade with WTO members, see Mattoo and Subramanian (2011).

11. Israel's export share is especially high in countries that import electronics, chemicals, and communication equipment—industries in which Israel has a significant comparative advantage.

12. An insightful toy model to think about trade barriers is as follows: Assume two symmetric countries. Each country specializes in production. Goods enter symmetrically into utility, with elasticity of substitution σ (>1) between the goods. There is only one factor of production—labor. It takes α units of labor to produce one unit of either country's good; it takes τ units of labor to transport that good to the other country. Both countries impose ad valorem tariffs at rate t. Then the ratio of imports to consumption of home good exports as a share of GDP is $v/(1+v)$, where

$$v = (1 + \tau/\alpha)^{1-\sigma}(1+t)^{-\sigma}.$$

The shutting down of trade (or the imposition of a [partial] trade embargo) is equivalent to a rise in tariff, or an increase of transportation cost. In either case trade shrinks. Then, reversing the autarkic policies by the opening up of trade would boost trade. The increase in productivity $1/\alpha$ weakens trade. See Krugman (2016). The model, however, does not capture the forces that led to the rise of Israel's trade with China over time.

Chapter 8

1. Why have European countries been unsuccessful in either encouraging high-skill immigration or in limiting the size of their welfare state? Razin and Sadka (2014) take a page out of the vast work on tax competition to provide insights. They argue that fiscal independence in a migration union like Schengen leads to policy distortions. Schengen members do not fully internalize the degree to which their generous welfare states attract immigrants, as the costs of immigration are borne by the union as a whole. Thus the need for fiscal unity in a common immigration zone is novel. See Ilzetzki (2016).

2. Until quite recently the academic literature treated migrants as substitutes for native workers. But, what if they were complements—if low-skilled migrants helped to boost the productivity of low-skilled natives? Ottaviano and Peri (2016) find that for workers with at least a high-school qualification, the wage effects of low-skill immigration are positive, if you drop the assumption that workers of the same age and education are perfect substitutes and that workers of one skill level do not affect the productivity of workers at other skill levels. The effect on the wages of high-school dropouts is only mildly negative. A paper by Mancorda, Manning, and Wadsworth (2012) similarly concludes that immigrants to Britain are imperfect substitutes for native-born workers, so they have little impact on native workers' job prospects or wages.

3. See Appendix 8A for some robustness tests.

4. Universities and colleges are the other important gatekeepers in the United States, through their selection of individuals for the F1 (student) or J1 (exchange visitor) visas (see Kerr et al. [2016]). While these visas do not offer long-term employment, U.S. firms often recruit graduates of U.S. schools, using visas like the H-1B. An advantage of employment-based immigration-policy regime compared to a points-based approach is that the job-market search process is more efficient in the former case. The employer-employee match is guaranteed to connect the immigrant talent with a productive and adequate job.

5. Kerr et al. (2016) give suggestive examples showing how global migration may be most pronounced for those at the very outer tail of the talent distribution.

Chapter 9

1. The demographic transition—a change from high to low rates of mortality and fertility—has been more dramatic in East Asia during the twentieth century than in any other region or historical period. East Asia's demographic transition resulted in its working-age population growing at a much faster rate than its dependent population, thereby expanding the per capita productive capacity of East Asian economies. This effect was not inevitable; rather, it occurred because East Asian countries had social, economic, and political institutions and policies that allowed them to realize the growth potential created by the transition.

2. The ultra-Orthodox Jews (Haredi) comprise 9.9 percent of Israel's overall population and close to 14 percent of the working-age population. The reason for the difference in these shares lies in the fact that this population is characterized by a large share of children and youth (below the age of fifteen).

3. One can make a comparison between the ultra-Orthodox Jewish communities across the world. Outside Israel (particularly in the United States), these communities have much lower fertility rates, and much greater supply of labor. Therefore, the exceptional fertility rate of the ultra-Orthodox Jewish does not necessarily have to do with their religious beliefs.

4. The demographic transition—a change from high to low rates of mortality and fertility—has been more dramatic in East Asia during the twentieth century than in any other region or historical period.

5. Razin and Sadka (1995) study the general-equilibrium welfare implications of child allowances.

6. The Communist Party introduced the one-child policy in 1979 to tackle population growth. It was scrapped in late 2015 following years of warnings from demographers over low birth rates and an aging population. China's national crude birth rate was 12.1 births per 1,000 people in 2015, down from 21 in 1960.

7. The Arabs comprise 20.8 percent of Israel's overall population and 18.7 percent of the working-age population. The reason for the difference in these shares lies in the fact that this population is characterized by a large share of children and youth (below the age of fifteen). The share of children aged 0–14 is 35 percent (versus 27.7 percent among Jews).

Chapter 10

1. The current economic costs of the Israeli settlements in the West Bank are hard to measure, because no one can forecast long-run implications or future scenarios—those that are derived from either the "one-state solution" or the "two-state solution." OECD (2010) reports that the population that lived in post-1967 areas in 2009 (greater Jerusalem included) was 775,000 people, which added 11.5 percent to the population of pre-1967 Israel. Subtracting from this figure 265,000 Palestinians from East Jerusalem, the population of the Israeli settlers in the West Bank (including a small number in the Golan) is 510,000—about 6.8 percent of the population of Israel. OECD calculates that this population receives 7.4 percent of the entire government consumption. Namely, this population receives a share of government spending (including defense and police) that is significantly larger than its actual share in the population of Israel.

2. A look at Israel's performance following the second intifada reveals a mixed picture. The dangerous security situation has combined with a global economic slowdown triggered by the bursting of the U.S. high-tech bubble to throw Israel into one of the worst recessions in its history. Israel's GDP contracted significantly. Unemployment reached over 10 percent at the beginning of 2001. Tourism dropped more than 50 percent from 2000 to 2001. Defense expenditures increased as government receipts have fallen, and the Israel shekel has lost value against the U.S. dollar. But, most of the economic decline is attributed to the high-tech sector weakness in the presence of the dot-com crisis.

3. "Intifada" means uprising in Arabic.

4. For a discussion of West Bank sovereignty and the matrix of control in the West Bank, see Appendix 10A.

5. The Palestinian-Israeli economic cooperation and trade relations are governed by the 1994 Paris Protocol, signed between the Palestine Liberation Organization (PLO), representing the Palestinian authority of the West Bank and the Gaza, and the government of Israel. The economic relationship between Israel and the Palestinian territories (before Hamas took control of Gaza) approximated a customs union. Differences in rates of indirect taxes, such as custom duties, tariffs, and VAT, were evidently inconsistent with free movement of goods between the two tax jurisdictions. What was agreed upon was a common customs envelope. It meant that with the VAT being a multistage sales tax, any tax savings achieved by purchasing inputs in the lower-tax jurisdiction would be corrected for by a higher effective tax rate being paid at the following stage. See Kleiman (1999).

6. See Edelstein (2011) for historical perspectives.

7. Average rates of growth of GDP per capita over the years 1997–2013 are: Palestine—1.5 percent; West Bank—2.5 percent; and Gaza—0.0 percent. See Arnon and Bamya (2015).

8. See Alper (2016) and Appendix 10A.

Part 4

1. Organized lobbying efforts for export and investment subsidies and importable industry protection, and capital-government cronyism, are evidently common across all variants of capitalistic systems, but they are more pronounced under deal-based market economies.

Chapter 11

1. Each book is from a different decade. An article by Michael Klein (2005) reviews six English-language books on the economy of Israel.

2. Credit to the central government increased at the whopping rate of 75 percent per annum between December 1948 and September 1951 (Patinkin [1958], pp. 112–113).

3. The surveyed books are:

Avi Ben-Bassat, ed., *The Israeli Economy, 1985–1998: From Government Intervention to Market Economics*, Cambridge, MA: MIT Press, 2002.
Yoram Ben-Porath, ed., *The Israeli Economy: Maturing Through Crises*, Cambridge, MA: Harvard University Press, 1986.
Nadav Halevi and Ruth Klinov-Malul, *The Economic Development of Israel*, Praeger Special Studies in International Economics and Development, published in cooperation with the Bank of Israel, New York: Frederick A. Praeger Publishers, 1968.
Leonardo Leiderman, ed., *Inflation and Disinflation in Israel*, Jerusalem: Bank of Israel, 1999.
Micha Michaely, *Foreign Trade Regimes and Economic Development: Israel*, New York: National Bureau of Economic Research, Columbia University Press, 1975.
Don Patinkin, *The Israel Economy: The First Decade*, Jerusalem: Maurice Falk Project for Economic Research in Israel, 1959.

Epilogue

1. The main factor behind these developments has been the devastating boom-bust cycle of the Irish real estate market, and the weakly regulated banking sector, which was acutely exposed to toxic assets that were traded over the globe. The unemployment rate in Ireland, which moved up immediately after the financial meltdown, recovered quickly, thanks to the relative strength of the UK labor market. See Lane (2011) for a comprehensive analysis of the Irish crisis. The nominal Irish gross domestic product as of 2017 exceeds the highest level it reached during the credit-bubble era. Emigration is slowing or reversing. Unemployment is also falling, from a peak of 15 percent at the height of the crisis to 8.4 percent in 2017.

2. On the question of how cutting trade and financial links affect Latin America export-led economies, Frieden (1991) observes that in Latin America "what sociopolitical harmony was restored by the export boom of the 1920s dissolved as foreign market collapsed with the Great Depression . . . After 1929, a succession of trade and financial supply and demand shocks spurred industrial development and social change. They also contributed to the rise of nationalistic populism throughout the continent . . . Effects of the crisis varied from country to country, but all of Latin America faced a combination of declining demand and falling terms of trade that seriously reduced its ability to import goods."

References

Abramitzky, Ran. 2011. "Lessons from the Kibbutz on the Equality-Incentives Trade-Off." *Journal of Economic Perspectives* 25 (Winter): 185–208.

Abramitzky, Ran, and Victor Lavy. 2014. "How Responsive Is Investment in Schooling to Changes in Redistributive Policies and in Returns?" *Econometrica* 82 (4): 1241–1272.

Alfaro, Laura, Areendam Chanda, Sebnem Kalemli-Ozcan, and Selin Sayek. 2004. "FDI and Economic Growth: The Role of Local Financial Markets." *Journal of International Economics* 64 (1): 89–112.

Aloni, Tslil. 2017. "Intergenerational Mobility in Israel." MA dissertation, School of Economics, Tel Aviv University.

Alper, Jeff. 2016. "The 94 Percent Solution: A Matrix of Control." www.merip.org/mer /mer216/94-percent-solution.

Anderson, James E., and Eric van Wincoop. 2003. "Gravity with Gravitas: A Solution to the Border Puzzle." *American Economic Review* 93 (1): 170–192.

Antras, Pol. 2004. "Advanced Topics in International Trade: Firms and International Trade." Lecture notes, Harvard University.

———. 2015. *Global Production: Firms, Contracts, and Trade Structure.* Princeton, NJ: Princeton University Press.

Arian, Alan, and Michal Shamir. 2002. "Abstaining and Voting in 2001." In *Elections in Israel—2001*, edited by Alan Arian and Michal Shamir, 150–175. Tel Aviv: Israel Democracy Institute.

Arnon, Arie, and Saeb Bamya, eds. 2015. *Economics and Politics in the Israeli-Palestinian Conflict.* Provence: AIX Group, Université Aix-Marseille.

Avner, Uri. 1975. "Voter Participation in the 1973 Election." In *Elections in Israel—1973*, edited by Alan Arian, 203–218. Tel Aviv: Academic Press.

Badinger, H. 2007. "Globalization, Taylor Rules, and Inflation." Mimeograph. Vienna: Wirtschaftsuniversität Wien.

Bank of Israel. 1991. "A Program for Absorbing One Million Olim." April (Hebrew).

———. 2006. *Annual Report.* Jerusalem.

Bean, Charles. 2006. "Globalization and Inflation." *Bank of England Quarterly Bulletin* Q4, 468–475.

Ben-Bassat, Avi, ed. 2002. *The Israeli Economy, 1985–1998: From Government Intervention to Market Economics.* Cambridge, MA: MIT Press.

Ben-David, Dan. 2007. "Soaring Minds: The Flight of Israel's Economists." CEPR Discussion Paper 6338, Center for Economic and Policy Research, Washington, DC.

———. 2008a. "Brain Drained: Soaring Minds." CEPR VOX, March 13. http://voxeu.org/article/academic-exodus.

———. 2008b. "Brain Drained: A Tale of Two Countries." CEPR Discussion Paper 6717, Center for Economic and Policy Research, Washington, DC.

———. 2015. *The Shoresh Handbook on Israel's Society and Economy.* Tel Aviv: Shoresh Institute.

Benhabib, Jess, and Boyan Jovanovic. 2012. "Optimal Migration: A World Perspective." *International Economic Review* 53 (2): 321–348.

Ben-Porath, Yoram. 1986. "The Entwined Growth of Population and Product, 1922–1982." In *The Israeli Economy: Maturing Through Crisis,* edited by Yoram Ben-Porath, 121–150. Cambridge, MA: Harvard University Press.

———, ed. 1986. *The Israeli Economy: Maturing Through Crises.* Cambridge, MA: Harvard University Press.

Bentolila, Samuel, Juan J. Dolado, and Juan F. Jimeno. 2007. "Does Immigration Affect the Phillips Curve? Some Evidence for Spain." *European Economic Review* 52 (November): 1398–1423.

Berman, Eli. 2000. "Sect, Subsidy, and Sacrifice: An Economist's View of Ultra-Orthodox Jews." *Quarterly Journal of Economics* 115 (3): 905–953.

Bernanke, Ben S. 1983. "Nonmonetary Effects of the Financial Crisis in the Propagation of the Great Depression." *American Economic Review* 73: 257–276.

———. 2016. "The Fed's Shifting Perspective on the Economy and Its Implications for Monetary Policy." Washington, DC: Brookings Institution.

Binyamini, Alon, and Assaf Razin. 2008. "Inflation-Output Tradeoff as Equilibrium Outcome of Globalization." *Israel Economic Review* 6 (1): 109–134.

Bird, Karen. 2011. "Voter Turnout among Immigrants and Visible Minorities in Comparative Perspective." In *The Political Representation of Immigrants and Minorities: Voters, Parties, and Parliaments in Liberal Democracies,* edited by Karen Bird, Thomas Saalfeld, and Andreas M. Wüst, 51–76. London: Routledge/ECPR.

Biru Paksha, Paul, and Anupam Das. 2012. "Export-Led Growth in India and the Role of Liberalization." *Margin: The Journal of Applied Economic Research* 6 (February): 1–26.

Blanchard, Olivier. 2016. "Currency Wars, Coordination, and Capital Controls." NBER Working Paper 22388, National Bureau of Economic Research, Cambridge, MA.

Blonigen, Bruce A. 1997. "Firm-Specific Assets and the Link between Exchange Rates and Foreign Direct Investment." *American Economic Review* 87 (3): 447–465.

Borensztein, Eduardo, Jose De Gregorio, and J. W. Lee. 1998. "How Does Foreign Direct Investment Affect Economic Growth?" *Journal of International Economics* 45:115–135.

Borio, Claudio, and Andrew Filardo. 2007. "Globalization and Inflation: New Cross-Country Evidence on the Global Determinants of Domestic Inflation." Unpublished Paper (March). Basel: Bank for International Settlements.

Borjas, George J. 1999. "The Economic Analysis of Immigration." *Handbook of Labor Economics* 3, part A, 1697–1760.

———. 2006. "Native Internal Migration and the Labor Market Impact of Immigration." *Journal of Human Resources* 41 (Spring): 221–258.

Bosworth, Barry, and Susan Collins. 1999. "Capital Flows to Developing Economies: Implications for Saving and Investment." *Brookings Papers on Economic Activity* 1:143–169.

Brainard, S. Lael. 1997. "An Empirical Assessment of the Proximity-Concentration Trade-off between Multinational Sales and Trade." *American Economic Review* 87 (4): 520–544.

Bransfetter, Lee. 2006. "Is Foreign Direct Investment a Channel of Knowledge Spillovers? Evidence from Japan's FDI in the United States." *Journal of International Economics* 68 (2): 325–344.

Bruno, V., and H. S. Shin. 2015. "Capital Flows and the Risk-Taking Channel of Monetary Policy." *Journal of Monetary Economics* 71:119–132.

Calvo, Guillermo. 1978. "On the Time Consistency of Optimal Policy in a Monetary Economy." *Econometrica* 46 (November): 1411–1428.

———. 1992. "Are High Interest Rates Effective for Stopping High Inflation? Some Skeptical Notes." *World Bank Economic Review* 6:55–69.

———. 2016. "From Chronic Inflation to Chronic Deflation: Focusing on Expectations and Liquidity Disarray Since WWWII." NBER Working Paper 22535, National Bureau of Economic Research, Cambridge, MA.

Calvo, Guillermo A., and Carlos A. Vegh. 2001. "Inflation Stabilization and BOP Crises in Developing Countries." In *Handbook of Macroeconomics*, edited by John Taylor and Michael Woodford, 1615–1669. Amsterdam: Elsevier.

Card, David. 1990. "The Impact of the Mariel Boatlift on the Miami Labor Market." *ILR Review* 43 (January): 245–257.

Caves, Richard E. 1971. "International Corporations: The Industrial Economics of Foreign Investment." *Economica* 38:1–27.

Cecchetti, Stephen, and Kim Schoenholtz. 2016. "A Primer on Helicopter Money." CEPR VOX, August 19. http://voxeu.org/article/primer-helicopter-money.

Central Bureau of Statistics. 1992. *Statistical Abstract of Israel* no. 43. Jerusalem: Government of Israel.

———. 2016. *Statistical Abstract*. Jerusalem: Government of Israel.

Cerutti, E., S. Claessens, and L. Laeven. 2015. "The Use and Effectiveness of Macro Prudential Policies: New Evidence." IMF Working Papers 15/61, International Monetary Fund, Washington, DC.

Chang, Roberto, and Andres Velasco. 2001. "A Model of Financial Crises in Emerging Markets." *Quarterly Journal of Economics* 116:489–517.

Chen, Nancy, Jean Imbs, and Andrew Scott. 2004. "Competition, Globalization and the Decline of Inflation." *Journal of International Economics* 63 (1): 93–118, 312.

Choukhmane, Taha, Nicholas Coeurdacier, and Keyu Jun. 2016. "The One-Child Policy and Household Savings." LSE mimeograph.

Clarida, Richard, J. 2008. "Reflections on Monetary Policy in the Open Economy." In *NBER International Seminar on Macroeconomics*, edited by Jeffrey Frankel and Christopher Pissarides, 67–83. Chicago: University of Chicago Press.

Coe, David, and Elhanan Helpman. 1995. "International R&D Spillovers." *European Economic Review* 39:859–887.

Coe, David T., Elhanan Helpman, and Alexander W. Hoffmaister. 2009. "International R&D Spillovers and Institutions." *European Economic Review* 53 (October): 723–741.

Cohen, Sarit, and Chang-Tai Hsieh. 2000. "Macroeconomic and Labor Market Impact of Russian Immigration in Israel." Unpublished mimeograph. Ramat Gan, Israel: Bar Ilan University.

Cukierman, Alex. 1988a. "Rapid Inflation—Deliberate Policy or Miscalculation?" Carnegie-Rochester Conference Series on Public Economic Policy, North-Holland, 29, pp. 11–26.

———. 1988b. "The End of High Israeli Inflation." In *Inflation Stabilization: The Experience of Argentina, Brazil, Bolivia, Mexico, and Israel*, edited by Michael Bruno, Guido Di Tella, Rudiger Dornbusch, and Stanley Fischer, 121–142. Cambridge, MA: MIT Press.

Dadush, Uri, Dipak Dasgupta, and Dilip Ratha. 2000. "The Role of Short-Term Debt in Recent Crises." *Finance and Development* 37:54–57.

Dahan, Momi. 2007. "Why Has the Labor-Force Participation Rate of Israel Men Fallen?" *Israel Economic Review* 5 (2): 95–128.

———. 2017. "Income Inequality in Israel: A Distinctive Evolution." Mimeograph (Hebrew).

de Haan, Jacob, and Jan-Egbert Sturm. 2016. "How Development and Liberalization of the Financial Sector Is Related to Income Inequality: Some New Evidence." BAFFI CAREF IN Centre Research Paper 2016–33, Milan.

de la Potterie, Bruno van Pottelsberghe, and Frank Lichtenberg. 2001. "Does Foreign Direct Investment Transfer Technology Across Borders?" *Review of Economics and Statistics* 83 (August), 490–497.

Diamond, W. Douglas, and Philip H. Dybvig. 1983. "Bank Runs, Deposit Insurance, and Liquidity." *Journal of Political Economy* 91 (3): 401–419.

Djankov, Simeon, and Bernard Hoekman. 2000. "Foreign Investment and Productivity Growth in Czech Enterprises." *World Bank Economic Review* 14 (1): 49–64.

Djankov, Simeon, Caralee McLiesh, and Andrei A. Shleifer. 2007. "Private Credit in 129 Countries." *Journal of Financial Economics*, 84 (2): 299–329.

Docquier, F., O. Lohest, and A. Marfouk. 2005. "Brain Drain in Developing Countries." Département des Sciences Économiques de l'Université catholique de Louvain Discussion Paper 2007-4. http://www.abdeslammarfouk.com/uploads/1/6/3/4/16347570/bddc.pdf.

Dornbusch, Rudiger, and Sebastian Edwards. 1989. "The Macroeconomics Populism in Latin America." WPS Working Paper 316, World Bank, Washington DC.

Eaton, Jonathan, and Samuel Kortum. 2002. "Technology, Geography, and Trade." *Econometrica* 70 (5): 1741–1779.

Eckstein, Zvi, Ofer Setty, and David Weiss. 2015. "Financial Risk and Unemployment." CEPR Working Paper DP10596, Center for Economic and Policy Research, Washington, DC.

Eckstein, Zvi, and Yoram Weiss. 2004. "On the Wage Growth of Immigrants: Israel, 1990–2000." *Journal of the European Economic Association* 2 (June): 665–695.

Edelstein, David M. 2011. *Occupational Hazards: Success and Failure in Military Occupation.* Ithaca, NY: Cornell University Press.

Eggertsson, Gauti B., and Paul Krugman. 2013. "Debt, Deleveraging, and the Liquidity Trap: A Fisher-Minsky-Koo Approach." *Quarterly Journal of Economics* 127 (3): 1469–1513.

Eggertsson, Gauti, Neil Mehrotra, and Lawrence Summers. 2016. "Secular Stagnation in the Open Economy." *American Economics Review, Papers and Proceedings* 106 (5): 503–507.

Eichengreen, Barry, and Kevin O'Rourke. 2010. "What Do the New Data Tell Us?" CEPR VOX, March 8. http://voxeu.org/article/tale-two-depressions-what-do-new-data-tell -us-february-2010-update.

Eilam, Nir. 2014. "The Fiscal Impact of Immigrants: The Case of Israel." MA thesis, Eitan Berglas School of Economic, Tel Aviv University.

European Commission. 2003. "The Brain Drain to the US: Challenges and Answers."

Feenstra, Robert C. 1999. "Facts and Fallacies about Foreign Direct Investment." In *International Capital Flows*, edited by Martin Feldstein, 34–56. Chicago: University of Chicago Press.

Fleming, Marcus. 1962. "Domestic Financial Policies under Fixed and under Floating Exchange Rates." IMF Staff Paper 9, November, 369–380. International Monetary Fund, Washington, DC.

Flood, Robert P., and Garber, Peter M. 1984. "Collapsing Exchange-Rate Regimes: Some Linear Examples." *Journal of International Economics* 17 (August): 1–13.

Fratzscher, M., M. Lo Duca, and R. Straub. 2013. "On the International Spillovers of US Quantitative Easing." ECB Working Paper No. 1557, Frankfurt, Germany.

Frieden, Jeffrey A. 1991. *Debt, Development, and Democracy: Modern Political Economy and Latin America, 1965–1985.* Princeton, NJ: Princeton University Press.

Friedlander, Dov. 2009. "Fertility in Israel: Is the Transition to Replacement in Sight?" In *Population Bulletin of the United Nations: Completing Fertility Transition.* United Nations. https://www.researchgate.net/profile/Dov_Friedlander.

Friedman, Milton. 1968. "The Role of Monetary Policy." *American Economic Review* 58: 1–17.

———. 1969. "The Optimum Quantity of Money." In *The Optimum Quantity of Money and Other Essays*, 1–50. Chicago: Adline.

———. 1971. "Government Revenue from Inflation." *Journal of Political Economy* 79 (4): 846–856.

Friedmann, Yoav. 2016. "The Information Technology Industries: Employees, Wages and Dealing with Shocks." *Israel Economic Review* 14 (1): 97–132.

Froot, Kenneth. A., and Jeremy C. Stein. 1991. "Exchange Rates and Foreign Direct Investment: An Imperfect Capital Markets Approach." *Quarterly Journal of Economics* 106 (5): 1191–1217.

Gali, Jordi. 2008. *Monetary Policy, Inflation, and the Business Cycle: An Introduction to the New Keynesian Framework*. Princeton, NJ: Princeton University Press.

Gertler, Mark, and Nobuhiro Kiyotaki. 2011. "Financial Intermediation of Credit Policy in Business Cycle Analysis." In *Handbook of Monetary Economics*, vol. 3B, edited by Benjamin M. Friedman and Michael Woodford, 45–90. Amsterdam: Elsevier.

Goldman, David F. 2013. "Israel's Demographic Miracle." Mimeograph.

Goldstein, Itay, and Assaf Razin. 2006. "An Information-Based Trade-off between Foreign Direct Investment and Foreign Portfolio Investment." *Journal of International Economics* 70:271–295.

———. 2015. "Three Branches of Theories of Financial Crises, Foundations and Trends in Finance." *Foundations and Trends in Finance*, no. 1, 1–66.

Gopinath, Gita. 2004. "Lending Booms, Sharp Reversals and the Real, Exchange Dynamics." *Journal of International Economics* 62 (1): 1.

Gopinath, Gita, and Oleg Itskhoky. 2008. "Frequency of Price Adjustment and Pass-through." NBER Working Paper 14200, National Bureau of Economic Research, Cambridge, MA.

Gopinath, Gita, and Roberto Rigobon. 2007. "Sticky Borders." *Quarterly Journal of Economics* 123 (2): 531–575.

Gordon, Robert. 2016. *The Rise and Fall of American Growth: The U.S. Standard of Living since the Civil War*. Princeton, NJ: Princeton University Press.

Gornick, Janet, and Markus Jäntti, eds. 2014. *Income Inequality: Economic Disparities and the Middle Class in Affluent Countries*. Stanford, CA: Stanford University Press.

Gould, Eric, and Omer Moav. 2007. "Israel's Brain Drain." *Israel Economic Review* 5 (1): 1–22.

Greenwood, Jeremy, and Boyan Jovanovic. 1990. "Financial Development, Growth, and the Distribution of Income." *Journal of Political Economy* 98:1076–1107.

Griffith, Rachel, and Helen Simpson. 2003. "Characteristics of Foreign Owned Firms in British Manufacturing." NBER Working Paper No. 9573 (March), National Bureau of Economic Research, Cambridge, MA.

Hale, Galina, Assaf Razin, and Hui Tong. 2014. "Stock Prices in the Presence of Liquidity Crises: The Effect of Creditor Protection." *Economica* 81 (April): 329–347.

Halevi, Nadav, and Ruth Klinov-Malul. [1968?]. *The Economic Development of Israel*. Praeger Special Studies in International Economics and Development, published in cooperation with the Bank of Israel. New York: Frederick A. Praeger Publishers.

Hanson, Gordon, R. Mataloni, and M. Slaughter. 2001. "Expansion Strategies of U.S. Multinational Firms." In *Brooking Trade Forum 2001*, edited by Dani Rodrick and Susan Collins, 245–282.

Hanson, H. Gordon, and Matthew J. Slaughter. 2016. "High-Skilled Immigration and the Rise of STEM Occupations in U.S. Employment." NBER Working Paper 22623, National Bureau of Economic Research, Cambridge, MA.

Head, Keith, and Thierry Mayer. 2016. In *Handbook of International Economics*, edited by Elhanan Helpman, Gita Gopinath, and Ken Rogoff, vol. 4, 23–45. Amsterdam: Elsevier.

Helpman, Elhanan. 1999. "R&D and Productivity: The International Connection." In *The Economics of Globalization: Policy Perspective from Public Economics*, edited by Assaf Razin and Efraim Sadka. Cambridge: Cambridge University Press.

———. 2003. "Israel Economic Growth: An International Comparison." *Israel Economic Review* 1:1–10.

———. 2004. *The Mystery of Economic Growth*. Cambridge, MA: Harvard University Press.

———. 2006. "Trade, FDI, and the Organization of Firms." NBER Working Paper 12091, National Bureau of Economic Research, Cambridge, MA.

Helpman, Elhanan, Marc Melitz, and Yona Rubinstein. 2008. *Quarterly Journal of Economics* 123 (2): 441–487.

Helpman, Elhanan, Mark Melitz, and Steve Yeaple. 2004. "Exports vs FDI." *American Economic Review* 94 (1), 300–316.

Holmstrom, Bengt, and Jean Tirole. 1997. "Financial Intermediation, Loanable Funds, and the Real Sector." *Quarterly Journal of Economics* 112:663–691.

Ihrig, J., Steven B. Kamin, Deborah Lindner, and Jaime Marquez. 2007. "Some Simple Tests of the Globalization and Inflation Hypothesis." Board of Governors of the Federal Reserve System, International Finance Discussion Papers.

Ilzetzki, Ethan. 2016. "Review of *Migration and the Welfare State: Why Is America Different from Europe?* by Assaf Razin and Efraim Sadka." *Israel Economic Review* 14 (1): 129–133.

Karni, Edi. 1983. "Revenue from Inflation." *Yediot Aharonot*, June 12.

Kerr, Sari Pekkala, William Kerr, Çaglar Özden, and Christopher Parsons. 2016. "Global Talent Flows." *Journal of Economic Perspectives* 30 (Fall): 3–30.

Keynes, John M. 1924. "Alfred Marshall, 1842–1924." *Economic Journal* 34 (135): 311–372.

Kleiman, Ephraim. 1999. "Fiscal Separation with Economic Integration: Israel and the Palestinian Authority." In *The Economics of Globalization: Policy Perspectives from Public Economic*, edited by Assaf Razin and Efraim Sadka, 219–240. Cambridge University Press.

Klein, Michael. 2005. "Studying Texts: A Gemara of the Israeli Economy." *Israel Economic Review* 3 (1): 66–82.

Krugman, Paul. 1979. "A Model of Balance-of-Payments Crises." *Journal of Money, Credit and Banking* 11 (August): 311–325.

———. 1998. "It's Baaack! Japan's Slump and the Return of the Liquidity Trap." In *Brookings Papers on Economic Activity* 2, 130–155. Washington, DC: Brooking Institution.

————. 1999. "Balance Sheets, the Transfer Problem, and Financial Crises." *International Tax and Public Finance* 6: 459–472.

————. 2000. "The Price of Globalization?" In *Global Economic Integration*, edited by Alan Greenspan, 201–225. Jackson Hole Symposium.

————. 2006. "A Few Notes on Income Inequality." *New York Times*, March 13. http://krugman.blogs.nytimes.com/2006/03/13/a-few-notes-on-income-inequality/?_r=0.

————. 2016. "Trade Plateaus." *The Conscience of a Liberal* (blog). http://krugman.blogs.nytimes.com/.

Krugman, Paul, Maurice Obstfeld, and Marc Melitz. 2015. *International Economics: Theory and Policy*. 10th ed. New York: Pearson.

Kung, James Kai-Sing, and Yi-Min Lin. 2007. "The Decline of Township-and-Village Enterprises in China's Economic Transition." *World Development* 35 (4): 569–584.

Kydland, Finn, and Edward C. Prescott. 1977. "Rules Rather than Discretion: The Inconsistency of Optimal Plans." *Journal of Political Economy* 85:473–493.

Lane, Philip. 1997. "Inflation in Open Economies." *Journal of International Economics* 42:327–347.

Lane, Philip R. 2011. "The Irish Crisis." CEPR Discussion Paper 8287, Centre for Economic Policy Research, London.

Lange, Oscar, and Fred M. Taylor. 1938. *On the Economic Theory of Socialism*. Ann Arbor: University of Michigan Press.

La Porta, Rafael, Florencio Lopez-de-Silanes, Andrei Shleifer, and Robert Vishny. 1998. "Law and finance." *Journal of Political Economy* 106:1113–1155.

Leiderman, Leonardo, ed. 1999. *Inflation and Disinflation in Israel*. Jerusalem: Bank of Israel.

Lipsey, Robert E. 2000. "The Role of Foreign Direct Investment in International Capital Flows." NBER Working Paper 7094, National Bureau of Economic Research, Cambridge, MA.

Loungani, Prakash, and Assaf Razin. 2001. "How Beneficial Is Foreign Direct Investment for Developing Countries." *Finance and Development* 38 (2): 20–44.

Loungani, Prakash, Assaf Razin, and Chi-Wa Yuen. 2001. "Capital Mobility and the Output-Inflation Tradeoff." *Journal of Development Economics* 64:255–274.

Lucas, Robert E. 1975. "An Equilibrium Model of the Business Cycle." *Journal of Political Economy* 83 (6): 1113–1144.

————. 2000. "Some Macroeconomics for the 21st Century." *Journal of Economic Perspectives* 14:159–168.

————. 2003. "Macroeconomic Priorities." *American Economic Review* 93:1–14.

————, ed. 2014. *International Handbook on Migration and Economic Development*. London: Edward Elgar.

Mancorda, Marco, Alan Manning, and Jonathan Wadsworth. 2012. "The Impact of Immigration on the Structure of Wages: Theory and Evidence from Britain." *Journal of the European Economic Association* 10 (February): 120–151.

Mankiw, N. Gregory. 2010. "The Trilemma of International Finance." *New York Times,* July 24. http://www.nytimes.com/2010/07/11/business/economy/11view.html.

Manski, Charles F., and Joram Mayshar. 2003. "Private Incentives and Social Interactions: Fertility Puzzles in Israel." *Journal of the European Economic Association* 1 (March): 181–211.

Markusen, Lames R. 2002. *Multinational Firms and the Theory of International Trade.* Cambridge, MA: MIT Press.

Mattoo, Aaditya, and Arvind Subramanian. 2011. "China and the World Trade System." Policy Research Working Paper 5897, World Bank, Washington, DC.

Meltzer, Allan H., and Scott F. Richard. 1981. "A Rational Theory of the Size of Government." *Journal of Political Economy* 89 (5): 914–927.

Michaely, Micha. 1975. *Foreign Trade Regimes and Economic Development: Israel, National Bureau of Economic Research.* New York: Columbia University Press.

Middle East Research and Information Project. 2000. *Report No. 216* (fall). Washington. DC: World Bank.

Miller, Edward M. 1977. "Risk, Uncertainty, and Divergence of Opinion." *Journal of Finance* 32 (September): 1151–1168.

Mishkin, Fredric S. 2007a. "Is Financial Globalization Beneficial?" *Journal of Money, Credit, and Banking* 39 (March–April): 259–294.

———. 2007b. Remarks given at the Annual Macro Conference, Federal Reserve Bank of San Francisco, San Francisco.

Mohar, Rinat. 2009." Israel's Foreign Trade: Gravity Model." Mimeograph, Bank of Israel (Hebrew).

Mundell, Robert A. 1963. "Capital Mobility and Stabilization Policy under Fixed and Flexible Exchange Rates." *Canadian Journal of Economics* 29:475–485.

Narodnoe Khoziastvo USSR. 1990. Moscow: Statisticka.

National Academy of Sciences. 1995. *Research-Doctorate Programs in the United States: Continuity and Change.* Washington, DC.

Neuman, Shoshana. 1999. "Aliyah to Israel: Immigration under Conditions of Adversity." IZA Discussion Paper 89, December, Bonn, Germany.

Obstfeld, Maurice, and Alan. M. Taylor. 2002. "Globalization and the Capital Markets." NBER Working Paper 8846, National Bureau of Economic Research, Cambridge, MA.

OECD. 2010. "Study on the Geographic Coverage of Israeli Data." OECD.Stat, http://stats.oecd.org/.

Oi, Jean. 1992. "Fiscal Reform and the Economic Foundations of Local State Corporatism." *World Politics* 45:99–126

Ottaviano, Gianmarco, and Giovanni Peri. 2016. "Rethinking the Effects of Immigration on Wages." NBER Working Paper No. 12497, National Bureau of Economic Research, Cambridge, MA.

Patinkin, Don. 1959. *The Israel Economy: The First Decade.* Jerusalem: Maurice Falk Project for Economic Research in Israel.

Peri, Giovanni. 2005. "Determinants of Knowledge Flows and Their Effect on Innovation." *Review of Economics and Statistics* 87 (May): 308–322.

———. 2016. "Immigrants, Productivity, and Labor Markets." *Journal of Economic Perspectives* 30 (Fall): 3–30.

Peri, Giovanni, Kevin Y. Shih, and Chad Sparber. 2014. "Foreign STEM Workers and Native Wages and Employment in U.S. Cities." NBER Working Paper 20093, National Bureau of Economic Research, Cambridge, MA.

Persson, Torsten, and Guido Tabelini. 1990. *Macroeconomic Policy, Credibility, and Politics.* London: Routledge.

Phelps, Edmund S. 1967. "Phillips Curves, Expectations of Inflation and Optimal Unemployment over Time." *Economica* 34 (135): 254–281.

Phillips, Alban W. 1958. "The Relation between Unemployment and the Rate of Change of Money Wage Rates in the United Kingdom, 1861–1957." *Economica* 25: 283–299.

Rampini, Adriano, and S. Viswanathan. 2011. "Financial Intermediary Capital." AFA 2013, San Diego Meetings Paper.

Razin, Assaf. 1995. "The Dynamic-Optimizing Approach to the Current Account: Theory and Evidence." In *Understanding Interdependence: The Macroeconomics of the Open Economy,* edited by Peter B. Kenen, 312–340. Princeton, NJ: Princeton University Press.

———. 2004. "The Contribution of FDI Flows to Domestic Investment in Capacity, and Vice Versa." In *Growth and Productivity in East Asia,* edited by Takatoshi Ito and Andrew K. Rose. NBER-East Asia Seminar on Economics, vol. 13, 149–167.

———. 2015. *Understanding Global Crises: An Emerging Paradigm.* Cambridge, MA: MIT Press.

Razin, Assaf, and Prakash Loungani. 2007. "Globalization and Equilibrium Inflation-Output Tradeoffs." In *NBER International Seminar on Macroeconomics 2005,* edited by Jeffrey Frankel and Christopher Pissarides, 171–192. Cambridge, MA: MIT Press.

Razin, Assaf, Yona Rubinstein, and Efraim Sadka. 2004. "Fixed Costs and FDI: The Conflicting Effects of Productivity Shocks." NBER Working Paper 10864, National Bureau of Economic Research, Cambridge, MA.

Razin, Assaf, and Efraim Sadka. 1993. *The Economy of Modern Israel: Malaise and Promise.* Chicago: University of Chicago Press.

———. 1995. *Population Economics.* Cambridge, MA: MIT Press.

———. 2003. *Labor, Capital and Finance: International Flows.* New York: Cambridge University Press.

———. 2007. *Foreign Direct Investment: Analysis of Aggregate Flows.* Princeton, NJ: Princeton University Press.

———. 2014. *Migration and the Welfare State: Why Is America Different from Europe?* London: Palgrave-MacMillan.

———. 2016. *How Migration Can Change Income Inequality?* CEPR Discussion Paper 11244, Center for Economic and Policy Research, Washington, DC.

Razin, Assaf, Efraim Sadka, and Benjarong Suwankiri. 2011. *Migration and the Welfare State: Political Economy Policy Formation.* Cambridge, MA: MIT Press.

Razin, Assaf, Efraim Sadka, and Phillip Swagel. 2002a "The Aging Population and the Size of the Welfare State." *Journal of Political Economy* 110 (August): 900–918.

———. 2002b. "Tax Burden and Migration: A Political Economy Theory and Evidence." *Journal of Public Economics* 85 (2): 167–190.

Razin, Assaf, and Jackline Wahba. 2015. "Welfare Magnet Hypothesis, Fiscal Burden, and Immigration Skill Selectivity." *Scandinavian Journal of Economics* 117 (April): 369–402.

Razin, Ofair, and Susan Collins. 1999. "Real Exchange Rate Misalignments and Growth." In *The Economics of Globalization: Policy Perspectives from Public Economics*, edited by Assaf Razin and Efraim Sadka, 75–92. Cambridge: Cambridge University Press.

Rey, Helene. 2015. "Dilemma Not Trilemma: Global Financial Cycles and Monetary Policy Independence." NBER Working Paper 21162, National Bureau of Economic Research, Cambridge, MA.

Rogoff, Kenneth. 2003. "Disinflation: An Unsung Benefit of Globalization?" *Finance and Development* 40 (December): 55–56.

———. 2004. *Economic Review: Federal Reserve Bank of Kansas City* 88 (4): 45–78.

Romer, D. 1993. "Openness and Inflation: Theory and Evidence." *Quarterly Journal of Economics* 107 (November): 869–904.

———. 1998. "A New Assessment of Openness and Inflation: Reply." *Quarterly Journal of Economics* 112 (May): 649–652.

Rosefielde, Steven, and Bruno Dallago. 2016. *Transformation and Crisis in Russia, Ukraine and Central Europe.* London: Routledge.

Rosefielde, Steven, and Stefan Hedlund. 2009. *Russia Since 1980: Wrestling with Westernization.* Cambridge: Cambridge University Press.

Sachs, Jeffrey. 2012a. "What I Did in Russia." March 14. http://jeffsachs.org/2012/03/what-i-did-in-russia/.

———. 2012b. "Toward an International Migration Regime." *American Economic Review: Papers & Proceedings* 106 (5): 451–455.

———. 2017. "Navigating the New Abnormal: The Populist Backlash." Project Syndicate, February 3, 2017.

Saito, Hisamitsu, and Toshiyuki Matsuura. 2016. "Agglomeration Economies, Productivity, and Quality Upgrading." RIETI Discussion Paper 16-E-085, Research Institute of Economy, Trade, and Industry, Tokyo.

Sargent, Thomas. J. 1999. *The Conquest of American Inflation.* Princeton, NJ: Princeton University Press.

Schneider, Martin, and Aaron Tornell. 2004. "Balance Sheet Effects, Bailout Guarantees and Financial Crises." *Review of Economic Studies* 71 (3): 883–913.

Sharaby, Linda. 2002. "Israel's Economic Growth: Success Without Security." *Middle East Review of International Affairs* 6 (September): 25–41.

Shiller, Robert, J. 2015. "The Housing Market Still Isn't Rational." *New York Times*, July 24.

Summers, Laurence. 2014. "Secular Stagnation? The Future Challenge for Economic Policy." Toronto: Institute for New Economic Thinking, April 12, 2014. https://www.ineteconomics.org/conference-session/secular-stagnation-the-future-challenge-for-economic-policy.

———. 2016. "Trump's Carrier Deal Could Permanently Damage American Capitalism." *Washington Post*, December 4.

Syrquin, Moses. 1985. "Economic Growth and Structural Change: An International Perspective." In *Israeli Economy: Maturing Through Crisis*, edited by Yoram Ben-Porath, 173–205. Cambridge, MA: Harvard University Press.

Tetlow, R., and B. Ironside. 2007. "Real-Time Model Uncertainty in the United States: The Fed, 1996–2003." *Journal of Money, Credit and Banking* 39 (October): 1533–1561.

Tinbergen, Jan. 1962. *Shaping the World Economy: Suggestions for an International Economic Policy*. New York: Twentieth Century Fund.

UN (United Nations). 2002. "Replacement Levels In Sight?" *Economic and Social Affairs, Population Bulletin of the United Nations*, special issue nos. 48/49. United Nations Population Division.

———. 2005. World Investment Report. New York.

Wong, C. P. W. 1988. "Interpreting Rural Industrial Growth in the Post-Mao Period." *Modern China* 14 (1): 25–61.

Wynne, Mark, A., and Erasmus K. Kersting. 2007. "Openness and Inflation." Federal Reserve Bank of Dallas, Staff Paper 2.

Yashiv, Eran, and Nitsa Kassir (Kaliner). 2011. "Patterns of Labor Force Participation Among Israeli Arabs." *Israel Economic Review* 9 (1): 53–101.

———. 2014. "The Labor Market for Israeli Arabs." INSS, Tel Aviv University. http://www.tau.ac.il/~yashiv/Israeli%20Arabs%20in%20the%20Labor%20Market%20—%20Policy%20Paper.pdf.

World Bank. 2009. *World Development Report (2009): Reshaping Economic Geography*. Washington, DC: World Bank.

Index